'The task of making Lacan's ideas approachable has alway ̲ ̲ ̲ ̲ a challenge. Hook brings his own unique approach to this task, interweaving popular cultural and Lacanian theory in an instructive way. It is via the words of Bill Clinton that we come to understand what "the unconscious structured like a language" might mean; via reference to an episode of *E.R.* that we come to appreciate how, for Lacan, "truth has the structure of fiction". And it doesn't end there: it is by means of the makeover show *How to Look Good Naked* that we understand how our own (imaginary) self-image is always mediated by the Other; with reference to colloquial speech ("Who's your daddy?") that Lacan's idea of "the Name-of-the-Father" is brought to life. Hook has developed and refined this material during more than a decade's worth of teaching . . . and it shows.'

— **Stephanie Swales**, University of Dallas, author of
Perversion: A Lacanian Approach to the Subject

SIX MOMENTS IN LACAN

Many first time readers of Jacques Lacan come to his work via psychology, a discipline that Lacan was notoriously antagonistic towards. *Six Moments in Lacan* takes up the dual challenge of introducing Lacanian psychoanalysis to an audience interested in psychology, while also stressing the fundamental differences between the two disciplines. Punctuated by lively examples, *Six Moments in Lacan* demonstrates the distinctive value of Lacanian concepts in approaching afresh topics such as communication, identity, otherness and inter-subjectivity.

Avoiding the jargon and wilful obscurity that so often accompanies expositions of Lacan's psychoanalytic theories, this book puts Lacanian ideas to work in practical and illuminating ways. A handful of concepts, drawn from distinct moments in Lacan's teaching, are contextualized and explained, and applied to the task of exploring the psychological and unconscious dimensions of everyday life. Notions such as the big Other, full versus empty speech, logical time, imaginary and symbolic identification and the idea of the master signifier are brought to life via popular cultural references. Revitalizing several Freudian and Lacanian concepts for everyday use, *Six Moments in Lacan* asks – and answers – a series of compelling questions:

- Why is it that each instance of speech implies a listener?
- Why is the notion of subjectivity inadequate when it comes to the 'trans-subjective' nature of language?
- Is it possible to elaborate a non-psychological theory of identification?
- Why is a Lacanian approach to the subject so at odds with models proposed by psychology?

Six Moments in Lacan provides an accessible and highly engaging introduction to Lacan and Lacanian psychoanalysis, aimed at early practitioners and students in psychoanalysis, psychotherapy and those studying upper undergraduate and postgraduate level psychology.

Derek Hook is an Associate Professor in Psychology at Duquesne University and an Extraordinary Professor in Psychology at the University of Pretoria. A former lecturer at the London School of Economics and Birkbeck College, he is the author of *A Critical Psychology of the Postcolonial* and *(Post)apartheid Conditions*.

SIX MOMENTS IN LACAN

Communication and Identification in Psychology and Psychoanalysis

Derek Hook

Routledge
Taylor & Francis Group

LONDON AND NEW YORK

First published 2018
by Routledge
2 Park Square, Milton Park, Abingdon, Oxon OX14 4RN

and by Routledge
711 Third Avenue, New York, NY 10017

Routledge is an imprint of the Taylor & Francis Group, an informa business

British Library Cataloguing in Publication Data
A catalogue record for this book is available from the British Library

Library of Congress Cataloging in Publication Data
A catalog record for this book has been requested

ISBN: 978-1-138-21160-5 (hbk)
ISBN: 978-1-138-21161-2 (pbk)
ISBN: 978-1-315-45261-6 (ebk)

Typeset in Bembo and Stone Sans
by Florence Production Ltd, Stoodleigh, Devon, UK

For Merryn, again

CONTENTS

FIGURES

ACKNOWLEDGEMENTS

I am indebted to the students who have taken my course on Lacanian psychoanalysis (at the London School of Economics, Birkbeck College and Duquesne University) for allowing me the opportunity to develop the material contained in this book. I am likewise indebted to colleagues at these and related institutions that have been kind enough to support my work. Thanks are also due to the Department of Psychosocial Studies at Birkbeck College, to the Departments of Psychology at Duquesne University and the University of Pretoria and the International Social Research Foundation for providing funding my work. A particular note of gratitude is owed to Calum Neill.

Earlier versions of several of the following chapters have appeared in the form of journal articles. Acknowledgements are due to these journals (and the associated editors) for permission to rework this material. Sections from Chapter 2 originally appeared as 'Nixon's "full speech": Imaginary and Symbolic registers of communication' in the *Journal of Theoretical and Philosophical Psychology*, 33, 1, 32–50. Copyright (c) 2013 by the American Psychological Association. Reproduced with permission. Chapter 3 is a much extended version of 'Towards a Lacanian Group Psychology: The Prisoner's Dilemma and the Trans-subjective' originally published in the *Journal for the Theory of Social Behaviour*, 43, 2, 115–132. Reprinted by permission of John Wiley & Sons, Inc. Chapter 4 expands material included in the paper 'Love, artificiality and mass identification', previously published in *Psychodynamic Practice*, 20, 2, 128–143. Reprinted by permission of Taylor & Francis, LLC. Sections of Chapter 6 were originally published as 'The subject of Psychology: A Lacanian critique' in the journal *Social & Personality Psychology Compass*, 11, 5. Reproduced with permission.

INTRODUCTION

Six moments in the history of a 'non-relation'

Psychoanalysis . . . as anti-psychology?

Many who teach Lacanian theory in university settings in the English-speaking world are obliged to do so from within the discipline of psychology. This immediately poses a significant problem: that of the fundamental incompatibility – the 'non-relation' – between Lacanian psychoanalysis and psychology.[1] This may at first seem a minor issue, a question of making adjustments here and there to avoid a conflation of these two disciplines. From a Lacanian perspective, this is decidedly *not* the case.

In a recent series of joint interviews, French intellectuals Alain Badiou and Élisabeth Roudinesco (2014) reflected on the legacy of Jacques Lacan. An unexpected feature of their discussions was the frequency with which the relation between psychoanalysis and psychology was broached. There is little ambiguity in how this relationship is characterized: from the standpoint of Lacanian psychoanalysis, psychology is the enemy. Roudinesco comments, for example that: 'Lacan never stopped criticizing psychology as a false science' (pp. 10–11).

> He opposed every form of identitarian closure that denies the alterity that constitutes us . . . he opposed the behaviourism and cognitivism that have reduced man to his naturality, reduced him to his biological being, to his body and his brain.
>
> (2014, pp. 28–29)

When, a few pages later, Roudinesco asks 'Are psychoanalysts destined to become psychologists . . .?' (p. 66), one cannot but wonder what she has in mind with this designation ('psychologists'). Her answer, with its obvious echo of Michel Foucault's critique of the discipline in *Discipline & Punish* Foucault (1977), is not long coming: psychologists are 'technicians of the soul' (p. 66).

Understood in this way, psychology (which, importantly, is inclusive of the psychotherapeutic) is naïvely positivistic (a misguided form of scientism). It fails to engage the Otherness that lies at the heart of subjectivity; it falls prey to the illusion that the human subject can be approached as a consistent, self-enclosed identity. Psychology, moreover, is necessarily tied to the objectives of a type of disciplinary normalization whereby – staying with Foucault – subjects must be assimilated into the contemporary judgements and values of society. A three-fold attack on the various forms of psychology's alleged reductionism (the respective reductionisms of behaviourism, cognitivism, and latterly, of neuroscience) is thus extended by means of a political critique which considers 'psychologism' a 'blatant ideological program' (p. 30).

The terms of this rejection of psychology are thrown into further perspective when Roudinesco responds to a prompt by her interviewer, Christine Goémé:

> *C.G.:* Isn't one of the most important aspects of the Lacanian enterprise the fact that it stands in the way of any and all psychologization of the subject?
>
> *É.R.:* Yes. The rejection of psychology is a constant in Lacan's work. Lacan had one hell of a horror for this discipline . . . for him, psychoanalysis was precisely an anti-psychology. He had contempt for the American school of 'ego psychology', focused as it was on the ego or self. He wanted more of the unconscious, more of the real, in order to avoid the pitfalls of the psychologization of existence that amounts to no more than the behaviourist domestication of consciences.
>
> (p. 52)

To the claims that psychology is a mode of human engineering and a false science that is unreceptive to the reality of the unconscious, we must now add three more allegations: 1) that it reduces the category of the subject to an ego, 2) that it studies behaviours so as better to regulate them and 3) that it is mechanistic (behaviourist) in its operations.

Badiou adds to Roudinesco's comments when he advances that Lacan was a 'ferocious adversary' of any adaptive (i.e. psychologized) vision of psychoanalysis that would be content

> with training the human animal to conform to its social environment, transforming it into an animal subjected to dominant values that would no longer have any reason to ensure . . . nonconformity [or] . . . excessive originality.
>
> (p. 21)

If the above criticisms seem exaggerated, a brief perusal of Lacan's various attacks on psychology assures us that the above comments do not misrepresent his position.

Pavón-Cuéllar's astute (2013) investigation of Lacan and social psychology provides a montage of such attacks. For Lacan, says Pavón-Cuéllar

> There is no 'possible accord' of psychoanalysis with psychology . . . Psychoanalysis 'contradicts' psychology . . . The 'dominion of validity of what is called "psychology" (reality) has nothing to do with the level (the signifier) upon which psychoanalysis rests' . . . Lacan finds between psychoanalysis and psychology . . . an essentially negative connection characterized by non-relation, distance, disagreement and contradiction.
>
> (p. 266)

Lacan's tirade against psychology was more than a matter of intellectual, ethical and philosophical divergences. It was occasioned by a threat alluded to by Badiou and Roudinesco (2014): the assimilation of psychoanalysis to conceptual and clinical domains of psychology. One could argue that in much of the English-speaking world *this has already happened*, that what we consider to be psychoanalysis has been effectively psychologized. Hence the imperative with which I begin this introduction to Lacan: that of setting Lacanian theory apart from psychology, of carefully specifying the differences between these approaches.

Lacan's early attacks escalate from snipes at the inadequate epistemological basis of psychology – 'psychology as "an error of perspective", as "poorly grounded", as adhering to an "illusion"' (Pavón-Cuéllar, 2013, p. 266) – to an excoriation of its aspirations to be a science and a condemnation of its ideological nature (and here I cite Pavón-Cuéllar at length):

> [I]n contrast to a psychoanalysis based on 'the relationship of subject to subject', psychological 'manoeuvring' reduces the 'subject' to an 'object' . . . [The] 'objects' of psychology . . . are nothing more than *objectified ideas* than can be converted into behavioural . . . or cerebral *material things* upon which all [the] 'materialism' of psychology is grounded . . . 'all psychological science is affected by the ideals of the society in which it is produced' . . . psychology displays 'its low uses of social exploitation' . . . by 'explaining' how 'to behave' in the 'society dominated by capital accumulation'.
>
> (pp. 266–267)

Lacan was clearly not content merely to ignore psychology. What was it though about the typical procedures and assumptions of psychology that so agitated Lacan, for whom the discipline had the potential to wholly deform psychoanalysis? Jacques-Alain Miller offers a concise answer. Ego psychology, he says (an illustrative case in point for our purposes here):

> lops off Freud's first topography [the model of the psyche as divided between unconscious, preconscious and consciousness], thus eliminating the very

> concept of the unconscious and its foundation in the structure of language
> and the function of speech . . . it establishes the ego as the truest agency.
>
> (Miller, 1996b, p. 307)[2]

Here it helps to add – to risk retelling an oft-told tale – that Lacanian psychoanalysis pivots on the role of the signifier, prioritizing, in other words, language and *speech* as the route of access to the unconscious. By centralizing the operations of the signifier, and doing so as way of engaging the productions of the unconscious, Lacanian theory departs from psychology in at least two fundamental ways. Not only is the conscious identity or individuality (or ego) of the subject dramatically decentralized and deprioritized – viewed in fact as a type of symptom or mirage – but so is *the whole field of meanings and (self-)understandings premised upon such an egoic (or 'imaginary') basis.*[3]

'Traversing the chasm'

How then are we to make our way through the mutual disregard and – certainly in Lacan's case – *outright animosity*, which has for so long has characterized the 'non-relation' between Lacanian psychoanalysis and psychology? [4] Perhaps simply by reiterating that Lacanian psychoanalysis is, in Roudenisco's phrase, an 'anti-psychology' and by concluding the case closed. There is much to support such a position. We have heard many reasons why Lacanian psychoanalysis cannot be assimilated into the psychological (psychology is hopelessly ego-focused, inattentive to the signifier, dismissive of the unconscious, objectifying in its procedures, etc.). Then again, we might ask: Is this the whole story? Is it the case that Lacan and his followers protest too much when they castigate and caricature psychology? Might Lacan and Lacanians in fact have a reluctant debt to psychology itself?

The psychological, after all, represents a heterogeneous disciplinary field. There are, arguably, modes of (critical, philosophical, human science) psychology and psychotherapeutic practice that embrace psychoanalytic ideas and which cannot summarily be categorized as necessarily at odds with Lacanian theory. Consider the comments of Yael Goldman Baldwin, who locates Lacanian psychoanalysis squarely within the remit of a human science psychology (opposed to *natural* science [quantitative, experimental, positivistic] psychology):

> Lacanian psychoanalysis provides a significant contribution to the field of
> psychology as a human science because of its emphasis on the exceptional
> importance of human speech . . . and because Lacanian psychoanalysis
> presupposes and entails an ethics of autonomy, meaning and responsibility
> . . . Lacanian psychoanalysis is a fine representative of how human science
> psychology can be pragmatically and productively put into clinical practice.
>
> (2016, pp. 306–307)

To this consideration we should add the fact that many component elements within Lacanian theory – notions of inter-subjectivity, the importance of speech, language and discourse – intersect, even if only tangentially, with concepts within the wider disciplinary field of psychology. Lacan, moreover, clearly adapted a number of psychological concepts in the fashioning of his psychoanalytic theories. The 'mirror-stage', no doubt his single most well-known theory, is derived largely from psychologist Henri Wallon's (1931) earlier conceptualization of the 'mirror test' (Neill, forthcoming; Nobus, 2017). The mirror stage likewise borrows from Charlotte Bühler the 'psychologically generalized' (Lacan, 2006, p. 147) notion of transitivism. (Transitivism is a notion that refers to what we might call 'over-extensions' of the ego: when another child is hit, for example, the perceiving child cries as if s/he'd similarly been struck).[5] Similarly, the Zeigarnik effect, glossed by Lacan as the 'psychological effect produced by an unfinished task' (p. 184), played an important role in theorizing the abrupt halts and suspensions of resolution characteristic of Lacanian clinical practice. [6] The debt to Wallon – who Lacan knew socially – is particularly noteworthy:

> Wallonian thinking played an early role in the development of Lacan's theory. Wallon wrote about the 'the symbol' and 'the image' . . . [which] Lacan was to build upon . . . to arrive at his conception of 'the Symbolic, the Imaginary' . . . Wallon . . . developed themes such as the prematurity of the human baby, transitivism, and the other . . . [considering also] the baby and the image in the mirror – all ideas that became central to Lacanian thinking . . . Among the Wallonian ideas he uses are those of functional anticipation . . . the construction of the body image, and that the recognition of oneself in the mirror comes at the start of the process whereby the child develops from . . . perceiving images to affixing labels and meaning to them.
>
> (Bailly, 2009, p. 22)

The argument can be made that whatever psychological resources are assimilated by Lacan don't remain 'psychological' for very long, for the reason that they are transformed and reformulated (or, following Billig [2006] *misapplied* and *distorted*) by psychoanalytic (re)conceptualization. Nonetheless, the counter-argument can likewise be posited: Lacan still owes a reluctant debt to psychology; the ideas he borrows and 're-invents' never completely transcend their origins as psychological concepts. 'It is . . . perplexing', writes Pavón-Cuéllar (forthcoming),

> to discover how the young Lacan so closely approaches the ego-psychological tendency that led in due course to the [wish] to purify psychoanalytical 'psychology'. . . . understood as an analysis of 'metapsychological propositions' . . . [T]his psychologistic standpoint was diametrically opposed to the mature Lacan's project of . . . going 'beyond psychology' and surpassing 'psychological prejudices'.

One of Lacan's biographers, David Macey, likewise suggests that the early Lacan's work was not as fundamentally opposed to the modes of psychological and biological thought he would subsequently reject:

> Didier Anzieu, who attended Lacan's [early] lecture[s] . . . recalls a talk on
> identification illustrated by the wielding of glass test tubes containing two
> different species of cricket . . . The fact that the behavior of locusts and
> sticklebacks [was] . . . used by Lacan to illustrate the process of identification
> in major papers of the 1950s is a reminder of how much his early theories
> owe to ethology and psychobiology and how little they owe to linguistics.
>
> (1993, p. 36)

None of this is to pave the way for a *rapprochement* between Lacanian theory
and psychology. Here I side with Malone and Friedlander (2000a), Parker (2003,
2015c) and Pavón-Cuéllar (2009, 2013, forthcoming), fellow travellers in the
investigation of Lacan and 'the psychological', who, despite noting the promising
literature exploring links between Lacanian theory and critical/social psychology
(Branney, 2008; Branney, Gough and Madill, 2009; Dashtipour, 2009, 2012;
Malone, 2012; Neill, 2013; Owens, 2009; Parker, 2001; Pavón-Cuéllar, 2010), do
not understate the irreconcilability of these two endeavours. My goal in complicating the 'non-relation' discussed above is simply to suggest that approaching
Lacanian theory from a background in psychology is perhaps not as outrageous as
many Lacanians would maintain. Perilous undertaking as this might be, it is nonetheless important given that certain forms of psychology – typically those of a
more critical, philosophical or human science bent – remain an important first point
of access for many subsequent students and practitioners of psychoanalysis and
Lacanian theory.

The fraught relation between these two bodies of theory may in fact prove
productive. By continually distinguishing Lacanian notions from (what might appear
to be) similar constructs in psychology, we have a better chance of grasping Lacanian
ideas in their distinctiveness. Indeed, a heightened critical and conceptual differentiation might result via such juxtaposition, from an awareness of the apparent
irreconcilability evinced between Lacanian and psychological theory. Non-
resolution and disharmony – two prevailing motifs within Lacanian theory – come
here to assume something of a pedagogical value.

I do not offer a systematic overview of Lacan's varied, often oblique (and typically
derogatory) references to psychology in what follows. I adopt a more selective,
strategic and (hopefully) proactive approach by concentrating on two themes of
pivotal importance to psychoanalysis and psychology alike, the topics of communication and identification. Doing so enables us to distil a series of apparent
intersections – and, as importantly, moments of *dissonance* – between Lacanian theory
and the psychological in a more focused manner. If communication sounds at first
a less than crucial concept in Lacanian theory, we might again refer to Jacques-
Alain Miller: 'Lacan continually worked on the structure of communication', he
notes, 'trying to be more and more precise . . . he always held to the thesis that
psychoanalytic experience makes an unusual use of the general structure of
communication' (1996a, p. 18).[7] Chapters 1, 2 – and to some extent Chapter 3 –
focus on the topic of communication from a distinctively Lacanian perspective.

The concept of identification is perhaps more obviously crucial to psychoanalysis. Speaking of Lacan's theorization of the notion of the imaginary up until his famous Rome Report of 1953, Sheridan (1981) observes: 'Lacan regarded the "imago" [an unconscious mental image influencing a subject's behaviour] as the proper study of psychology and identification as the fundamental psychical process' (p. 279). While Lacan's view on the imago would change over time – the term being eventually dropped from his analytical vocabulary altogether – as the domain of the symbolic increasingly took precedence over that of the imaginary, his attention to identification would nevertheless remain constant. Concentrating on the topic of identification allows us to throw into perspective a series of critical contrasts between Lacanian and psychological conceptualizations. Indeed, more than virtually any other Lacanian problematic it demonstrates the shifts that Lacan's own early thinking underwent in departing from the register of imaginary to resolutely non-psychological symbolic processes of subject formation. Identification is the central theme of Chapters 4 and 5.

Improvising Lacan

In a 2010 interview Slavoj Žižek offered an insightful remark on how we might read Lacan's seminars. Lacan's position in the seminars was not that of the master or even the analyst: 'Lacan . . . defined his own position in his seminars . . . like this: it is not that he is analysing the public; the public is his audience, his big Other, and he literally improvises there' (Žižek, Aristodemou and Frosh, 2010, p. 425). Lacan, in Žižek's view, struggles, extemporizes in the seminars, returning repeatedly to earlier material to correct or supersede the analogues and formulas of previous years. One has this sense in reading the seminars – particularly in respect of Lacan's answers to questions from his audience – that he is in the process of developing, *experimenting* even with various extensions of Freudian thought. This then – contrary perhaps to the 'ideology of Lacanian dogmatism' (Roudinesco, 2014, p. 52) – provides a model for how we might go about introducing and applying Lacanian theory.

Several qualifications are necessary at the outset of any attempt to introduce Lacanian concepts and link them – however tangentially – to another field of conceptualization. First off, a point about periodization: rather than overloading the complexity of theoretical issues by transposing concepts from multiple periods of Lacan's teaching, I have opted – with a few digressions – to focus on Lacan's work in the 1950s in which notions of the symbolic order, the Other, the signifier, inter-subjectivity and the ideas of communication and identification are all clearly prioritized. The 'six moments' in Lacan's work that have supplied the book with its title and that I have taken as springboards for further elucidation and extrapolation are virtually all drawn from this phase of his teaching.

A second qualification concerns the very nature of producing an introductory text: to reduce the complexity of Lacanian thought in favour of clarity and intro-duction, notes Thom (1981), always runs the risk of misleading assimilations.

In opting for an expository approach, I take just such a risk. This danger is potentially redoubled, particularly so when we take to heart Parker's warning that 'The effort to render Lacanian concepts intelligible to an audience of psychologists may thus perform the very problem [it wishes to avoid]', namely 'that Lacan may be thought to be compatible with psychology' (Parker, 2015c, p. 14). I remain open to the charges that what follows is not only simplification, but that it is too 'psychological' by far. My response in each case would be to note that what is presented here is the first step in a journey of progressive distanciations. This seems one of the hallmarks of Lacan's own successive theorizations within psychoanalytic theory: one conceptual step marks its distance from a familiar horizon of thought only to itself be re-worked, and surpassed in a further round of conceptual revisions.

Despite all the foregoing talk of psychology, I have offered nothing by way of a definition. My own preference would be to invoke the term beyond the constraints of any strict or orthodox disciplinary allegiance. The psychological, as I prefer to understand it, is something of a heterogeneous domain, less than rigidly demarcated by the disciplinary codes that seem increasingly to regulate the field. It refers, in an open-ended way, to engagements with human subjectivity, understood via a variety of theoretical, 'critical' and preferably philosophically informed perspectives. [8] All this being said, it remains nevertheless crucial to specify more precisely what I have in mind when referring to psychology as it exists in its disciplinary-codified and hegemonic forms. I follow Ian Parker here, who in his own investigation of the incompatibility between Lacanian theory and psychology speaks of the later as 'the academic and professional domain of theory and practice developed in Western, specifically Anglo-American culture to describe and explain behavioural and mental processes' (2015c, p. 12). If the breadth of this definition sets up the potential of straw-man arguments, let me stress that my aim here is not so much a systematic engagement with (or critique of) psychology as the attempt to refine the concepts and terms of practice of what – at least for Lacan – might be properly called 'psychoanalytic'.

From (Lacanian) moment to moment

Our itinerary of various moments in Lacan begins with a discussion of the concept of 'the big Other' within the context of inter-subjective communication. This Other can be approached in multiple ways, as: the third point which grounds and makes dialogue possible; the assumed point of knowledge and/or authority in discourse ('the subject supposed to know'); and the trans-subjective network of assumed rules governing social behaviour. The chapter provides examples of these aspects of the Other, brought into contrast with George Herbert Mead's (1934) idea of 'the generalized other', and Erving Goffman's (1959) dramaturgical idea of the presentation of self in everyday life. It explores also how many of our commonplace conceptualizations of communication might be challenged by a theorization that allows for no purely 'intra-psychic' life beyond the horizon of the symbolic. Crucial here is the distinction between imaginary and symbolic registers of communication, which function, respectively, to sustain the ego's images of itself, and – more disruptively – to link the subject to a *trans-subjective* order of truth.

Chapter 2 explores the transformative potential of inter-subjective communication, enlarging upon Lacanian notions of the symbolic order, the L-Schema (treated here as Lacan's map of the communicative interchange) and the distinction between 'full' and empty 'speech'. The chapter offers a brief Lacanian engagement with Richard Nixon's admission of Watergate wrongdoings in his famous interviews with David Frost. This example helps animate a number of psychoanalytic concepts – the ideas of founding speech, symbolic registration and the twofold movement of the symbolic – which contrast interestingly with themes in the social psychology of communication, particularly Austin's (1962) notion of speech acts, Pinker's (2007) discussion of indirect speech and Frankfurt's (2005) analysis of bullshit.

Lacan's fascination with the logical conundrum of the prisoner's dilemma takes centre stage in Chapter 3. An investigation of this puzzle provides a means of advancing the Lacanian argument that we need to grasp a logical succession of modes of subjectivity: from subjectivity and inter-subjectivity to a form of *trans-subjective social logic*. Whereas the first of these two modes have been studied in much detail in social psychology (Gillespie and Cornish, 2009; Gillespie and Richardson, 2011), the third, the level of the *trans-subjective*, remains largely neglected. This is problematic, for it is only when the level of trans-subjective social logic is reached that the big Other starts to function and a form of 'social objectivity' becomes possible. The trans-subjective, moreover, proves to be a condition of possibility for the operations of the unconscious. The distinction between the *inter-subjective* and the *trans-subjective* is also vital in appreciating the difference between symbolic and imaginary forms of identification, that is, in understanding how various symbolic gestures – acts of a performative or declarative sort – are important *non-psychological* bases for the making of psychological (or imaginary) identification.

Drawing on Freud's (1921) account of group psychology ('massenpsychologie') and prompted by the growing literature on collective emotion, Chapter 4 considers the phenomenon of mass identification from two interlinked perspectives. The first of these concerns the Freudian idea of libidinal (or affective) ties of attachment. The second, more overtly Lacanian perspective, focuses on the role of symbolic elements, and the distinction between (lateral) imaginary ideal-ego as opposed to (hierarchical) symbolic ego-ideal values. The closing section of the chapter insists upon a Lacanian prioritization of the symbolic and structural above the affective and poses two questions. It is the case, first, that a 'detour through the Other' qualifies many of our most powerful affective experiences? Second, is it so that a degree of artificiality (instances of ritualized enactment, overtly symbolic coding, etc.) is a precondition of the 'authenticity' of emotion?

Chapter 5 questions whether two of Lacan's key theoretical constructs – the master signifier and the notion of the unary trait – enable us to advance what we might call a 'non-psychological' theory of identification. I show, through a discussion of a celebrated master signifier (the name 'Mandela'), how symbolic identifications can be understood less on the basis of the internalization of psychological objects/images than through the operation of master signifiers which function, as nodal points in signification, to anchor a given discourse or subjective libidinal economy. Similarly, the unary trait, as minimal differential element occurring within symbolic identifications, is better characterized as linguistic than in any way psychological, subsisting as it does in the trace or inscription effects of signifiers rather than any purely psychological operation. We are left then with an intriguing depiction of how a type of subjectivity emerges not by means of psychology, defined in the sense of imaginary operations, but as the result of operation of language.

The final chapter picks up and develops several key discontinuities in the psychology/psychoanalysis 'non-relation' that pivot on Lacan's understanding of the subject. I argue that the latter concept – perhaps the most difficult notion within Lacan's work – proves something of a centrepiece in the anti-psychological trajectory of his psychoanalytic theorization. The objective of the chapter is not to systematically work through all of Lacan's criticisms of psychology. The aim is rather to register a selection of such critiques – including the ideas that psychology is 'objectivistic', overly ego-focused, that it wrongly presumes natural scientific, biological, developmental and adaptive perspectives – and to situate them as retrospective backdrop to the explorations of Lacanian theory contained in the foregoing chapters. One can read the trajectory of Lacan's teaching as an ever more assertive and systematic excision of all facets of the psychological. This closing chapter argues that this exclusion of the psychological is particularly pronounced when it comes to the topic of the subject. Indeed, given psychology's multiple 'objectivations', along with its inability to bring the de-natured and divided subject of speech and the signifier into view, we can understand why, for Lacan, there is no – and can be no – *subject* of psychology.

Notes

1   If teaching Lacanian theory within psychology brings with it a variety of problems (to be enumerated throughout the course of this book) there are also, potentially, problems with teaching Lacan outside of the domain of clinical practice: namely that Freudian/ Lacanian concepts are distanced from the field of application for which they were designed and where, arguably, they are most effective and relevant.

2   While Miller (1996b) is admittedly targeting ego psychology here, his comments could be said to stand as of paradigmatic importance for psychology as a whole.

3   Hence, as Samuels (1996) reiterates, the importance of free association as a type of symbolic activity through which one attempts to go beyond the defences of the ego to attain unconscious desires and thoughts.

4   This is not a one-sided story: psychology as a whole has proved, unsurprisingly, unreceptive to Lacan. For a signal instance, see Billig's (2006) damning rejection of Lacan's misuses of psychology.

5   To cite Lacan's (2006) own words: it was Bühler who 'in observing the behaviour of a child with its playmate . . . recognized this transitivism in the striking form of a child being truly captured by another's image' (p. 147).

6   As Parker (2003) notes, the concept was in fact introduced into psychoanalysis by Daniel Lagache in the context of discussions of transference rather than by Lacan himself although it has subsequently found a home in Lacanian theorization.

7   This is not to overlook Lacan's critique of several assumptions underlying the very conceptualization of (intentional, successful, ego-centred) 'communication' as such, something discussed in some detail in Chapter 1.

8   One might cite here a series of journals which maintain a commitment to critical trends in theoretical psychology while remaining receptive to Lacanian theory: *Journal of Philosophical and Theoretical Psychology*; *Frontiers in Psychology*; *Psychoanalysis, Culture & Society*; *Psychology in Society*; *Subjectivity*; and *Theory and Psychology*.

1

IN THE FIELD OF THE OTHER

Towards a Lacanian theory of communication

Lacan, it is often noted, was something of an intellectual magpie, a thinker who was interested, as Élisabeth Roudinesco (2014) emphasizes, in *everything*. One of the disciplinary areas that influenced Lacan's early work was communications theory. Analytical terms derived from this field (notions of entropy, cybernetics, etc.) punctuate his work of the early 1950s, particularly Seminar II. What then, does a Lacanian theory of communication – or indeed, of *non-communication* – look like? I noted in the introduction of this book that the notion of communication is of crucial importance in both psychoanalysis and psychology. It is hence via a Lacanian conceptualization of communication that we can begin addressing our general theme of the relation between Lacanian theory and the psychological.

The central contention of this chapter, broadly stated, is that Lacanian psycho-analysis provides a unique means of distinguishing two fundamental registers of communication. The first of these occurs along what Lacan dubs the 'imaginary axis'. This is the domain of inter-subjectivity that serves the ego and functions to support and consolidate the images subjects use to substantiate themselves. The second register – far more disturbing and unpredictable – occurs along the symbolic axis. It links the subject to a *trans-subjective* order of truth, it provides them with a set of socio-symbolic co-ordinates, and it ties them into a variety of roles and social contracts. Importantly, it entails the radical alterity of what Lacan refers to as 'the Other'.

There is a specific analytical device that Lacanian theory offers in respect of the conceptualization of communication. Drawing on the inspiration of earlier diagrammatic portrayals of the communicative process (such as that of Shannon and Weaver, 1949), Lacan devised a rudimentary schema with which he hoped to differentiate the noise of everyday *imaginary* (or 'empty') speech from the disruptive potential of a form of *symbolic* (or 'full') speech. The latter was, in Lacan's view, capable of delivering truth and – as one would hope of the psychoanalytical process – effecting change in its speakers. One of my objectives here is to provide an outline of the device in question, namely Lacan's 'L-Schema', a conceptual map that allows us to isolate the key elements underlying imaginary as opposed to symbolic modes of exchange.[1]

The symbolic third

Where to begin then with a Lacanian theorization of communication? Perhaps with an elementary assertion: any dialogue, any form of inter-subjectivity, needs to be grounded in something other than the standpoints of its individual participants. Any dialogue, that is to say, presupposes a third party. This much is evident in the case of two people from different cultural backgrounds who meet for the first time and are able to converse, simply by virtue of sharing the same language. Such a common feature – a quite literal *lingua franca* – cannot originate in or belong to either person; it must be 'Other', heterogeneous to both.

Communication, as such, always entails *a third point of reference*, a 'third place in discourse', which is external to both speaker and listener. This 'third place' typically functions implicitly, discretely, even though it often *feels* as if there really are only two perspectives involved in any dialogical interchange. Then again, when meaning breaks down or when conflict emerges, the importance of this third becomes apparent. The role of such an external authority – take for example a code of ethics or a set of institutional procedures – provides a means of settling disagreements. It is via a *symbolic*, which is to say an extra-subjective, point of appeal that a means of adjudicating such conflicts becomes possible.

Should we wish to diagrammatize this principle of a third, we might opt to superimpose a vertical upon a horizontal axis (see Figure 1.1). The horizontal axis represents the one-to-one exchange of inter-subjective dialogue. The vertical axis – which both stands outside of and anchors this line of exchange – stands for the symbolic axis of human exchange. It includes reference to an external third, and it is to be contrasted with the imaginary axis of such inter-subjective dialogues occurring between an ego and its others. The Lacanian name for this third, which functions as an amassed collection of social conventions and laws, indeed, as an embodiment of authority and/or truth, is the Other (capital 'O' so as to distinguish it from those others who function as effective alter egos).[2]

Here it helps to reinforce the elementary distinction, insisted upon by Lacan in Seminar III, between the other as inter-subjective counterpart and *the* symbolic Other. The former concerns those who count as reflections of my own ego and who might function as my own mirror image. It is in respect of such others that I will experience both aggressive rivalries and idealized relations of narcissistic love. Such imaginary others are *ego-equivalents* with whom inter-subjective relations are possible. The big Other by contrast, the third place, stands beyond the realm of imaginary identifications; it exists outside of the frame of such games of mirrored wholeness and antagonism. Lacan offers the following distinction:

> There is the other as imaginary. It's here in the imaginary relation with the other that traditional *Selbst-Bewusstein* or self-consciousness is instituted . . . There is also the Other who speaks from my place, apparently this Other who is within me. This is an Other of a totally different nature from my other, my counterpart.
>
> (1993, p. 241)

'Can I get a witness?'

The Other operates not only as a locus of intelligibility but as a principle of appeal. It signifies the prospect – indeed, the apparent *inescapability* – of symbolic mediation (hence, diagrammatically, the diagonal lines linking each communicator to the Other). The Other, furthermore, plays a role in affirming subjective experience, making it a 'confirmed reality'. We can take up this idea in reference to what might seem a rather prosaic example. What is the first thing we do upon receiving 'big news'? If – presuming for the time being that it is good news – we receive it in a private capacity, surely our first impulse is to share it with some Other? While there is an obvious interpersonal element here – wanting to share happy news with those one cares about – there is also a broader form of symbolic registration at work. It is as if in 'logging' the news it is confirmed, made official. In the case of bad news, of course, the opposite may hold: we may try and withhold the news from others – indeed from *the* Other – waiting for the appropriate time to share it, if sharing it all.[3]

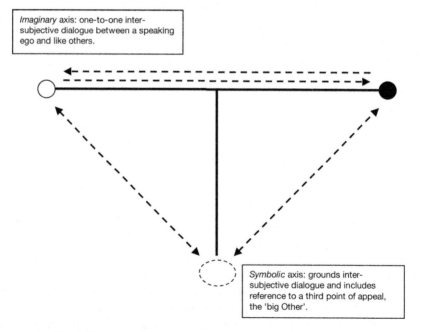

Imaginary axis: one-to-one inter-subjective dialogue between a speaking ego and like others.

Symbolic axis: grounds inter-subjective dialogue and includes reference to a third point of appeal, the 'big Other'.

FIGURE 1.1 Symbolic and imaginary axes of communicative activity

Consider the "record-breaking" performances of athletes that cannot be recognized as such because they occurred within training as opposed to under formal conditions of competition. One or two witnesses or other participants in the training session will not count. A verifying authority needs to be present, an Other that amounts to more than any singular form of subjectivity. The very notion of a *record*, inasmuch as it presumes not just a type of witnessing, but a *form of verification and historical documentation*, implies precisely this notion of an authorizing Other.

Some years ago at a picnic I watched two children they went around the garden, gathering a variety of natural specimens (flowers, oddly shaped stones, dead bugs, etc.), which they then brought to show their father. The given 'find' would only count as such once it had been recognized by him. What was in question was more than just a naming operation, or the settling of a dispute (although it was to some degree this also: the children's deliberations over what they had found were only settled once their father supplied the appropriate signifier). It involved also a validation of sorts, and not only of what had been found, but of the children themselves.

This is, of course, a continual parental task, the *marking* of the achievements of one's children ('Well done!', 'Good job!' 'You did it, you clever thing!'), and it gives us a clue to the oft-repeated request made by children: 'Look at me mommy!' I initially found the related parental remark 'Look at you!' somewhat puzzling. The social function of the remark – that of exclaiming upon, underlining an achievement of the child's – seemed clear enough. Yet there was an obvious redundancy involved: in making such a comment one is obviously already involved in doing the looking – why then the need again to issue the imperative to look? Why indeed, unless of course the request to look is *directed at someone else, to a point of recognition* existing beyond that of the perspectives of the child and parent alike?

The consensus-establishing function of the big Other is also of interest here. We might refer back to our example of two people in dialogue: if inter-subjectivity were merely a matter of two conversing subjectivities trying to make sense of one another, then conflicts would be intractable. Two opposed perspectives, each unable to make recourse to anything other than their own frame of reference, would surely result in irresolvable conflicts. This is the terrain of Lacan's imaginary register.[4] This domain is as much characterized by the ego's self-love as by its limitless potential for rivalry and aggression. Given that in such circumstances there is no principle of external mediation, and that only one side can ultimately win, we are left with what amounts to a Hegelian 'struggle to the death'. We might take the example here of legal conflicts, or, more particularly, the apparent intractability of divorce disputes and custody battles. Things get hopelessly muddied in such a rivalry of competing egos; there are two conflicting versions of events, each of which is anchored into its own self-interested subjective reality. The only thing that can be ascertained with objective certainty here is the principle of the relevant law.

Third-party appeals

One way of understanding the alterity of the big Other, that is, the fact that it cannot be fixed at the level of inter-subjectivity, is simply to stress that this Other encapsulates the entirety of the symbolic domain. This is the Other as the 'treasury of the signifier', as the sum total of signifying elements, expressions and utterances within a given language or cultural milieu. We can enlarge upon this, insisting that the symbolic Other is akin to the amassed roles, rules and unwritten obligations that define a given societal situation. The Other can thus be viewed as an alienating system, an always-already-existing collectivity of signifiers that the subject needs to accommodate themselves to. It is the ever-shifting constellation of norms and social values with which there can be no automatic or harmonious fit.

The distance of this Lacanian coneptualization from everyday conceptions of psychological subjectivity, from notions of the self, is pronounced. We are here confronted with a kind of supra-agency – be it that of language, the entire accumulated mass of 'the social' – which speaks through, or over us, which appears to *determine* the subject. In the tussle between psychological subjectivity and the role of determining structure, the Lacanian notion of the Other is on the side of structure. Ed Pluth underlines this when he insists that 'Lacan's attention to the symbolic register forces us to account for the subject's origin in terms of signifiers that have a place that is external to or beyond the child . . . [an origin] "in" the Other functioning as a "transcendental locus"' (forthcoming).

Picture two sporting teams engaged in a competition. This situation provides us with an effective sketch of the narcissistic ego-logic of the imaginary register. Despite the likeness, the equivalence between players – each team member has an opposing number on the other side - both teams want to defeat their opponent. Platitudes aside, there is no concession from either side that the opposing team might be as deserving of recognition or that the question of who wins is a matter of indifference to them.

Now although things sometimes get out of hand in such contests – scuffles between players, aggressive exchanges, etc. – such bad-tempered interchanges are, as a rule, brought to an end by the intervention of a referee. Unlawful confrontations of this sort are cut short; calls for verification from the Other quickly take precedence. Protestations of unfairness, appeals for a decision ('Penalty!', 'Off-side!'), are thus addressed to the figure who oversees the game.[5] What must be noted here is that this Other – who embodies the rules of the game, who is *the* point of appeal for the players – cannot be assimilated into the 'horizontal' level of the one-to-one interactions of the competing players. Simply put: the Other remains necessarily beyond the level of dyadic inter-subjectivity. A referee would not be able to adjudicate, to make crucial judgements ('Goal!', 'No goal!'), to provide a type of symbolic registration, if this were not the case.

In terms of the *symbolic* axis of communication then, to reiterate the point made above, we are concerned with something more than merely *taking another's perspective*, which, after all, would not remove us from the level of imaginary inter-subjectivity. We cannot, for example, imagine a referee, who in order to make a crucial decision, adopts an empathic posture, and puts him or herself in the subjective position of one of the players . . .

So, what is often taken as an ideal of communicative efficacy (or indeed, as a rudimentary ethical gesture) – the attempt to 'see something from the other's point of view' – is not necessarily a goal of effective communicative change. It is likewise, from a Lacanian perspective at least, decidedly not an ethical ideal. That is to say: there is no easy stepping outside of ego-subjectivity within the perspective of the ego itself; there is no imaginary assumption of 'how the other sees it' that succeeds in bracketing one's own ego. This paradox should be emphasized: the attempt to 'put myself in the shoes of an other' occurs *via one's own ego*, so the very gesture of empathic inter-subjectivity really only reaffirms my ego (i.e. the logic here is that of how *I think* they see it).

A maxim of Lacanian clinical practice comes to the fore here: it is only via the Other, by means of the symbolic enunciations that patients make, that they and what they are speaking about (however indirectly) can be approached in a (relatively) ego-bracketed fashion.[6] Michael Miller (2011) accordingly stresses that clinicians should be attuned not to the *inferred content* of a patient's discourse, but 'to the letter' of *actually enunciated* speech. Such a literal approach, he stresses, involves less of a leap of theoretical faith than does an approach 'which takes as its source the inferred content of the patient's speech and behaviour' (p. 52). Inferring contents, distilling apparent themes, or making interpretive assumptions about what patients say, invariably says more about the analyst's own ego than it does about the patient.

It is for these reasons that Lacanian clinicians remain wary of attempts to see things from the perspective of others and avoid making assumptions about what their patients are thinking or feeling. In such instances, the other becomes all too easily a prop for the (clinician's) ego's own self-realization.[7] Hence the Lacanian critique of 'counter-transference' as a means of interpreting the patient's current emotional state (i.e. comments such as: 'I am feeling anxious in this setting, which makes me wonder if *you* are feeling agitated'). For Lacan these are at basis ego-centred interpretations that foreground the clinician's own ego even while claiming access to the other.[8]

'(To) whom am I speaking?'

I have stressed both the omnipresence of the Other in communication (the Other as a 'hovering interlocutor' that makes dialogue work) and the role of the Other as 'the subject supposed to know', that is, the Other as principle of truth or authority. The Other can also be said to exist in appeals to posterity, as the dimension of history. This idea can be further elaborated via a series of examples.

Who, we might ask, are the epitaphs on tombstones addressed to? Obviously, at the most direct and circumscribed level, they are addressed to the loved ones of the departed person, those people who gathered at his or her funeral, and their immediate community. Then again, it would seem that such epitaphs are also addressed to an Other audience that exceeds the amassed subjectivity of a given time and place. This is one of the reasons that Lacan's notion of the Other cannot be viewed as the equivalent of social psychology's 'generalized other' (Mead, 1934) (discussed in more detail below); we are not merely dealing with an aggregate of subjectivities here.

Something else is present in the Other, an element of the historical beyond. The Other is always characterized by the impossibility of full comprehension, by the prospect of a future exceeding our own situation. What holds for funereal rites likewise holds for obituaries: why the need to publish an announcement of the death (or for that matter, the birth) of persons that, insofar as the vast majority of the public is concerned, remain unknown? Who are such messages directed towards, other than to the Other of history itself?

Consider the Place Vendôme Column, erected in Paris in 1805 to celebrate Napoleon's military victories. A long historical sequence is depicted: a series of Napoleon's campaigns unfold in a spiralling bas-relief of 425 bronze plates stretching from the base of the column to the tip. In and of itself, this architectural form seems less than puzzling, until we ask the question: who would ever be in a position to read the narrative events thus depicted?

The answer is *no one*, unless an elaborate system of scaffolding was to be constructed around the structure such that spectators could effectively climb around the column, reading its images sequentially, from bottom to top. The same holds of any number of historical monuments which bear inscriptions that are often impossible to read with the naked eye. Although such monuments are located in public places, and are meant to have an impact on their audience, their primary addressee supersedes the empirical bounds of any one given set of spectators. Monuments of this sort are messages to no one else so much as the Other of history itself. This example helps emphasize that the messages we send are never directed exclusively to one singular (or obviously-intended) recipient. Their itinerary always involves the prospect of an Other addressee.

This lesson of an extra-subjective recipient applies also to our everyday social activities and to the domain of 'intra-subjective' thinking. Both such situations involve implicitly addressing an extra-subjective interlocutor, an Other. The question then deserves to be asked of virtually any 'private' signification I indulge in: 'To whom am I (implicitly) speaking?' and, perhaps as importantly, 'What is it that I want to let them know?', 'What message am I performing for them?'.

This provides one way of applying Lacan's notion that 'a letter always reaches its destination': what is ostensibly a purely subjective message, an utterance meant seemingly for no one but myself is nevertheless legible to big Other, who assuredly receives the letter, even though in retrospect we might prefer it had never been sent.

A second degree of Otherness

In May 1957, Lacan offered an intriguing description of the Other, which has been adeptly paraphrased by Muller and Richardson (1982) as follows:

> ... who 'is this other to whom I am more attached than to myself, since, at the heart of my assent to my own identity it is still he who agitates me'? ... Evidently it is not an 'other' subject, nor is it to be discovered through an 'awareness of others' ... In terms of other subjects, the 'other' in question here 'can be understood only at a second degree of otherness', through which it is still in a 'position of mediating' between me and other subjects. ... As such it is the 'guarantor of the truth' and of 'good faith'.
>
> (p. 172)

Several aspects of this description deserve our attention, particularly perhaps the idea of the Other as existing 'at the heart of my assent to my own identity' (p. 172). The paradox here seems clear enough – the radical alterity of this Other stands – so it appears – between the subject and their own subjectivity. Malcolm Bowie offers a useful formulation here, stressing that Lacan's Other includes both 'short-range' and 'long-range' definitions: '[I]t designates now one member of the dialectical couple "Subject-Other" and now the limitless field and over-riding condition in which both members find themselves ... [of] "alterity", "otherness"' (Bowie, 1991, p. 83). Up until now I have stressed the second facet of Bowie's description, the idea that the Other occupies a point outside psychological inter-subjectivity. This helps us avoid a potential misreading – and indeed, a psychologiza-tion – of the notion of the Other. This is the idea that the Other might be reduced to an individual's perspective, viewed merely as extension of a given subject's personality.

For Lacanian theory it is not the case that we each possess our own self-determined Other. The Other cannot be reduced in this way, it cannot be 'privatized', extracted from the symbolic order that it encapsulates. Given that this issue strikes to the heart of the relation between Lacan and the psychological, it is worth underlining this fact: the Other is not a 'psychological' concept; *it cannot be collapsed into the imaginary (or egoic) individuality of any singular subject.*

The Other arises from symbolic activity, from speech, from communicative behaviours, from the use of signifiers. The Other then, is not, and never can be a sub-category of the ego. It pays here to turn to Lacan's own descriptions of this concept. When, in 'The Instance of the Letter in the Unconscious' Lacan invokes the notion of the Other, he stresses 'the radical ex-centricity of one to himself with which man is confronted', along with the fact of 'a radical heteronomy gaping within man' (Lacan, cited in Muller and Richardson, pp. 171–172) brought about by the use of language, signifiers.[9]

Our example of competing sports teams helps reiterate the point: the players cannot each abide solely by the parameters of their 'own Other'. If each were to play according to their own rules, the game would collapse into a state of chaos. Interestingly, it is often just this – the issue of agreed upon rules – that proves a sticking point in the co-operative games of young children. The big Other has not yet adequately taken root in such situations, and as such rule-structured games often fail, because children prefer to make their own rules rather than following the rules of the Other.

Is it not however inevitable that the Other will at same level be 'individualized'? We need here to be attentive to the difference between the symbolic order, that is, the functioning of language, the system of laws, the network of roles, on the one hand, and how the subject grapples with this anonymous system, how a workable (but never fully knowable) version of this symbolic is installed *for them* on the other. So, while it is true that the Other can be approached as the symbolic domain *as particularized for the subject*, no such Other – at least in a non-psychotic universe – is 'private', cut adrift from the symbolic network that we share with others. So it remains true of course that the various members of a team may have differing *interpretations* of the rules of the game, and very different *impressions* of the referee. Ultimately however there must be a functional Other, a discrete locus of judgement and authority if the game is to work at all. By virtue of the fact that we are communicating at all, that a rudimentary symbolic sociality (a 'rules of engagement') is in place, we can be sure that an Other – a nexus of conventions irreducible to singular subjectivity – is already functioning.

On 'meta-truth'. . . . and the Other that lacks

Before leaving our sporting example we should draw attention to a type of truth-of-consensus that is in operation in such contexts. As every sports fan knows, what 'counts' according to a referee's decision does not necessarily reflect what actually occurred on the playing field. The Other, simply put, is sometimes in error. Apparently authoritative yet nonetheless inconsistent, the Other – as Lacan's later (2007) work insists – is imperfect, lacking, subject to error. So what ultimately 'goes down in history' regards a sporting event is not what (I might think) *really* happened. It is what the referee declares that stands as the historical record. There is a kind of over-riding 'meta-truth' at work here, because even if we disagree with the referee's decision, what we do not dispute is the parameters of the rules of the game or, indeed, the referee's mandate to implement them.

Can there be a kind of temporary slippage between the (little) other and the big Other? Absolutely. Another subject may fleetingly occupy the position of the Other for a subject. This is true of persons who occupy positions of authority, who – like the referee – dispense judgements or embody the law or truth. We might cite also here the case of the stranger who interrupts an intensely private conversation, and who thus represents the presence of appropriate social norms of conversation and decorum.[10] These examples, incidentally, underline an important qualification: we should not fix the Other in any one personage, or view it in a static way as embodied only in certain lofty or powerful figures. The notion of the Other must, by contrast, be grasped as a *functional principle* rather than as concretely personified or historically fixed position.

Moreover, the Other, although typically afforded a general stability – in the lives of neurotic as opposed to psychotic subjects that is – is never whole or complete ('fully knowable'). Which is to say: the Other emerges rather in a state of constant re-negotiation, indeed, as a question or effect of authority posed by *signifiers* rather than subjects. We can provide two examples of the 're-negotiation' of the Other. The governing bodies of given sports often revise the rules the game. Similarly, theological debates are – under certain conditions – permitted in respect of the meaning of key passages of holy texts. These examples underline the point of how crucial the function of the Other is in social and symbolic societies. As Borch-Jacobsen (1991) stresses, it is this symbolic factor, the framework of convention, of consensual rules and regulating principles, that enables a pacification of fractious human relations, that makes the transformation of a state of 'egos at war' into genuine social ties possible.

The trans-individual versus the 'intra-psychic'

What is by now perhaps apparent is that there is, for Lacan, no purely 'intra-psychic' domain that exists beyond the range of the symbolic. The Other is indivisible from human subjectivity and psychical functioning as such. Malone and Friedlander (2000b) make the same argument in respect of the notion of 'the self': 'Subjective structures are not situated within "the self" – they function trans-individually' (p. 8). This idea, that the unconscious is not intra-psychic, but is *external, distributed*, apparent in the operations of spoken language, has a pragmatic clinical implication. Clinicians should not appeal to some or other reality beyond that of speech itself. Parker (2015c) extends this, insisting that we should oppose conceptualizations that treat the unconscious as if it is '"preverbal" or "inside" the individual . . . [or] located in the brain' (p. 20). Hence the value of Lacan's oft-repeated dictums that 'the unconscious is the discourse of the Other (i.e. that it is not "inside" the subject), that it is a discourse, and that it is structured like a language (i.e. that it is not "preverbal")' (Parker, 2015a, pp. 79–80). Moreover:

> The claim that we should search under the surface of spoken interaction and excavate a deeper reality behind language serves to mislead us as to where the unconscious is and how it works.
>
> (Parker, 2015c, p. 10)

This is not to say that individuals do not see and experience themselves in such imaginary ways, that is, as endowed with rich forms of individual subjectivity that escape the horizon of the Other's influence. Such views are the stuff of the ego, productions of a type of imaginary misrecognition (or *méconnaissance*). Despite the ego's convictions to the contrary, the subject cannot exempt themselves from symbolic mediation.[11] From a Lacanian standpoint, in even the most pronounced circumstances of separation or exclusion we remain accompanied by a kind of 'hovering interlocutor'.[12] The Other can be understood as the very medium of symbolic pronouncement, the symbolic means through which our communications to others – and indeed, to ourselves (our 'own' thoughts, ideas) – are possible.

We might develop this idea in a rhetorical fashion, asking: How come even my most 'brute', immediate, ostensibly 'non-mediated' responses take on an immanently *symbolic* form ('Oh God!', 'Jesus Christ!')? Why is it that even in my most private moments – say of frustration or anger – I nonetheless utilize 'public language' (or signs, or gestures)? Why would some 'private' word, some made-up term or gesture all of my own not suffice? Furthermore: why is it that in such situations – of often intense affective intensity – I remain still caught up in the process of making meaning – at least potentially – for some Other? A related issue: why is it that a private outburst of rage, assuredly seen by no one, is so typically accompanied (certainly for the neurotic subject) by the reflexivity of 'how it may have been seen'?

What is being insisted upon here – a notably 'extra-psychological' position – is the radical contingency, the *externality* of even our most private expressions. We have a sense in the above examples of how meaning might be said to come from the Other. Any act of signification is only intelligible, only indeed *possible* against a background framework of rules and presuppositions that co-determines my meaning.

The impossibility of escaping the Other is nicely explored in the Robert Redford film *All Is Lost* (2013). Redford plays a solo yachtsman who is hundreds of miles out at sea when he realizes that his vessel is slowly sinking. Despite the solitary conditions of his plight, his attempts to remedy – and make sense of – his situation invariably invoke the Other. This occurs both in his desperate bids at communication (he places a message in a bottle and throws it out to sea) and in his expressions (such as the scream of frustration with which he signals the futility of his attempts to save himself).

We might take the question of profanity here. An offensive word, if it is to function as such, must *offend*, which is to say that it must *be understood*, first (a 'private' word of my own making won't do), and be understood, furthermore, precisely *as offending* some Other. If no one is there to be scandalized by a given obscenity, then it doesn't effectively work as an obscenity. The world of profanity requires stable conventions of meaning, a consensus as to what is generally offensive. To trade insults likewise requires a shared agreement between involved parties that the degrading signifiers in question are *actually insulting*. That is to say: in using profane language, as in indulging in offensive actions of gestures, one demonstrates an implicit understanding of the Other. Neither such instance of communication can be said to work without a mutual point of reference, without the Other as site of agreed meaning.

The theatre of the everyday

While the Other for Lacan functions both so as to co-ordinate communicative efforts (as the third in any dialogue) and as providing the medium of communication (as the treasury of the signifier), it also remains, as already noted, 'incomplete'. What I mean to reiterate here is that – to put it in Lacanian jargon – the Other itself *lacks* (indeed, *desires*). The Other, moreover, constantly elicits questions and affirmations on the part of its subjects; it is the focus of considerable guess-work and subjective speculation. Dany Nobus (2000) asserts that 'the big Other is nothing but the dimension of . . . others that remains unknown to the speaker', adding that 'the Other entails the recognized, yet never fully ascertained aspect of [one's] . . . addressee' (p. 12). Stavrakakis (2007) likewise highlights that the Other is, by definition, unsatisfying, alienating:

> it is exactly this impossibility, this lack in the Other, which keeps desire – and history – alive. We never get what we have been promised, what we were expecting from the Other, but that's exactly why we keep longing for it.
>
> (p. 47)

This implies a further crucial idea: we as subjects constantly call upon, reiterate and thus reinstate the Other. Žižek (2006) insists that the Other is, strictly speaking, virtual in nature; the Other, he affirms, is a (trans)subjective presupposition which exists only insofar as we *act as if it exists*. We need the Other, no doubt, but the Other likewise needs believing subjects if it is to operate as a functional principle. Just as the Other cannot be reduced to the (imaginary, ego-dimension of the) subject, so the Other itself cannot be said to exist *without* subjects.

'Generalized' versus the symbolic Other

A brief digression is warranted here, so as to properly distinguish Lacan's symbolic Other from an intersecting yet importantly different conceptualization, namely that of the 'generalized Other' as developed by George Herbert Mead (1934). Mead's classic formulation is as follows:

> The organized community or social group which gives to the individual his unity of self may be called 'the generalized other'. The attitude of the generalized other is the attitude of the whole community.
>
> (1934, p. 154)

This succinct formulation is followed by a striking passage:

> If the given human individual is to develop a self in the fullest sense, it is not sufficient for him merely to take the attitudes of other human individuals towards himself and towards one another . . . [Nor is it sufficient] to bring that social process as a whole into his individual experience merely in these terms: he must also, in the same way that he takes the attitudes of other individuals towards himself and towards one another, *take their attitudes*

> *towards the various phases or aspects of the common social activity or set of social*
> *undertakings in which, as members of an organized society or social group, they are*
> all engaged . . . [H]e must then . . . generaliz[e] these individual attitudes of
> that organized society or social group itself, as a whole.
>
> (Mead, 1934, pp. 154–155, *emphasis added*)

In Mead (1934) then, as in Lacan, there is a sense that society, the social mass, in all its complexities and diversity, needs a stand-in, a set of workable suppositions accommodated in the figure of a hypothetical other.

That the presumed other might be reliably knowable, able to confer stability, or, indeed, afford *a unity of self*, is clearly where their respective conceptualizations part ways. For Mead (1934), this generalized other provides the basis for a type of cognitive mapping of the social, a way of knowing and orienting the self. While this might be said to hold true also, to a degree, for Lacan, the key difference is that for him, such assurances are never long-lasting. So while it is true that the Other must attain a temporary degree of stability – certainly so for neurotic or non-psychotic subjects – the factor of the ultimate unknowability of the Other, the fact that the Other keeps subjects guessing, querying, wondering – indeed, *fantasizing* – is a fundamental aspect of the psychoanalytic concept.

Lacan's Other is never wholly reassuring; the proximity of the Other (or, of *the desire of the Other*, to be more precise) is one of the Lacanian formulas of anxiety (Lacan, 2014). The notion of the Other, moreover, typically invokes a variety of dimensions, such as a desire for recognition, the aspect of the historical beyond and (as we will go on to see) the factor of the symbolic registration, that are absent in Mead's theorization.

Nevertheless, Mead's (1934) conceptualization does offer something of interest from a Lacanian perspective. He perspicaciously distinguishes three levels of sociality: the inter-subjectivity of attitude-formation; the development of a schema of the social whole; and, importantly, a sense of how the attitudes of others are deployed and understood *in relation to how such others participate within shared social activities*. This third level of social activity – the engagement of others with the Other, as we might put it – will be a key concern in Chapter 3 where I retrace Lacan's discussion of the Prisoner's Dilemma.

We may conclude then that while Mead (1934) provides the basis of a nuanced engagement with subjectivity, his conceptualization remains primarily psycho-logical in nature. Indeed, inasmuch as it is concerned with the development of attitudes, his generalized other remains largely within the horizon of the imaginary, an imaginary aggregation of the community.[13] Lacan's notion, by contrast, is predominantly symbolic in nature; it is concerned with symbolic processes, the operation of the signifier and the functionality of language. Moreover, Lacan's concept involves desire; as will be explained further as we continue, it is a *desiring* Other that the subject relates to in terms of their own desire and lack.

As we will see time and time again – an assertion which speaks to our general theme of the relation between Lacanian psychoanalysis and the psychological –

Lacan prefers explanations of 'the signifier' (of language and structure) over explanations of psychological attributes and processes. We should as such complete a further step in our account of the Other by approaching it first and foremost as an effect of symbolic processes and language. We should likewise be wary of reducing the Other to the psychological stuff of attributions, self-reflexivity and attitudes. Mead's (1934) concept, as firmly (social) psychological in nature, and as reliant on just such psychological thinking, clearly cannot be characterized in the same way as Lacan's big Other. The generalized other is clearly not a primarily linguistic or language-based phenomenon.

The locus of speaking

We can recap much of the foregoing discussion by highlighting two intertwined lines of enquiry. The first concerns the irreducibility of the symbolic for human subjectivity and the associated idea that in speaking, in *signifying*, I open myself up to an Other horizon of intelligibility.[14] The second has to do with the constant presence of a symbolic addressee or 'hovering interlocutor', that is, with the presumption of an external site or recipient to which my social acts are implicitly directed. If the first of these themes stresses an internal locus of the Other, the second implies something decidedly exterior to the subject. Where then should we situate the Other: inside or outside the subject?

Stressing the role of the Other-as-language (as symbolic functioning) helps make sense of the apparent contradiction between the Other as *external* point of reception and inherent possibility *within* the speaking subject. The Other, notes Leader (2000), is not only the set of elements that make up the symbolic world the subject is born into, it is also the symbolic place which is present *each time that someone speaks*. We have thus the Other apparently 'inside' us, as the foreign language – or 'mOther tongue' to use Fink's (1995) helpful phrase – that we rely upon in our attempts at expression. And yet there is also the 'outside' Other, the Other as the set of communicative rules and symbolic codes which forms the grounds and basis of all attempts at meaning-making. This, we might say, is the Other as a *locus of listening*:

> The Other is a place *from which you are heard*, from which you are recognized. The Other is thus the place of language, external to the speaker, and yet, since he or she is a speaker, internal at the same time.
>
> (Leader, 2000, p. 60)

It helps in grasping this apparent double location of the Other to draw attention to how each act of speaking presupposes a point of reception, a place of intelligibility from which the speaker might – however imperfectly – be understood. This is a constant refrain in Lacan: each instance of speech presupposes a listener, a recipient, an interlocutor or, perhaps more directly, a 'frame of listening'. 'To speak is first of all to speak to others', Lacan states in 1955 (1993, p. 36). To which he later adds: '[T]here is no speech without a response . . . even if it meets only with silence' (2006, p. 216). Even an internal monologue presupposes a field of reception, an addressee. An act of speaking instantiates an Other; the structural position of speech *is*, in this sense, the Other.

An interesting developmental perspective can be introduced here. Leader (2003) cites a series of studies from linguistics and child psychology that concentrate on the period during which the Other starts to operate within the speech of children. The use of connectives, he comments, often indexes the presence of the Other: when children start to use terms such as 'and' and 'but' it indicates the supposed presence of another speaker. This, interestingly, is supported by studies of linguistic development. Ruth Weir's (1962) research on 'crib speech', as cited by Leader, demonstrates that the 'private' monologues of infants typically takes the form of dialogues, despite that they are, in effect, single-person dialogues. Weir (1962) noted that the crib speech of infants contained a high frequency of imperatives (i.e. verbs used in giving orders, making requests). The gradual internalization of such imperatives – which we can consider as speech coming from the Other – was evident when infants begin *addressing themselves* in this way, indeed, when imperatives come to be transformed into declaratives (i.e. self-based declarations). The proto-sociality of such early speech is striking, and the Lacanian conclusion is clear: the Other has begun to play its part in the self-dialoguing speech of the infant.

Focusing on the role of the Other in a patient's discourse (and, as importantly, the role of the *desiring* or *enjoying* Other), can prove useful, diagnostically. While I cannot hope to do justice to this topic here – doing so would require a considerable detour to describe the various Lacanian diagnostic structures (psychosis, neurosis, perversion, etc.) (see Fink, 1997; Nobus, 2000; Rodriguez, 2004; Swales, 2012; Verhaeghe, 2004) – a few scattered examples may serve in lieu of a more systematic engagement. Left to speak on their own, neurotic patients tend to maintain the rhythms of conversational turn-taking; they anticipate contributions, interjections and questions on the part of their listener. The Other, in short, is a consistent and stable presence. In the speech of psychotic patients, by contrast, one would expect to find that the Other has been less securely installed, indeed that meaning is not anchored in conventional understandings (as in schizophrenia) or indeed that the big Other function has taken on an excessive, persecutory and overtly *externalized* role (paranoia).[15] Speaking more generally of psychosis, Gherovici and Steinkoler (2015) note that

> The psychotic is spoken by the Other, as manifested in the delusions, usually experienced as thoughts coming from the exterior, imposing themselves from without. The psychotic is subjected to the Other without mediation through intruding ideas, hallucinations, voices, imposed thoughts and commands.
>
> (p. 30)

The Other is very differently present in the speech of the hysterical subject, who does whatever they can to make themselves the object of the Other's desire and fascination. In becoming the object of the Other's desire the hysteric attempt to master this desire, and, as importantly, to maintain it, extending it wherever possible in the form of an unfulfilled desire, making possible thus their own role as desired object, desire's lack (Fink, 1997). The obsessional neurotic also adopts a distinctive posture, refuting not just the contingencies of their own lack and thereby their own desire, but also the desire and the lack of the Other. The obsessional wishes to negate and refute the possibility of lack in the Other least it open up to many uncertainties, too many unsettling desires, in their own lives. Hence the presenting picture of the obsessional as – to paraphrase Fink (1997) – as ostensibly whole, complete, someone who does not suffer lack, a person who fiercely refuses to see themselves as in any way dependent on the Other.[16]

Let us return though to the question of the location of the Other. Lacan's concept seems to collapse the intuitive inside/outside distinction. The Other is inherent in all of our expressive attempts, no matter how personalized or private. This much is difficult to deny, for such expressive attempts are, after all, based on the use of 'borrowed' signifiers that are never simply internal to or solely possessed by individual subjects. Yet, given the 'unowned' nature of such signifiers – which typically possess a lengthy history far surpassing the subject's own comprehension – even their most carefully crafted utterances remain, in a very significant sense, foreign.[17] The issue then is not whether the Other is 'in' or 'out', but how the inside/outside distinction needs to be rethought in terms of a trans-subjective unconscious that is simultaneously neither (in any exclusive sense) and both.

Renata Salecl (1998) adds an informative gloss on the issue of the location of Other. The big Other, she says, is the symbolic structure in which the subject is always-already embedded; it is not, as such, a positive social fact:

> it is quasi-transcendental, and forms the frame structuring our perception of reality; its status is normative, it is a world of symbolic rules and codes. As such, it also does not belong to the psychic level: it is a radically external, non-psychological universe of symbolic codes regulating our psychic self-experience. It is a mistake either to internalize the big Other and reduce it to a psychological fact, or to externalize the big Other and reduce it to institutions in social reality.
>
> (Salecl, 1998, p. 17)

The Other, explained in such terms, exists indivisibly between the psychical and the structural; it occurs at the shifting intersection between the subjective and the societal, without being reducible to either.

Statement/enunciation

Emphasizing the importance of the role of the Other as addressee adds a degree of complexity to how we may have understood the determining role of *the receiver* of given communication. The message I send is always in part a function of *whom it is sent to*. This recipient plays a determining role in its success; they make something of it, recognize something in it, and through it, they make something of me. This sets up a kind of anxious reverberation, not only the anticipation of *how I am might be understood*, but also in the terms of the feedback effect of *what I might have meant* now that I am aware of how the other has apprehended my words. Or, in Sharpe's formulation, 'my speech is received via the Other . . . I get back meaning via my speech's reception' (2004, p. 50).

This role of Other as relay mechanism is implicit in Lacan's assertion that 'in human speech the sender is always a receiver at the same time . . . one hears the sound of one's own words' (1993, p. 24). Similarly: 'What I seek in speech is the response of the other' (2006, p. 247). The Other hence plays the part of intermediary, and not only in how I understand myself, but in terms of the communications intended for others that are also nonetheless unexpectedly directed to myself. This gives us a better grasp of the *return*-effect of a signal and a better appreciation of how one's intended message is only a fraction of what is effectively communicated.

This facet of the Other, the factor of 'how I am heard', always entails the potential of over-interpretation. There is a convergence here between Lacanian notions of the symbolic, and the traditional emphasis in Freudian psychoanalysis on the ambiguity of meaning and intention, slips of the tongue, and so on. The breadth of how I might be heard always exceeds the more delimited field of my (conscious) statement, whether by virtue of the tonal variations of my voice, my accent or the 'materiality' of how I speak (different patterns of pronunciation, types of verbal emphasis, etc.). I will be understood differently in varying contexts, whether due to the fact that the phrases or idioms I use may have different connotations to what I had presumed, or simply by virtue of the contingencies of the context within which I am speaking.

This is also how to understand the conceptual overlap between the Other understood *as* symbolic order and the idea of the unconscious as 'discourse of the Other'. These are essentially variants on the same idea. In both such cases we are concerned with the impossibility of ever fully controlling the implications of one's speech within the social field. The perennial disparity between speakers' statements and the enunciative dimension of how such content is performed and/or heard is thus a condition of possibility for the emergence of the Lacanian unconscious.

To offer such a conceptualization of communication is not, importantly, to imply that some transparent form of communication exists, or to intimate that there could ideally be some perfect communicative utterance that is direct, unmediated by ambiguity and mishearing. The incommensurability between statement and enunciation (between the *content* of a given communication and the performative conditions under which it is *enunciated*) is structural. Indeed, it is this constitutive split which dictates that the subject is barred, never fully transparent unto themselves. The fact of this gap or irreconcilability – an instance of the Lacanian 'real' – cannot be overcome. It qualifies all communication and it ensures that a type of disjunction characterizes each instance of speaking.

Miscommunication as the rule

Erving Goffman's (1959) theory of impression management likewise calls attention to how the complex signalling machinery of human interaction always leaves the message-sender open to a type of double-reading. This is the distinction between the (relatively controlled) expressions a communicator consciously uses, and the (less domesticated) expressivities they inadvertently 'give off'. There is an obvious parallel here with the discussion of the modalities of statement and enunciation discussed above.

A fundamental asymmetry underlies interpretative exchanges, Goffman (1959) insists, which gives *the listener* a distinct advantage. This power-differential arises as a result of the interpretative latitude afforded the recipient of communications, who is able to scrutinize any of the multiple (and particularly *unintended*) forms of expressivity given off by the person who is speaking. This directs us to what for psychoanalysis is a structural necessity of communication: the 'bandwidth' of a speaker's potential meanings is always wider than the bare minimum needed at any given moment to deliver a minimal message.

We have then a stronger thesis than the idea that ambiguity and misunderstanding are unfortunate yet inevitable by-products of any communicative attempt. Rather, what we might take to be 'successful communication' is never secure, but is rather something of an accident, the unlikely outcome of a potentially huge range of signals, over-readings and ambiguous significations that are present in each communicative situation. That we may have learnt to screen-out the seemingly redundant or inadvertent components of everyday communication – bracketing the polysemic nature of speech, the multiple interpretative trajectories inherent in any utterance – does not mean that pure, uncomplicated communication is possible. Hence the Lacanian assertion that our communicative attempts are always qualified by types of failure, by an over-arching impossibility; it is this very impossibility of us ever transparently 'saying it all' or fully understanding one another that keeps us talking.

Anxious speech

The Lacanian insistence on the necessary disjuncture between statement and enunciation may appear unfounded, certainly so from the ego's perspective on its own linguistic productions. The ego views its words as under its control; as far as it is concerned, there is no fundamental disparity between the dimensions of statement and enunciation. This comforting illusion is called into question by Verhaeghe's (2001) assertion: 'when I speak I do not know what I am going to say, unless I have learned it by heart or am reading my speech from a paper' (p. 22). To appreciate this state of affairs, we should move away from idealized notions whereby we imagine a subject's experiences as perfectly mapped by and conveyed through their words,[18] and consider a different and less comforting paradigm of speech production.

Let us think for a few moments about nervous speech, about how difficult it is to be in control of our words under trying circumstances. Take for instance the tense conditions of a job interview, or those 'we have to talk' moments, such as when a relationship is in crisis, or, better yet, when one has to bring a relationship to an end. It is not surprising that we often rehearse what we are going to say in such situations – not just the argument, but crucial phrases also – or indeed that inopportune phrases sometimes emerge ('I didn't mean it like that', 'You're twisting my words!'). In such pressurized circumstances there is always the possibility of our words seeming to betray us, the prospect that we say the wrong thing. Anyone who has been through a sequence of job interviews knows this: don't speak too much: the longer you speak, the more chance there is of some unintended meaning coming to the fore.

Another example: in responding to formal legal charges, or in respect of talking to the press in relation to such charges, lawyers invariably ask their clients to read a prepared statement rather than to speak 'off the cuff'. Such a strategy confirms that we cannot trust our words; offering a spontaneous reaction, 'speaking our minds' is a high-risk strategy. Speaking under pressurized situations is no doubt different from less anxiety-provoking circumstances, and yet the former can be taken as paradigmatic in a sense: the possibility of speaking beyond one's self is a condition of speaking as such. It is just this inherent potential of speaking that psychoanalysis attempts to utilize via the technique of free association. The analyst's request to their patient that they free associate tacitly transmits the following message:

> If you speak without thinking about what you say, you will end up saying something that you never expected to say. That is a knowledge that concerns you and nobody else; it is a knowledge of vital importance to you, as it refers to your desires and the secret forms of enjoyment that you have and of which you are not aware.
>
> (Rodriguez, 2004, p. 4)

On (not) informing the Other

The fact of the Other as an omnipresent interlocutor provides an interesting means of understanding declarative statements. It helps us appreciate the *force* of speech-acts (Austin, 1962) whose performative enactment always exceeds the literal meaning of the words spoken. When, for example, public oaths are made, when someone states a fact 'for the record', or makes a verbal contract before a series of witnesses ('I swear to tell the truth and nothing but the truth. . .'), we have more than the inter-subjectivity of speech, but a type of history making (indeed, precisely a *declaration*). The implication of this idea is that communication, particularly in its performative, declarative and institutional capacities, is constantly involved in types of symbolic registration, in alerting the Other, be it to the fact of my stupid accident (the function of my 'Darn it!') or to the occurrence of a historical event (hence the obvious redundancy of newspaper headlines announcing something that everyone already knows – 'Royal couple wed', 'New president inaugurated', etc.).

This is not of course to say that we don't often attempt to bypass such instances of symbolic registration. A number of examples of attempting *not* to inform the Other can be found in the work of psychologist Steven Pinker, who addresses this general topic – clearly not in any psychoanalytic or Lacanian way – via the topic of indirect speech. Pinker (2007) describes a number of scenarios in which a degree of deliberate ambiguity (or 'indirect speech') is utilized such that symbolic registration is put on hold. In each case the key protagonist is involved in a risky gambit, and the use of ambiguity enables them to 'save face' in Goffman's (1967) phrase, so as to potentially preserve an existing set of social roles.

In the first example, drawn from the film *Fargo*, a driver who is pulled over by a police officer for an infraction hands over his license along with a 50-dollar bill, suggesting that they 'take care of this now'. The benefits of such a strategy are obvious: rather than the risk entailed by a more explicit offer of a bribe – which of course is itself illegal, and could make matters considerably worse for the driver – his ambiguity provides an alternative explanation should the offer be rebuffed. It suspends the full implications of this act: the Other has not been properly informed of what has gone on. Pinker's comment on the discretion of veiled bribes brings to the fore this dimension of evasion:

> Somehow the implicated nature of the bribe allowed both sides to pretend that they could deny that they had transacted a bribe, as if they thought a hidden tape recorder might be running and they could be indicted by a prosecutor in court.
>
> (2007, p. 400)[19]

A second example drawn from Pinker concerns the enactment of the sexual come-on, as in the much parodied line, in which a potential suitor asks his partner after a first date: 'Would you like to come up and see my etchings?' That the partner can decline the (implicit) offer smuggled into this question by taking it literally – 'Etchings really aren't my thing' – means that the embarrassment of a failed pass can be avoided.

In both of these cases the fact of being able to offer something in a tacit manner – of momentarily bypassing the symbolic registration of the event – is vital. Stated in a more direct way, the bribe, the pass, would have changed things. The definition of the situation, the *status* of the act, would have been different, as indeed would the *relationship* between the two individuals. In the case of an explicit bribe, the act becomes a crime; the admission of desire where previously a merely platonic relationship had existed changes the roles and obligations of the protagonists.

Neither of these acts, once properly performed, can be undone. Let us imagine that the couple in question worked together, and that she was not interested in a sexual relationship with him: by virtue of suspending the symbolic impact of this event, the given social space between the two can be preserved, the structure of their given relationship (friendly co-workers) remains intact. This is the benefit of not informing the Other: things can go on as they were, the participants can preserve the social roles they had prior to the encounter, as if nothing had happened.

Of course, none of the participants in these scenarios is really deceived by what is going on – the real target of deception is the extra-subjective Other. Pinker misses this when he asks 'Why do people feel that indirect speech lets them get away with . . . hypocrisy in a way that plain speech would not . . .? I don't know' (p. 416). The Lacanian answer is that you can of course get away with hypocrisy, provided no adequate symbolic registration of the event occurs, so long, in other words, as the Other doesn't get wind of it.[20]

The ways of desire

I have intimated that the Other is never fully intact or whole, indeed, that the Other is neither disinterested nor satisfied. More simply put: the Other *desires*. There is a certain magnetism or fascination that underscores the subject's relation to the Other who is perceived as holding the truth – or the authority – that the subject either wants or aspires to. This, the goal of supposed knowledge and truth, is a powerful motor of subjectivity, hence Lacan's reference to the Other – understood here as an important instrument of the clinic – as 'the subject supposed to know'.

Such an Other is, understandably, quite typically the target of love, and as frequently, of deep resentment. For clinicians, the parameters of such a relationship, with its negative and positive polarities, will be immediately recognizable. This is a transference relationship, one in which the projections and fantasies of subjects are mobilized; this is the powerfully affective relationship which engages the subject's unconscious and which makes the psychotherapeutic relationship effectively work.[21]

We understand better in this respect how the Other acts as a principle of co-ordination, as a means through which the subject gains their bearings. What one needs in such situations is not merely a static set of ideas, a fixed set of symbolic co-ordinates, but a more animated and dynamic sense of what it is that the *Other is actively imagined to want* (and to want *of me*).

Lacan links the topics of the Other and desire explicitly in Seminar V, noting there that

> the very reason why . . . [the Other] is opaque to us. . . . is because there is something in him that we do not know, and which separates us from his response to our demand, and it is nothing other than what is called his desire.
>
> (1957–1958, session of 25 June 1958, p. 4)

There is also a cryptic comment in *The instance of the letter in the unconscious* where Lacan connects the concepts of the Other, desire and the unconscious:

> If I have said that the unconscious is the Other's discourse (with a capital O), it is in order to indicate the beyond in which the recognition of desire is tied to the desire for recognition. In other words, this other is the Other that [is] . . . bound up with the desire for recognition.
>
> (2006, p. 436)

This, the question of the Other's desire/recognition, is not a minor or uncomplicated issue. Lacan's reference to 'the recognition of desire' as linked to 'the desire for recognition' makes it apparent that a dialectical relationship is in play. What this means is that in the subject-Other relation, desire is always ambiguous and complex, never exclusively the subject's own, but always desire *for* the Other, desire *as* the Other (desiring what the Other desires), and, furthermore, a form of desire that is entangled in the desire *to be desired* and *recognized* by the Other.

Readers familiar with Lacan will hear in this the echo of his famous aphorism, adapted from Hegel, namely: 'Desire is the desire of the Other'. Calum Neill (2014) offers an illuminating discussion of this famous Lacanian maxim. The preposition 'of' in the foregoing statement, he observes, marks a rich ambiguity which allows us to appreciate something of the complexity of the relation of desire as it obtains between subject and Other:

> The subject's desire is the desire of the Other insofar as it is the desire for the Other to desire him or her. It is the subject's desire to be the object of the Other's desire. This would entail the desire to be recognized by the Other. It is perhaps primarily this sense of *desire of the Other* that we can understand in the relationship between the infant and mother. The child wants to be the object of the mother's desire, it wants the mother to desire it.
>
> (Neill, 2014, p. 40)

Expanding briefly on the above, the 'desire of the Other' comprises the following: desire *for* the Other (wanting the Other); desiring *as* the Other (desire for what the Other desires); desire for the Other *as Other* (the Otherness of what is desired, the always unsatisfied nature of desire); and desire *for the desire of* the Other (to be desired and recognized by the Other).

Suffice to say then that for Lacan the subject's most intimate subjective functions – those of desire – are inseparable from the Other. Calling attention to the factor of desire not only foregrounds the 'motivational' factor implicit in the Other. It likewise emphasizes the dimension of the unconscious – evident also in the unknowable, enigmatic quality of the Other – and thereby ensures that the Other is an essentially psychoanalytic concept.

We may supplement this (perhaps overly abstract) account by referring to a somewhat more grounded interpretation of the role of the Other offered by Lacan in 'On a Question Prior to any Possible Treatment of Psychosis'. The Other there is defined as: 'the locus from which the question of his [the subject's] existence may arise' (2006, p. 459). Furthermore:

> The fact that the question of his existence envelops the subject, props him up, invades him . . . is revealed to the analyst by the tensions, suspense, and fantasies that he encounters . . . [T]his question is articulated in the Other.
>
> (Lacan, 2006, p. 459)

Stijn Vanheule (2011) offers what I take to be the best exposition of this idea. At the level of the unconscious, each speaking subject is confronted with a rudimentary question concerning its own identity:

> 'Who am I?' is the question all humans are unconsciously confronted with, and for which no inherent answer is readily available . . . this question relates to three issues: one's 'sex'; one's 'contingency in being' . . . and 'the relational signifiers of love and procreation' . . . The question of *the subject's sex* concerns whether one is a man or a woman, as well as the question of how one gives shape to sexual identity. The matter of *contingency in being* refers to the fortuity of life, and to the question [of] what life means in the light of death. The *relational signifiers* in their turn point to the question of what it is that really connects people in love, and to the question of parenthood.
>
> (Vanheule, 2011, p. 64)

To avoid misunderstanding: such questions are not intellectual or even conscious in nature. They should be approached rather as lived 'existential' propositions and concerns, as (unconsciously) enacted questions. Vanheule adds:

> [T]he subject is not defined as a reflective entity that asks [these] questions, but as an entity that is created because . . . [such] questions are articulated . . . The question produces the subject and not the other way around.
>
> (2011, p. 64)

Parle-être: The speaking being, subject of the signifier

Vanheule (2011) provides a Lacanian corrective to perspectives that prioritize the subject over the Other. Such approaches – which would presumably include all of humanistic or ego-focused psychology – invariably confer a far greater sense of agency to the subject than to symbolic processes. Here, once again, we confront another parting of ways between psychology and Lacanianism. For Lacanian theory it is not the case that the Other is belatedly appended to a subject who until then had enjoyed a pre-symbolic existence. Nor is it the case that anything like an equally weighted or symmetrical relationship exists between subject and Other.[22] Diagrammatically, we might represent this state of affairs not as subject and Other as two closely aligned or even overlapping 'partners in dialogue'. The Lacanian subject (certainly in his '*Structuralist*' phase) would better be represented as occupying a space entirely within the encompassing field constituted by the Other. The subject as speaking being (Lacan's '*parle-être*'), 'comes to', *begins*, and is always-already within, the symbolic. Lacan makes no bones about it: 'the condition of the subject', he says, 'depends on what unfolds in the Other' (2006, pp. 458–459). The Other precedes and over-determines us as speaking beings; it speaks through and over us even – perhaps particularly – in those moments when we feel we are completely in possession of 'our' language.

This is the radical shift in perspective we need to adopt if we are to follow Lacan's lead, one in which the agency of the symbolic takes precedence over the agency of the subject. This is Joël Dor's (1998) position, when, in good Lacanian fashion, he insists not only on the primacy of the signifier, but on 'the *domination of the subject by the signifier*' (p. 49).

Outlining the L-Schema

We may now turn our attention to Lacan's map of the communicative interchange, that is, to his L-Schema which extends (via the addition of several extra terms) the elementary diagram of communication provided above (Figure 1.1). The L-Schema, says Lacan, 'represents the interruption of full speech between the subject and the Other and its detour through the two egos, o and o', and their imaginary relations' (1993, p. 14).

On a first line of approach then, we can treat the schema as a diagram of communication where Subject (S) and ego (o) – two facets of the individual contained on the left-hand side – are conversing with another ego (o') (on the top right). As established above, any ego to other interaction brings into play another principle of Otherness, the 'big Other' (bottom right). We are thus able to account for the four corners of the schema. These four corners represent the four nodal points of *a single subject's subjectivity*. Such a subject is 'drawn to the four corners of the schema', says Lacan, from 'S', his or her 'ineffable and stupid existence', to o', the position of their objects (alter egos or 'little others'), on to o, the place of their ego, his/her form 'as reflected in the form of [their] . . . objects', to, finally, O, the Other, 'the locus from which the question of [their] existence may arise for [them]' (Lacan, 2006, p. 459).

Given the psychoanalytic emphasis on the split nature of the subject and upon the fleeting quality of unconscious events which suddenly emerge and then disappear, it is not surprising that the subject is viewed as *a set of relations* rather than as a single, unified entity. This affirms something reiterated above, namely that there is always a split between the *content* of what the ego consciously says (the statement) and the act of speaking (the enunciation) which remains linked of course to the consideration of *how they are heard* (the place of the Other).[23]

A question appears: if we assume that the ego is the seat of identifications, the functional basis of the rational individual, then why does Lacan place it only in the third position of the schema (at the bottom left)? In this respect it helps to trace the communicative event as a movement across the positions of the schema. There is an initial moment of speaking (at S) which connects the subject to an other, an *alter ego* which supplies the images and desires that will provide the basis of the subject's ego (the ongoing process of identifications that give it its 'identity').

Such an 'identity' – never fully secured or self-enclosed – maintains always an alienating destiny. With the ego it is never the case of an original or integral 'me', but always instead an amalgamation of images and reflections that have been assumed

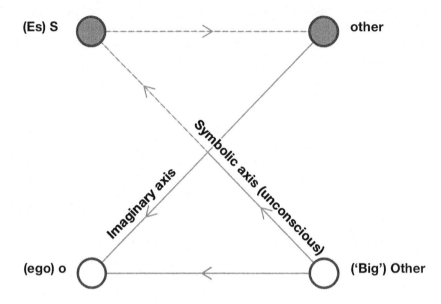

FIGURE 1.2 Lacan's L-Schema

so as to lend a degree of bodily and psychological (or ego) coherence. Such images are a means of ensuring a modicum of consistency to what would otherwise be the fragmentary experience of existence.

It is by virtue of the outside-in nature of the ego's constitution that, for Lacan, a form of alienation proves an inescapable condition of human subjectivity. There is thus a structural basis to the psychical and epistemological trend to misrecognition. This is what underlies the *méconnaissance* of distorted forms of knowing that are always routed via others,[24] and that are delimited by the ego's priorities of self-substantiation. We have then an answer to the question as to why the alter ego (o') comes first: because, simply put, as the originating source of the subject's identifications, it invariably does come first. These are the conditions for a constitutive form of aggressivity with an other who is always more authentic at being me, oddly, than I am. Such a narcissistic rivalry is part and parcel of any primary identification, a foundational element of human subjectivity. In Lacan's own terms:

> The human ego is the other . . . because in the beginning the subject is closer to the form of the other than to the emergence of his own tendency. He is originally an inchoate collection of desires . . . the initial synthesis of the ego is essentially an *alter ego*, it is alienated. The desiring human subject is constructed around a centre which is the other insofar as he gives the subject his unity, and the first encounter with the object is with the object of the other's desire.

(1993, p. 39)

There is no easy means of transcending this deadlock. The imaginary content of the ego is always-already derived from the other, which means that any attempt to assert the status of my existence or my desire *as primary* necessitates the elimination of this other. Of course to eradicate the other means that one loses the basis of one's own identifications, and along with it, the possibility of the recognition that this other provides.

The impasse is writ large: if I am to make any claims regards the uniqueness, the authenticity of my desire, the other must be done away with, as the enemy of my self-realization. Then again, this other is of desperate importance, for without them my ego has no existence. Such an imaginary relation 'always implies struggles, the impossibility of coexistence with the other' (Lacan, 1993, p. 40). The narcissistic flavour of this register of human subjectivity should by now be abundantly clear, as should its explanatory value for a variety of forms of cultural chauvinism, forms of 'in-group favouritism'.[25] This imaginary impasse is not the end of the story however. For this fundamental and competitive rivalry, which entails a 'primary and essential struggle to the death' (Lacan, 1993, p 40), is precisely 'what is overcome in speech insofar as it involves a third party' (p. 39).

The failure of successful communication

The psychoanalytic account of the aggressivity of imaginary inter-subjectivity stands in stark contrast to the inter-subjective ideal of different individuals and groups attempting to 'adopt the perspective of the other'. There are some important implications here for how one might think of inter-group conflict and communication.

Importantly, in speaking of ego-functioning we are not speaking exclusively of a given individual's ego, but, insofar as the ego can be understood as *a system of identifications* or a sequence of likeable ideal images, we are also considering the basis of a societal or cultural group. In fact, we could approach this issue the other way around: unless a mass of individuals shares such a set of idealizing images – and is thus, as we might put it, 'narcissistically bound' – there is no effective, *lived* group identity, none of the affective quality that typically characterizes group-membership.

We have already established that for psychoanalysis a type of inter-subjective confusion characterizes the very condition of human subjectivity. In outlining our supposed 'identities' we continually cast the net both too widely and not widely enough, including as essential parts of our egos that which *comes from others* (alienating, ego-substantiating images) and excluding that which characterizes the actual (fragmentary, inchoate) state of the ego. Put differently, we might say that two trends – two types of misrecognition – pertain to all ego identifications: problems of the over- and under-extension. First: we constantly misrecognize ourselves in those ideal (ego-affirming) features of others (a type of over-extension of the ego).[26] Second: we fail to recognize that the negative, denigrating (ego-threatening) attributes that we assume exist in others, belong to us (a type of under-extension of the ego). This flux between the over- and under-extension of the ego complicates the possibility of any absolute differentiation between different individuals and groups alike. Hence the impasse identified above: others (or other groups) are always vehicles for – *extensions of* – an ego, just as they exist at the very core of an ego, as its foundational basis.

Aside then from the antagonisms of recognition and denigration that characterize *imaginary* inter-group relations, we should turn our attention also to communicative moments between cultures. Colette Soler (1996) approaches this question in an interesting way, via the notion of *comprehension by way of identification*. On the imaginary axis, the operations of projection and ego-understanding predominate (the subject sees facets of their ego in the other, interprets the other on the basis of their own ego). This means that the other is approached most fundamentally via the means of identification. I understand cultural otherness fundamentally through a narcissistic (ego-based) frame of reference (the *méconnaissance* of ego misrecognitions), which, despite the illusions of certain select identifications ('they're just like me'), cannot but involve elements of alterity. After all, not all of the other can be assimilated into the interpretative scope of one's own ego.

This provides a means of thinking about cultural insularity: in attempting to understand others – and in attempting to be understood by others – one uses one's ego, one thinks by way of one's identifications. Problems in communication are often thought to arise due to differences in culture, because the participants lack a similar frame of reference. Initially Soler seems to agree: 'Successful communication always depends on a certain level of identification' (1996, p. 45). When you speak with someone with a similar background and who shares the same interests, you speak fluently together. Having said this, we need to pay attention to *what is lost* in apparently 'successful' communication, namely, the particularity or singularity of each person:

> Though you may understand an alter ego very well, there is always a fundamental difference between the two subjects. Successful communication eliminates the possibility of making your particularity appear.
>
> (Soler, 1996, p. 45)

What we typically take to be successful communication – the sense of two egos resonating with one another – is in fact rather the indication that there has been a failure to engage those qualities of the other not easily assimilated into the terms of the ego's self-understanding. So, although this form of communication (i.e. comprehension by way of identification) no doubt has its place in everyday sociality, it also eliminates particularity. It collapses what is unique about the subject into the ego's logic of the other-as-me. How then are we to access what remains of this singularity? Soler's answer is instructive. One finds the remains of this singularity in the failure of one's communicative actions: 'Singularity' she says, 'is obliged to manifest itself through the failure of common action' (p. 45).

A trans-subjective order of truth

I have spent some time outlining the above state of affairs to make clear that from a Lacanian perspective the conditions for the mutuality of recognition *do not exist* at the level of imaginary inter-subjectivity. This impossibility of resolution sheds some light on the volatility of those communicative interchanges in which recognition is refuted.

Any communicative engagement, insofar as it occurs on this imaginary axis, has the potential to flare up into rivalry, into modes of aggressive confrontation in which the goals of asserting the ego and claiming the other's recognition eclipse the objectives of consensual understanding. One should note that the ego-substantiation in question is served not only by explicit rivalry, but by a variety of means in which the narcissistic field of the subject's ego is bolstered. There is an apparent paradox here: excessive devotion to the other as the vehicle for my own narcissistic ego-gratification – as in the false altruism of self-lauding charitable acts – likewise derails the possibility of transformative communication. Rather than posing any challenge to the ego, the other here is essentially a 'means of me'.

A Lacanian approach to communication is aware that the imperatives of ego-recognition and ego-substantiation are always able to over-ride other communicative agendas (such as those of establishing forms of consensus, gaining understandings that lies beyond the horizon of one's own ego). More important than the message being conveyed – at least in the imaginary register – is the *implicit request made for recognition*. Such an imperative, on the side of message-senders and receivers alike, routinely supersedes the possibility of any real communicative gains or change.

This imaginary deadlock is unsurpassable, without the intervention of the symbolic, of the big Other. It is the possibility of appeals to the symbolic order (via the Other) that enables the establishment of truces, contracts, forms of alliance and mediated agreements. It is in this way that we have the basis for a properly *trans-subjective* order of truth. What Lacan is so keen to impress upon us in his work of the 1950s is that *the structure of communication itself* installs such a reference-point. Language, speech – and the spoken interchange of psychoanalysis itself – establish an order of truth, and provide the basis for potentially transformative social contracts and exchanges.[27]

The vector of the unconscious

Returning then to the L-Schema: having discussed the other-ego (o'–o) relation in some detail, we may now turn our attention to the diagonal that bisects this axis, that is, to the Other-subject (O–S) relation, the vector so clearly prioritized by Lacan. As opposed to the egoic speech of the imaginary axis, this relation holds a properly transformative – which is also to say *disruptive* – communicative potential.

The S – which phonetically invokes 'Es', as in Freud's 'Das Es' (the id) – indicates the place of the speaking subject. This is the subject of language, and the subject of the unconscious, who, by communicating within a given socio-symbolic context and by necessarily utilizing the codes, signifiers and language(s) supplied by the Other, constantly produces more in their communicative attempts than what had been consciously intended. As we have already seen, we cannot treat the subject as the first or primary term in this four-part structure. After all, the moment of speaking is always-already conditioned by the factor of the Other, by the fact of the symbolic system which I draw upon to express myself, and in terms of which I am heard. The starting point of the schema would thus be – counter-intuitively – at the bottom right, in the fourth position of the diagram, the only position, incidentally, that emits signals in two directions (it is the source of the ego's constant attempt to understand its symbolic location, its social role(s) (the O – o trajectory) and the necessary precondition for any attempt to use language, to express one's self in symbolic terms (the direction of O to S)).

The arrow from the bottom right to the top left thus gives us the vector of the unconscious. This diagonal implies that the possibility of the symbolic *speaking the subject* – a variation on both Freud's notion of over-determination and the '*Structuralist*' credo that the 'subject is spoken' – is a necessary precondition of speaking at all. This vector also implies that the unconscious must be understood via the symbolic order, via the fact of the trans-subjective factor of the Other, a fact which entails a far stronger symbolic (and societal) dimension than is typically accorded the notion of the unconscious. There is of course considerable resistance to this field of unintended messages and significations that stems from the Other. As well-defended and repressed egos, we typically reject such signals and trans-missions out of hand, or feel compromised by them. We are, in short, well trained in ignoring this 'channel' of significations, which, like a continual newsfeed, is constantly producing new and unintended significations, instances of a type of knowledge that we don't know we know.

We might identify here an apparent shortcoming of Lacan's diagram, one that allows us to return to our earlier discussion regarding the ambiguous inside/outside location of the Other. One potential limitation of the diagram is that the symbolic S–O axis, the trajectory of the unconscious, seems to necessarily separate S and O as opposite poles in a given line of transmission. While one appreciates why Lacan opts for such a schematization – it shows how the O 'feeds' the subject with signifiers, how significations performed before the Other give voice to unconscious impulses – it also however runs the risk of polarizing the Other and the uncon-scious. Differently put: the diagram might seem to support the notion that there is an internal unconscious ('Es' as 'id') as opposed to an external site of the Other. Part of what I argued above in respect of the inside/outside location of the Other is that the big Other concept, once properly understood, collapses such distinctions. The same holds here: S and O represent not so much opposite poles in a line of transmission, as a convergence of the Other as it emerges simultaneously as act of enunciation (what I say) and as site of its reception (how I am heard). In short: S and Other might be said to occupy the same place.[28]

All this being said, what Lacan's diagram certainly succeeds in illustrating is that the Other-subject line of transmission is continually disrupted, denied or simply bypassed by the production of ego meanings. The Other-subject axis, although crucial to the production of subjective truth and change, is constantly re-channelled by the cross-axis (o'–o) of other-ego exchanges. The dotted diagonal line connecting the middle of the diagram to the top-left corner indicates as much: any possibility of ego-disruptive or symbolic speech is re-routed and assimilated into the ego's characteristic function of misrecognition. The truth potential of Other significations produced on this axis are continually deflected; the provocative powers of full speech are caught up and carried away by what Lacan calls the 'wall of language' (namely, the defensive strength of the o'–o axis).

Now that we have explicated the basic terms of the L-Schema and readied it for use as a map upon which we might trace various instances of communicative interchange, a series of further questions emerge. What are the conditions under which the truth potential of Other speech is most effectively elicited? How does the 'full' speech of such Other transmissions break through the defensive barrier of 'empty speech' (Lacan's 'wall of language')? These are questions that are perhaps best broached through an empirical illustration; it is to just such an example that we turn in the following chapter.

The Freudian big Other

Before concluding, allow me to register a prospective objection. For readers approaching the above Lacanian postulates from a background in classical psycho-analysis, many of the foregoing notions – perhaps particularly the concept of the big Other – may appear more '*Structuralist*' than Freudian in nature. The claim might thus be made that the Freudian unconscious has yet to be adequately factored into this account. I want to briefly respond to this issue by linking the notion of the Other, as sketched above, to a more overtly Freudian understanding.

In a short introductory text on Freud, psychoanalyst Josh Cohen (2005) cites one of Freud's most well-known descriptions of unconscious phenomenon:

> all the acts and manifestations which I notice in myself and do not know how to link up with the rest of my mental life must be judged as if they belonged to someone else: they must be explained by a mental life ascribed to this person.
>
> (Freud, 1911, p. 169)

Cohen (2005) paraphrases Freud's reflections as follows:

> when 'I' speak, I am simultaneously and unknowingly ventriloquizing this someone else, someone both radically distant from and tantalizingly close to me. It is this 'someone else' that goes by the name of the unconscious.
>
> (pp. 60–61)

This is one of those moments where a Lacanian idea (the symbolic Other) that has been developed via recourse to decidedly non-psychoanalytic theorizations suddenly chimes with a foundational Freudian concept. Who is this 'radically distant' someone speaking through us? The Lacanian answer is the big Other, and this idea – certainly inasmuch as it stresses how the subject is continually 'being spoken' by intended significations – perfectly augments Freud's above description of the unconscious.[29]

This idea can be reinforced by referring back to Lacan's description cited above, in which he stresses that the Other, while lying at the heart 'of my own assent to my own identity', must be understood along the lines of a second degree of Otherness. The Lacanian accent here is unavoidable: the Other is less an internal person (a kind of personified id) than it is a type of Other discourse that can be heard in the equivocations and polyphonies of the subject's speech.

The same argument is made in an astute commentary by Muller and Richardson (1982), who adeptly paraphrase Lacan:

> Freud's 'Other scene', the dimension of the unconscious, this other place, is what Lacan calls the 'Other' . . . How does it function in relation to the subject? As a kind of discourse, bits of which emerge into our conscious life 'in certain privileged moments, in dreams, slips of the tongue . . . flashes of wit' . . . The Other is thus 'the locus from which the question of [the subject's] existence may be presented to him' . . . The question as it emerges from the Other is a genuine putting of the subject into question.
>
> (1982, pp. 208–210)

We can now understand why Lacan speaks of the unconscious as 'the discourse of the Other'. It is this discourse, which is to say, *the signifying field* in all its ambiguities and unintended enunciations, in all its attempted evasions and slippages of meaning, this signifying field *as it is spoken by the subject*, that, in effect, *is* the unconscious.

The elusive subject

If, in the foregoing discussion, the notion of the subject seemed less than coherent or complete, then this is not without good reason. The idea of the subject is one of the most challenging and elusive concepts in Lacanian theory, and something of this elusiveness is dramatized in the L-Schema, where we confront the impossibility of locating the subject in any one point of the diagram. As intimated above, the subject here seems akin to a pulse in the circuit of a diagram, an instance of speaking, an enunicative event.

We have made good progress thus far in outlining a series of rudimentary Lacanian concepts, yet much of what we have gained will be lost if we end up assimilating these concepts to a non-psychoanalytic view of subjectivity which for the most part equates 'the subject' with the ego. Lacanian psychoanalysis is focused on treating the ego *as symptom*, as a symptom which exists – and which proves a crucial challenge in psychoanalytic work – yet that exists precisely as a defensive formation. The ego, as Lacan tirelessly insists, is a type of systematic illusion that gives the appearance of substance and coherence.

What then is the subject? It is not the subject as conscious individual, as ego, as mind or as the substantialized entity (a self) that, from a standpoint in psychology, we expect to find. Perhaps the closest we can come here to grasping this Lacanian notion is simply by noting the affinity of the subject with the unconscious and with acts of speaking. This being said, we need to be wary of granting an automatic primacy to the subject *who speaks* instead of appreciating how in speaking there is *the possibility of a subject*. Jamieson Webster (forthcoming) puts this well: 'When speech functions as an act, when it deploys meaning by summoning the symbolic, it brings a subject into being.' The subject here, paradoxically enough, is contingent on an act of speaking, rather than speaking itself being contingent on an already existing category of the subject.

The idea bears repeating: the Lacanian subject is irreducible to – and, it seems, hopelessly at odds with – psychological modes of conceptualization.[30] Nowhere else, I would argue, is the recalcitrance of Lacanian theory regards any hopes of assimilation to psychology more pronounced. Even the notion of the unconscious, seems, at least in contrast to the idea of the subject-*as-lack*, as *event-in-speech*, familiar, not hopelessly at odds with psychology. We have become so accustomed to thinking of the subject as a self, a consistent presence – an identity – that Lacan's idea of the subject cannot but strike us untenable. This conceptual challenge is not easily surmounted. Time and time again, notwithstanding a professed dedication to Lacanian theory, or a clinical focus on the unconscious as enunciated in speech, one finds the evidence of conceptual slippage where talk of 'the subject' has slowly gravitated back to something 'egoic' in nature. Even as we glimpse the notion of the subject, it slips away from us, a subtle realignment occurs, and the subject has again taken on the parameters of the ego.

We might view this problem not simply along the lines of a lapse in scholarly or clinical attentions, but as symptomatic of the 'impossibility' of psychoanalytic theory. The evasiveness of this notion of the subject, the fact that it strikes us as so difficult to process, so resistant to comprehension, this itself is indicative of how *counter-egoic* the concept is. One has the sense in approaching this theory that one is – perhaps particularly so, given a background in psychology – disposed *to not understand* Lacanian theory. There is a related argument that Lacan repeatedly affirms in his *Écrits*, not infrequently in respect of psychology itself: in adopting the disposition of scientific neutrality we forget our own egoic standpoint. We neglect the fact that our will-to-know is conditioned by the imaginary, that is, by certain systematic defences and forms of mis-knowing which exist precisely to bolster our own egos.[31] And what we maintain regards the Lacanian view of the subject – that it is counter-egoic, resistant to comprehension – holds also more generally for Lacanian psychoanalytic theory, particularly, we might add, for those approaching it from the discipline of psychology.

Notes

1 Alan Sheridan, one of the earliest translators of Lacan's works into English, offers a helpful definition of the imaginary as that pertaining to the world of the *imago*, namely 'the world, the register, the dimension of images, conscious or unconscious, perceived or imagined' (1977, p. ix). The imaginary is the domain of fantasy, of the stabilizing or ego-consoling production of images 'identity' affirming reflections, the register in which signifier and signifier appear to coalesce, and where effects of meaning, understanding, identity and wholeness predominate.

2 Dolar defines the Other as

> the hypothetical authority that upholds the structure and the supposed addressee of any act of speech, beyond interlocution or intersubjectivity, the third in any dialogue.
>
> (1999, p. 87)

3 The attempt to withhold something from the Other is in also some respects the attempt to withhold it from one's self; hence the importance in the psychotherapeutic realm of the therapist/analyst *not* remaining complicit in such attempts at avoiding symbolic registration.

4 The omnipresence of this imaginary dimension within psychic life was already signalled by Freud in his (1914) 'On Narcissism'.

5 This is particularly clear in the game of cricket. When a bowler believes he has forced a batsman into conceding a wicket, he directs his charge of 'Out!' not to his opponent but directly to the umpire.

6 It is for this reason that the notion of empathy does not serve as a viable ethical concept in Lacanian psychoanalysis. A Lacanian clinical stance eschews the ideal of inter-subjective (ego) empathy, foregrounding instead the irreducible singularity of the other as inassimilable to the clinician's egoic understandings. Such an approach begs an interesting line of speculation: might we conceptualize an altogether different *non-egoic* form of 'empathy' realized, that is to say, at a different level to that of imaginary inter-subjectivity? Might it be possible to think 'empathy' in the ethical register of the subject's alterity to itself (to its own unconscious)? The ethical problematic is thus displaced from the level of conscious inter-subjective speculation to an engagement with the Other. Recast in this way, the subject's challenge of 'empathy' becomes that of the relationship to its own Otherness. We approach here what Lacan has in mind with his reading of Freud's programmatic statement '*Wo Es war, soll Ich werden*' (namely: 'Where It (the unconscious) was, there must I (the subject) come into being') (Neill, 2014). The real question then – to frame matters in the terms of a perhaps impossible ethical challenge – is how do we 'empathize' with the unconscious?

7 A powerful example is to be found in the domain of critical race theory. The point here is sometimes made that it is in the very moment that the white subject professes their love for various racial/cultural others that racism is re-enacted. Why? Because this love entails the narcissistic use of the (racial/cultural) other as a prop to the identity of the ostensibly 'loving' white subject.

8 It is along these lines that Miller (2011) offers a critique of those forms of American psychoanalysis that have come to be focused on 'communication between egos as the curative factor in psychoanalytic treatment' (p. 3). In such a situation:

> The analyst's ego communicates with, becomes a model for, and props up the ego of his analysand; that is, the psychoanalyst has been relegated to influencing the patient to be more like him.
>
> (p. 3)

9 Bowie (1991) adds an interesting note here, paraphrasing Lacan to stress the particular role of *speech* in the constitution of the Other: 'as soon as language takes . . . the form of speech it reassumes its intersubjective character: it becomes a "third locus" ' (Bowie,

1991, p. 82). The idea is that while the Other may be taken as the amassed collection of the entirety of a given language, it is in *speech* that the Other as 'third locus' is most overtly realized.

10 In the following chapter's examination of David Frost's interview of Nixon, we will see another example. There is a crucial moment when Frost, Nixon's interlocutor, his imaginary other and rival in dialogue, seemingly assumes the role of the big Other.

11 A technical note: I distinguish here between the 'extra-discursive' (*jouissance*, moments of 'the real') and the idea of the 'extra-symbolic', noting that the former is a constant factor in human subjectivity while the latter is an abstraction which makes little sense within the terms of Lacanian theory.

12 We might take up a tangential strand here: the case of solitary confinement may express something of the suffering of being forcefully separated from imaginary supports (inter-subjective acknowledgement/mirroring), a situation where one increasingly fails to exist – at least of the imaginary level – inasmuch as one is not reflected.

13 For a less overtly psychological conceptualization than Mead's that retains some family resemblance to both such notions of the Other, one might consider Garfinkel's (1967) symbolic interactionist description of shared social knowledge as the 'socially-sanctioned-facts-of-life-in-society-that-any-bona-fide-member-of-society-knows' (p. 77). This shared knowledge functions as the 'grounds of inference and action that people use in their everyday affairs and which they assume that others use in the same way' (p. 77). Garfinkel's concept thus overlaps with at least one dimension of Lacan's big Other.

14 We might think of this insistence on the irreducibility of the symbolic for subjectivity as a variation on Wittgenstein's declaration that there can be no such thing as a private language.

15 It is worth noting that one of Lacan's earliest extended discussions of the concept of the Other occurs in his seminar on psychosis (Seminar III), in the context of a series of reflections on paranoia. The clinical utility of the concept is here immediately apparent: the Other here has taken on a radically externalized and typically persecutory form. Seminar III includes a pithy formulation in which the essential mechanism of psychosis is glossed as the 'reduction of the Other, the big Other, the Other as locus of the word, to the imaginary Other' (Lacan, cited by Parker, 2015a, p. 70).

16 The role of the Other is likewise evident in cases of perversion. The perverse subject feels themselves to be the instrument of the Other's *jouissance* (Swales, 2012). 'It is patent,' says Lacan, 'that the sadist seeks the Other's anxiety' (2014, p. 177). Braunstein likewise asserts that the pervert dedicates their life to a type of excessive libidinal enjoyment (*jouissance*) 'that can only be understood in its relation with the Other . . . it could not even exist without the subjective division of the "victim"' (2003, p. 108).

17 Judith Butler articulates something of this situation – albeit in a context not focused on psychoanalytic theory – when she offers that

> speaking is always in some ways the speaking of a stranger through and as oneself, the . . . reiteration of a language that one never chose, that one does not find as an instrument to be used, but that one is, as it were, used by.
>
> (2000, p. 116)

18 The narcissistic enjoyment that arises from such perceptions of a perfect match between our experiences and our words – when we feel eloquent, articulate, that we have expressed ourselves well – follows the same rudimentary model of the child's jubilant assumption of their image in the mirror stage. In both such instances there is a moment of imaginary misrecognition that bolsters the ego by means of an elementary externalization. In both such cases the imaginary dialectic enables the (mis)recognizing subject to conclude that this external form – be it image or spoken words – is the 'I'.

19 The quasi-legal dimension of the Other foregrounded in this example can be emphasized by referring to Lorenza Chiesa (2007), who, reading Lacan's notion of the symbolic order as adapted from the '*Structuralist*' social anthropology of Lévi-Strauss, notes how the symbolic order (and thus, by extension, the Other) is akin to the *legal fabric of human culture*.

20 Importantly however, to highlight such (typically farcical) attempts to sidestep the Other is by no means to suggest that they always *succeed*. One could even argue that the elaborate decoy of attempting to avoid symbolic registration itself instantiates an Other (an 'Other to be deceived'). The point to emphasize here – an idea that Žižek (2005, 2006) makes time and time again – is that communicative exchanges can be analysed via an awareness of the multiple redundant declarative acts and gestures that are continuously reinstated so as to re-substantiate (or to avoid) laws and institutions.

21 Or, more in tune with Freud's comments on the topic: transference is what makes the psychotherapeutic relationship both possible and impossible.

22 Lacan (1979) carefully qualifies the nature of this relationship in Seminar XI, as circular but non-reciprocal. The questioning engagement of the subject to the Other ('What do you want of me?') is circular, but in a precise sense: it moves 'from the subject called to the Other, to the subject of that which he has himself seen appear in the field of the Other' (p. 207). This circularity *does not* imply a two-way process, it is 'circular, but, of its nature, without reciprocity. Because it is circular, it is dissymmetrical' (1979, p. 207).

23 One could extrapolate from this psychoanalytic basis (the statement/enunciation split) a rudimentary analytical model applicable to a far broader realm of communications. That is to say: virtually any communicative instance could – theoretically at least – be broken down into three analytical categories of communicative intent, enunciative act and its various interpretations. Such a model would provide three (potentially overlapping) types of misunderstanding. To avoid confusion, however: in a Lacanian framework, the last two of these categories (enunciations and mis-hearings) necessarily coincide; they are both facets of the Other. Both fit within the broader consideration of 'how I am heard'; they represent a convergence thus of the Other as both 'internal' (apparent in the act of speaking) and 'external' (how it is received).

24 That knowing, and indeed *desiring* objects is something that is necessarily routed via others, provides an important foundation for Lacan's (2006) claim about the fundamentally paranoiac nature of imaginary forms of knowledge.

25 This Hegelian logic is epitomized – as Frantz Fanon (1952/1986) has long since noted – in the dynamics of racism. The disparaged and resented other, who the racist subject wishes would be done away with is, in fact vital to the consolidation of their identity. Without this other providing the basis for the racist subject to assert – and ideally have recognized – their apparent superiority, this racist subject would not be able to claim a superior status in the first place.

26 The Lacanian term for what I am terming the over-extension of the ego is – as readers of Lacan's mirror stage paper know – 'transitivism'.

27 Hence Lacan's insistence in papers such as 'The function and field of speech and language in psychoanalysis' on the ideas of *symbol-as-pact* and the *symbolic-as-law*.

28 We can better appreciate thus Lacan's later turn to topological constructions: what cannot be easily represented in such a two-dimensional schema (namely that while S and O are in some sense different, representing respectively the site of enunciation and the Other site of reception), they nonetheless occupy the same place. A little bit of typological formalization might help here: the diagram might work better if rendered in three dimensions, 'rolled' in such a way that we could see how S and O positions on the diagram effectively overlap.

29 It is interesting to note how frequently this occurs: a Lacanian concept, which at first strikes one as a foreign supplement to Freudian theory, suddenly becomes the basis for the self-same assertion put forward, albeit in a different conceptual register, by Freud himself. This, as adherents of Lacanian theory would claim, gives us reason to consider many Lacanian concepts as containing the 'extimate' truth of Freudian theory.

30 I elaborate this argument in detail in Chapter 6.

31 This is an elementary point, but one worth reiterating inasmuch as it goes beyond the routine warnings against excessive subjectivity in qualitative research: we forget, in being objective researchers in the domain of the 'psychological', that it is our own egos – imaginary vessels of misrecognition *par excellence* – that are put into operation as a means of comprehending and understanding what we see.

2

NIXON'S 'FULL' SPEECH

The impotence of talk

If there is one common assumption that unites both the divergent traditions of psychoanalysis and the domain of psychotherapeutic culture more generally, it is the idea that speaking – putting one's difficulties and emotions into words – exercises a curative effect. This apparently self-evident truth often overlooks an inconvenient problem. Crucial as speech is, it often leads us nowhere. We need here to pay heed to Joël Dor's (1999) warning that the 'realm of speech is saturated with lies and contaminated with imaginary constructions; it is . . . the very place in which fantasies unfold . . . the place in which the subject reveals his own blindness' (p. 4).

This poses a question: how are we to understand those types of everyday communication in which a great deal is spoken by the participants, but effectively nothing new is heard or learnt, and no change is affected? The goal of this chapter, building on the framework established in Chapter 1, is to advance our understanding of particular modes of speech predominating within symbolic and imaginary registers of expression. Such an attention to (symbolic) 'full' as opposed to (imaginary) 'empty' speech provides a crucial means – at least for Lacanian psychoanalysis – of distinguishing between effective and ineffective therapeutic interactions, and by extrapolation, between transformative as opposed to non-transformative modes of communication. The illustrative device that we will draw upon to illustrate these ideas is, as the chapter's title suggests, an instance of speech uttered by former US President Richard Nixon in his interviews with British journalist David Frost in 1977. In order to appreciate the example, however, we will first need to introduce a series of further associated psychoanalytic, psychological and philosophical concepts so we are well placed to appreciate what Lacan, perhaps somewhat idealistically, has in mind with the concept of full speech.

'Let's talk about me'

We have all had the experience of watching two people talking, despite that both are effectively really only talking about – and listening to – themselves. Lacan confronts this problem of substance-less speech, the dead-end alley of self-proclaiming talk, with his notion of 'empty speech'. It is not hard to guess why he would prioritize this issue: an obvious clinical imperative lies with avoiding such a situation, where talking too much leads us away from truth. Any number of colloquial terms evoke the type of talk I have in mind here, the idea for example that someone has 'verbal diarrhoea', that they are ceaselessly blathering, 'gassing on' or that they talking *at* me rather than *to* me.

This ego-led type of interpersonal communication is well depicted in an episode of the US TV show *The Sopranos*. The lead character, Tony, is forced to take a hiatus from his therapy, and at first struggles to find a suitable listener to take her place. It quickly becomes apparent that her replacement, an old friend of Tony's, is not up to the task: although he listens at first, he uses the pauses in Tony's speech to insert stories and complaints of his own – in other words, he listens and responds with his ego. Their resulting conversation is like a comedic parody of a dialogue: their respective narratives hardly connect; they speak over one another, paying little if any attention to what the other is saying; any break in the other's speech becomes the opportunity for their counterpart to rehearse something about themselves. We have the situation, in short, where two speakers, seemingly involved in a dialogue, are actually involved in two self-enclosed monologues, each using the other as a communicative vehicle for a story they are telling themselves about themselves. In his 1961–1962 seminar on Identification, Lacan coins a term for this tendency to reduce everything to the perspective of me: 'mihilism'.

In such exchanges each participant is locked into a narcissistic closed-circuit of ego speech in which the only thing that matters is how this communicative content rebounds off their own imaginary sense of self. The familiar phrase, that someone is 'speaking shit' comes to mind – not in the sense of flagrant dishonesty, but in the sense of speech that one misleads oneself with, attempting thereby to secure or comfort one's self, to reduce one's anxiety, to make one's self feel whole. Importantly, what I am attempting to invoke is not something that can be reduced to impoliteness or a banal form of self-centredness. As will become apparent as we continue, such an ego-centred or 'imaginary' dimension of communication is not merely an anomaly, an irritating aspect of everyday speech that blocks true dialogue. This empty speech should be viewed rather as a constant tendency within communicative exchange between people, an impasse of dialogue that is *inherent to inter-subjective dialogue itself.*

This discussion of the problems underlying the imaginary register of communication sounds a note of caution regards the popularity of types of narrative analysis in psychology, particularly when such narrative analyses are deployed to ostensibly critical ends. Now while it is true that not all narrative forms can be limited to the function of empty speech, it is also the case that soliciting narratives from research subjects typically elicits the story *an ego wants to tell about itself*, which, in Lacanian terms, is for the most part a defensive and/or idealized formation, an index of the ego's fundamental imaginary alienation. Hence Lacan's description of empty speech as speech in which 'the subject seems to be talking in vain about someone who, even if he were his dead ringer, can never become one with the assumption of his desire' (2006, p. 211).

Personal narratives often exemplify the imaginary functioning of empty speech: much narrative form typically works to create wholeness, cohesion, to provide the continuity of a storyline, the closure of a narrative arc (the resolution of crisis or challenge) along with the basis of a viable imaginary identification (a protagonist). Hence the priority in Lacanian psychoanalytic treatments afforded to disrupting ego-narratives, overturning the imaginary powers of self-narration, via free association, the abrupt halting of sessions and so on.[1]

To this discussion of empty speech we must make a vital qualification. The imaginary dimension to speech is not only a problem; it is also absolutely necessary to communication, it is a precondition for dialogue to occur at all. As Soler (1996) argues, empty speech affords a means of connecting with others, it calls out for the recognition that they can provide, it contains the prospects of a type of imaginary mediation – that one might be understood, loved – but it is, in itself, insufficient for transformation, for symbolic forms of truth.

Empty speech and bullshit

There is a family resemblance of sorts between Lacan's notion of empty speech and Harry Frankfurt's (2005) conceptualization of bullshit. Frankfurt's philosophical analysis of the notion asserts that bullshit is neither simply careless, unplanned talk nor merely a case of lying. The bullshit of advertisers and politicians is, after all, anything but careless; it is often carefully crafted, strategically designed. An effective lie, moreover, necessarily retains some proximity to what is true, not only in the sense that successful lies are often interwoven within a series of truths, but in the more fundamental sense that the liar presumably needs to know what is true in order to design their deception.

Says Frankfurt: 'The liar is inescapably concerned with truth values . . . he must design his falsehood under the guidance of truth' (2005, pp. 51–52). For Frankfurt this is not the case in the 'hot air', the 'empty talk' of bullshit, which is produced without any concern for the truth. It is this detachment from the frame of the truthful – which even lies must remain strategically connected to – that particularly vexes Frankfurt. Hence his argument that bullshit is more the enemy of truth than are lies. With bullshit it is more a case of *fakery* than outright falsity, more an instance of *bluffing* than of intended dishonesty, which means that the bullshitter need not necessarily get things wrong, or even that what he or she says is factually untrue. Essentially anything goes – truths and falsities alike – in the narrative that the bullshit artist spins, so long as it serves their interests. 'The bullshitter may not deceive us, or even intend to do so, either about the facts or about what he takes the facts to be . . . he attempt[s] to deceive us about . . . his enterprise' (2005, p. 54).

What Frankfurt misses is the factor of ego-benefit, the ego-gratification that comes from speech of this sort. Bullshit, we might note, offering here an opportunity to expand upon Frankfurt's (2005) analysis, is essentially *ego-led speech*. With this hypothesis we are better placed to account for the omnipresence of this type of talk, and indeed, for its over-riding purpose, namely its *identity-substantiating function*. This reason outstrips a series of Frankfurt's speculations (the pleasures of bullshit in and of itself, etc.).[2] The key Lacanian insight in this respect concerns the fact that there is no essential self or ego, no integral substance to the 'I'. In light of this assertion we might better appreciate the insistence of this 'ego-serving speech': it is continually produced so as to provide some support, some content, for this mirage-like entity of the ego which is more than anything else a collection of images.

Heidegger's truth in discourse

We have arrived at a longstanding opposition in the philosophy of communication: the tension between instrumentality and truth. Given that a crucial antecedent to Lacan's empty/full speech distinction is found in Heidegger's (1927) opposition between '*Rede*' (or discourse) and '*Gerede*' (idle talk), it is worthwhile briefly introducing these concepts. In speaking of *Gerede* Heidegger is considering a type of intelligibility that is on display in everyday communicative interchanges. More specifically, if we break the contents of communication down into *the objects that it focuses on* (the objects that we speak about) and *the claims or positions we assert* relative to such objects, then idle talk is preoccupied predominantly with the latter. At its most basic *Gerede* is that mode of communication in which our interest in *making claims* or *establishing positions* relative to these objects over-rides any insight into the objects themselves. Rather than attempting to grasp the underlying truth of such objects, the communicative interchange remains pre-occupied with what is asserted *by means of* the objects in question. These objects are thus swept up and passed about on the current of various activities (claiming, arguing, asserting), without themselves ever being adequately interrogated or understood. The instrumentality of talk about things loses its way vis-à-vis its objects; a lack of interrogation sets in; an acceptance of what has already been said – of what one already 'knows' – prevails. Our talk thus becomes increasingly unsubstantiated, cut adrift both from its objects and from any adequate epistemological grounding.

If *Gerede* contains a rudimentary sense-making ability, a type of intelligibility, then so does *Rede*, although of a higher order. *Rede* is accorded an important place in Heidegger's philosophy, he considers it to be both a foundation for language – that is, it is the existential and ontological basis for language to work – and the means for the articulation of a superior type of intelligibility. '[T]he intelligibility of Being-in-the-world,' he says '*expresses itself as discourse*' (1927, p. 204). *Rede* must be separated from mere assertions about things, from a focus on properties and attributes. With *Rede* we are interested in how things might be disclosed in their

Being. *Rede* is thus never simply *about* something. It imparts to us rather a given object *and the necessary framework of understanding* that enables us a more significant apprehension or appreciation of the object. So, on the one hand we have an assertion about something (*Gerede*), a strategic speech act, and on the other a framework that underlies and enables this speech act to work (*Rede*) that makes possible a deeper intelligibility of things. How then are we to understand the workings of the latter as a precondition, as a 'basis of activation' necessary for speech acts to come into operation?

With the notion of *Rede* Heidegger is not driving after some pre-linguistic internal essence of objects in and of themselves. This however leaves us with an apparent problem: how to reconcile the requirements of the notion of *Rede* – able to adequately reveal or 'disclose' objects – without making the assumption that we can bypass language? If we turn to Heidegger's example of the heaviness of a hammer, we can see that this assertion (its heaviness) would not function if the surrounding terms had no meaning. The horizon of meaning thus established ensures that we can correctly isolate certain objects as hammers, and say whether or not they are heavy. Clearly, such statements are in one sense reliant upon the facts concerning the relevant object. However – and this is the crucial point – the verification of this facts-to-statements relation must entail an understanding of these 'framework elements' – that is, of what it is to be a hammer and what it is to be heavy – *without* these elements being derived simply from investigations of the 'actually existing' world. What counts then is not the attempt to match up the empirical world with ostensible facts – which of course would be potentially never ending – but a familiarity with the foregoing horizon of intelligibility we have at our disposal. This horizon of intelligibility is of course nothing but the framework of understanding offered to us by language, by *Rede*. Heidegger scholar Stephen Mulhall describes this situation:

> [S]ince this framework articulates what it is for something to count as a specific type of entity, it specifies the essential nature of things: to know the criteria governing the use of the term hammer just *is* to know what must be true of an entity if it is to count as a hammer . . . To grasp this framework is thus not just to grasp certain facts about our uses of words; it is also to grasp the essence of things. At this level, linguistic meaning and the meaning of entities are one and the same thing: the former discloses the latter.
>
> (p. 93)

It is for this reason that Heidegger (1927) can contend that '*Discourse is existentially primordial with state-of-mind and understanding*', indeed, that '[t]he intelligibility of something has always-already been articulated even before there is any appropriate interpretation of it' (p. 203).

For a psychoanalytic orientation eager to emphasise the role of the symbolic and to draw attention to the capacity of verbal communication to attain truth, one can appreciate the importance of Heidegger's theorization. If full speech is understood along the lines of *Rede*, we can see its potential, at least theoretically, for moving beyond the status quo of those un-interrogated types of everyday presumed 'knowledge' which remain in use without being properly apprehended. This trajectory towards truth within typically unexamined contents of communication is of clear importance when it comes to thinking about clinical methodology. The same holds true of the idea that there might be types of 'truth-activation' enabled by discourse, such that we see in full speech a form of 'speech which transforms the speaker in the very act of speaking' (1990, p. 141), to quote John Forrester. Or, as Lacan himself puts in the 17 March 1954 session of Seminar II: 'Full speech is speech which aims at, which forms, the truth . . . Full speech is speech which performs. One of the subjects finds himself, afterwards, other than he was before' (Lacan, 1988a, p. 107).

We can thus identify a clear convergence between Heidegger and Lacan in respect of the transformative function of communicative discourse. Heidegger maintains a commitment to discourse (or *Rede*) as able to reveal the truth, to disclose the 'Being-there' [Dasein] of its objects. In Lacan the notion of full speech provides a case of communicative interaction that disrupts the making of ego-attributions and ego-affirmations, destabilizing thus the constant reiteration of an established set of imaginary misrecognitions in favour of pointing to types of knowledge the subject didn't know they had.[3]

Communicating to sustain images

Having evoked a sense of empty speech and its rudimentary objectives, it helps to turn to a consideration of the particular attributes of this type of speech and its overall function. The evocative nature of language takes centre stage here. Although speech – and communicative behaviour more generally – holds out the potential of truth, it brings with it also the trappings of illusion; it enables us to believe in what we invoke. This is the imaginary aspect of language which functions to supply an illusory object status to what is in fact insubstantial. One is reminded of the seductive charms of rhetoric: the greater your powers of expression, the more I *feel* that I know *exactly what you're talking about*, that I share the same image, the same vision.

Clearly, one of Lacan's clinical objectives in prioritizing what he calls full speech is to bring to the fore the symbolic aspect of spoken interchange that may momentarily dissipate the illusory, figurative properties of language. He is thus able to present us with an opposition between two different forms of truth. There is, first, what is true within the confines of a given discourse (within the horizon of a particular mode of knowing, a type of intelligibility, the apparent 'adequacy to the thing' of a certain representation). In addition to this there is the truth made apparent by the pact established by the speech situation itself: the designated, symbolic roles conferred by a particular structure of interaction, for example, a consensus established as ratified by a form of symbolic registration. It is easy enough then to anticipate that much of language use, and certainly that of everyday talk, is often of an intermediary type – 'intermediate discourse' says Lacan (2006, p. 291) – cobbled together of both such aspects, both such claims to truth. Lacan (2006) hence offers the following injunction for clinical practice: that we need extract (full) speech from (empty) discourse.[4]

Lacan's 'imaginary register' is often discussed in ways that prioritize the visual: the imaginary is typically thought of as the domain of idealizing (and rivalrous) images, in terms of the mirrored reflections and identifications that buttress the ego, that lend it apparent coherence and stability. As I hope is by now apparent, we need to broaden this frame of reference to include also that aspect of language which functions – in a gestalt-like way – to lend to perception a sense of wholeness. To this we should add the imaginary function of *immediate comprehension*, which entails an insistence on attributing ego-centred meanings as a primary means of understanding. Lacan has in mind here nothing less than the tendency to automatic misrecognition, that is, the assimilation of something new within the narcissistic terms of what an ego already understands of itself.[5] Language is thus a crucial device in the making of imaginary constructions. Hence the idea, already introduced, that a subject, as it were, *speaks him- or herself into being*, into believing he or she is a substantial entity: this is the notion of empty speech as a way of shoring-up, lending consistency to, an ego; talking here is a project of imaginary *self-making*.

Ears wide shut

The image-making capacity of empty speech leads us away from difficult truths and introduces a set of systemic distortions into the subject's communications, distortions of what an ego *would like to hear and believe*. Hence the links so frequently found in psychoanalytic texts between subjective truth and what disturbs, discomforts, causes anxiety. Authentic speech, intimates Lacan (1998b) provokes anxiety, certainly so inasmuch as it is directed at a non-subjectifiable Other, an Other who can never be second-guessed, and who is always in part unrecognizable, impossible to anticipate.

We should not sidestep the factor of anxiety incurred by the Other (so emphasized by Lacan (2014) in Seminar X), that is, the fact of the persecutory element of the symbolic which, via this Other, constantly scrutinizes and terrorizes the subject. Of course – and this connects our current discussion to the topic of the unconscious in Lacan – the anxious dimension of communication resides not simply in the Other. What we might call a 'hypothesis game' exists between the subject and the Other. As discussed in the previous chapter, the Other is the target of the subject's ongoing existential attempts to affirm the meaning of their own socio-symbolic position and to guess what is wanted of them. This incessant questioning and answering process – an asymmetrical process, which as Verhaeghe (2001) stresses, takes place between a divided subject and a barred Other – is one way of conceptualizing the unconscious productions of the subject.[6]

Back though to the topic of empty speech: there is an abiding suspicion that what furnishes the ego with a comforting image of the world, or gratifies its inherent narcissism, necessarily involves a swerve away from reality. This much is apparent in Freud's (1917) comments on reality testing in *Mourning and Melancholia*. One would be correct in supposing that a somewhat bleak vision underlies Freudian epistemology in this respect, especially given the connection he poses between grasping the objective state of things and the giving up of more flattering images of one's self. This is a theme we will return to, the idea that there are few subjective truths that do not emerge without running against the grain of resistance, without difficulty, denial and refutation, hence no doubt Lacan's (2006) aside: 'Full speech . . . is hard work . . . laborious to articulate', painful to the subject (p. 515).

An important psychoanalytic maxim to bear in mind when analysing inter-subjective communication: talk is continually conditioned by the tendency (on the part of both speakers) to affirm the ego, to protect and insulate it against what it finds unpalatable, and to mobilize defences against hearing anything too disruptive. These defences involve an epistemological dimension already alluded to, namely the systematic distortions whereby the ego hears on the basis of what is already 'known' by, pertinent to, or reflective of its own interests (the state thus of 'having ears *in order not to hear*' (Lacan, 2006, p. 211). We might then overlay Piaget's long-standing concepts of assimilation and accommodation – which distinguish between the cognitive operations of fitting of new experiences into existing schemas and the construction of altogether new structures of understanding – with a properly psychoanalytic dimension: we may as such speak of *imaginary* assimilation and *symbolic* accommodation.

This underlines once again the challenges behind communicating at all: in sending a message the subject is typically more concerned with affirming an ideal image of its ego, with winning the gratifications of the recognition of others, than with what is being communicated *per se*. Frankfurt's (2005) example of a 4th of July orator who goes on in bombastic fashion about the greatness of America, its illustrious and heroic history, is instructive in this respect. What this speaker really cares about notes Frankfurt, is what people think of *him*, as a patriot, someone who reflects deeply on the origin of his country. The listener's disposition is likewise conditioned – the case, one might say, of 'having an ego for ears' – by how what is being said might serve to affirm their ego, what they know, what they might be able to tell others about themselves.

Subject ≠ ego

We have spent a good deal of time outlining something that Lacan (1988a) insists on in Seminar I, namely that 'the *ego* is an imaginary function' (p. 193). Crucially however – and the point is vital if we are to succeeding in differentiating Lacanian theory from the forms of psychology that he spends so much time attacking – the ego 'is not to be confused with the subject' (1988a, p. 193). Why should this be the case? Unusually, Lacan's response to this question is relatively straightforward:

We are necessarily obliged to admit the speaking subject as subject. But why? For one simple reason – because he can lie. That is, he is distinct from what he says. Well the dimension of the subject, the speaking subject *qua* deceiver, is what Freud discovered for us in the unconscious.

(p. 194)

In stressing the speaking subject of the unconscious as deceiver, Lacan is not concerned with the lie as a moral problem or an instance of conscious deception. He is instead drawing attention to the phenomenon of subjective inconsistency and division. He is alluding to the repeated clinical evidence that the ego is neither whole nor self-totalizing, but is instead constantly interrupted in speech by a *knowledge that it does not know it knows*. It is this that tells us that there is something – the subject – that exceeds the parameters of the ego, and that remains, as it were, un-objectified. In this respect the subject and the instance of unconscious enunciation are equated, certainly so inasmuch both lie beyond what the ego would claim as its own. This is one of the first occasions where Lacan invokes the unconscious by means of a variation on what will subsequently become a shorthand form of reference, namely the idea that 'it speaks' (*ça parle*):

Freud shows us that in the human subject there is something which speaks, which speaks in the full sense of the word . . . without the contribution of consciousness.

(1988a, p. 194)

Why this is so crucial to a consideration of Lacan's 'non-relation' with psych-ology, is that it is psychology – and psychoanalytic ego psychology in particular – that Lacan accuses of having regressed to an era prior to Freud's discovery of the unconscious. The result of this regressive gesture is that the ego is re-prioritized as the central concept and governing principle of psychic life. As Lewis (2008) notes of this backsliding move of the ego psychologists: 'this reduced psychoanalysis to a mere psychology, a science of the conscious ego', when the whole point of psychoanalysis *was precisely to unseat the ego*, to dislodge it from its prior position of sovereignty within the psyche, to thus 'resituate the ego in a wider psychic economy which preceded it and within which it was generated' (p. 19).

Not only is the subject situated definitively beyond the categories of the ego, it also exists beyond the ego's categories of knowing, that is, it outstrips epistemological strategies that rely on a type of objectification. There is thus a twofold error in conflating subject and ego. Such a conflation will prove a failure in the clinic, first, for subjectivity is greater in its component aspects than the ego ('The ego . . . is only one element in the . . . relations of the subject' (Lacan, 1988a, p. 194)). Prioritizing the ego will lead us to repeatedly overlook the unconscious. Second, no scientific approach that insists upon the fixity of stable objects of know-ledge can work here, for the subject of the unconscious eludes any encapsulation as object.[7]

'What do we call a subject?' Lacan asks, before going on to answer himself: 'Quite precisely, what, in the development of objectivation, is outside of the object' (p. 194). This, in short order, is why psychology is in his view inept, not up to the task of grappling with the subject: it retains an epistemology that requires coherent or regularly occurring objects of study. This alone makes it an unsuitable and ill-prepared discipline with which to access the constantly changing productions of the unconscious. The unconscious, after all, is incessantly finding new ways of transmitting itself; such plasticity – never-ending formal innovation – is what is required if systems of repression are, however momentarily, to be eluded.

A further consideration comes into play here. The epistemic posture of scientific psychology – the attempt to know, to understand, to fix in place what it attempts to study – is further mismatched to the subject of the unconscious because the unconscious is by its nature fleeting, transitory. It appears in acts – flashes of wit, slips of the tongue, symptomatic behaviours – and is, as such, not a substantial entity but rather a type of event. We cannot seize it as a type of permanence. The unconscious, by contrast – to borrow a characterization that Lacan will go on to offer in Seminar XI, that is certainly borne out by clinical experience – 'opens and closes'.

Existing beyond the horizons of object knowledge and, as we might put it, 'object-permanence', the unconscious is decidedly a non-psychological entity. Lacan's brief critique of the ideals of science in Seminar I thus pertains directly to his attack of the psychological:

> the ideal of science is to reduce the object to what can be closed and fastened within a system of interacting forces. In the end the object is only ever like that for science . . . [However] when it comes to organized beings, the scientist finds himself obliged after all to imply that action exists. Certainly one can always consider an organized being as an object, but as long as one grants it the status of the organism, one retains, if only implicitly, the idea that it is a subject.

> (p. 194)

There is a phenomenological dimension to Lacan's anti-objectivist position which is both crucial to appreciate and easy to miss. Jacques-Alain Miller's (1996a, 1996b, 1996c) discussion of Lacan's orientation prior to 1953 highlights the role of phenomenology for the young psychoanalyst. 'Phenomenology was of capital importance to Lacan as it introduced anti-objectivism' (Miller, 1996a, p. 11). This would prove foundational both for Lacan's theorization of the unconscious and for his notion of the subject. The phenomenology of Husserl, Sartre and Merleau-Ponty insists upon the fundamental non-objectivist status of the unconscious, remarks Miller (1996c). Consciousness is a vehicle through which we gain access to the world and not an object within. Hence one 'must not describe or analyse self-consciousness with the same categories you use to describe objects in the world' (p. 27c). In trying to describe the life of consciousness, none of the categories you use to describe the world is useful or adequate. You may have a category with which to describe an object in the world – 'substance' or some such term – but if you accept the idea of consciousness, there is no objectivist or positive category with which to describe it.

(Miller, 1996c, p. 27)

Characteristically of course, Lacan never imports a foregoing philosophical idea without in some way changing it, and the phenomenological perspective above is no exception. 'The Lacanian twist' here, 'is to transfer the phenomenological view of consciousness to the concept of the subject' (Miller, 1996c, p. 27) which is resolutely anti-objectivist. As if anticipating that the influence of phenomenology upon Lacan's theorization of the subject will one day be sidelined, Miller adds, for good measure, that 'Lacan transfers the whole of phenomenological analysis to the subject of the unconscious, and much of Lacan's teaching is a reformulation of this phenomenological theme in psychoanalysis' (1996c, p. 27).

Moving away from this phenomenological influence, it is worth noting that in Lacan's above (Seminar I) critique of objectifying sciences one can find the seeds of the proclamation that he will issue a decade later, that 'the status of the unconscious . . . is ethical' (p. 33, XI). We can refer to this idea both to reiterate the terms of the 1950s critique – the error of viewing the unconscious as an epistemological category, the fallacy of thinking it in ontological terms (a form of being, a substance) – and to add a crucial additional element. That is to say, in clarifying the ethical horizon within which the unconscious should be approached, Lacan is signalling that the real priority lies with engaging the unconscious as an *act* of the subject, which in turn engenders an attention to change, and an awareness of the unconscious itself as possessed of a paradoxical order of agency. It is for this ethical reason that Fink (2014a) insists that the essential aim of analysis lies not with understanding, with gaining insight, or some form of self-reflexive knowledge, but with *subjective change*, which, as he repeatedly insists, does not require the assent – or the consciousness – of the ego.

The subject must thus be thought not merely as beyond the confines of the ego, but beyond the terrain also of *consciousness*, which is of course one of traditional psychology's privileged concepts. Consciousness and the ego *both* stand in the way of the agency of the subject of the unconscious. What this means in effect is that Lacan assumes an *ethical* stance against psychology – ethical here defined in terms of facilitating change in the subject – inasmuch as these objectifications (the objects of conscious and the ego itself as a type of object) are, for Lacan, what we might call 'counter-agentic'. Lewis plays out aspects of this argument in an informative comparison of the 'subjectal' and the 'objectal':

That of which the subject is conscious is always an object for consciousness: that of which we cannot become conscious is therefore a 'subject' . . . The only genuine subject is one that has not been objectified, it is a subject that is acting, an agent, and if one is speaking of a subject that is involved with language this means a speaking subject . . . If the unconscious subject is fundamentally and always unconscious – subjectal – it can enter conscious awareness – objectality – only in a form that distorts its true nature . . . The subject can become an object for consciousness only in the form of 'symptoms'.

(2008, p. 21)

This sets the bar high for clinicians: the subject is known only via symptoms, in distorted form, via the – constantly changing – formations of the unconscious. The unconscious, contrary to crude caricatures of psychoanalysis, most certainly does not speak in formulaic terms. Nor does it adhere to a rudimentary set of codes or symbols. It would be an inept unconscious, after all, that attempts to express facets of unconscious desire in terms which are culturally all too familiar or that might be readily decoded.

Classical Freudian symbols no longer suit us, if, that is, their apparent signification is all too predictable in a culture saturated with such interpretations. In this sense the unconscious learns, or adapts from one era to another, so as better to cipher its missives. Hence Grose's (2014) observation that analysts need to grapple with 'an unconscious that is constantly pushed to invent its own language . . . [its own] means of articulating itself' (p. 20). This is an unconscious that utilizes an idiosyncratic and inconsistent set of 'symbols' (or, more appropriately, signifiers), an unconscious that in Grose's words 'replaces a father with a curtain because that's the best means it can find at the time' (p. 20). If it is the case then that each speaking subject uses language in a highly distinctive, indeed unique manner, then it should come as no surprise that the analyst has the challenge of hearing 'an unconscious that's totally different in each person' (Grose, 2014, p. 20), an unconscious that operates as a kind of private language.

'I did not have sexual relations with that woman'

This brief discussion of the unconscious leads us to consider what might be the most profitable listening strategies for a Freudian/Lacanian clinician. Helpful here is Lacan's (2006) oft-repeated declaration that the unconscious is *structured like a language*. One way of exploring this difficult pronouncement is by making reference to Bill Clinton's infamous insistence: 'I did not have sexual relations with that woman'. We find support from an unlikely source here, namely discursive psychology's attempts at a revised understanding of 'Freudian repression' (Billig, 1999). Proponents of discursive psychology emphasize that it is quite possible for an audience to hear in given expressions something quite different to what the speaker had intended.

This possibility of unintended hearing arises for the dual reason that all expressions leave some things unsaid and what is said can be understood in more than one way . . . Expressions do not exhaust the possibility of their meaning.

(Durrheim, Mtose and Brown, 2010, pp. 174–175)

Although many social psychological engagements with the notion of repression are explicitly anti-Lacanian (Billig, 1999, 2006), the above understanding fits perfectly with a Lacanian approach. From a Lacanian perspective, every statement brings in its wake a series of variations. Every utterance, in other words, exists within a horizon of associated yet differing formulations. What is conveyed in a communicative exchange, after all, is not merely a minimal, stripped-to-the-core message, but also a number of subsidiary prospective significations. This alerts us to a point of Lacanian psychoanalytic technique: the idea that the facilitation of a series of lateral significations may take priority over the aiming of extracting a single over-arching message.

'OK, so you say that you did not have sexual relations with *that* woman. Well, what other woman *did* you have sexual relations with?' Such would be one response to Clinton's statement. Another, taking into account the legal ambiguity of Clinton's appeal to 'sexual relations': 'You didn't have "sexual *relations*" . . . Well perhaps you could tell us about what sexual interactions/activities/practices you *did* engage in?'

In short: any communicative statement conveys along with it a matrix of alternative hearings. There is a framework of intelligibility that accompanies any statement, a framework which accordingly supports multiple grammatical permutations of such a statement. It helps, in making the point, to underscore the provisional nature of any message. How a message is framed by the contingencies of its context; how it is related to the imagined intent of the speaker; the conditions of how it was uttered, performed and why: all of these considerations mean that a message remains – even if perfectly legible – 'incomplete', open to 'unintended hearings'.

This idea, that a message ('I did not have sexual relations with that woman') brings with it a grid of grammatical permutations, is worth demonstrating. For a start, following Freud's suggestion regards the role of negation in how clinicians listen to their patients we could replace the relevant negation, substituting 'I did not have sexual relations with . . .', with 'I *did* have sexual relations with . . .'. Similarly, we could subject the statement to substitutions of object and verb (i.e. 'I did not have sex with "a" [. . . *but with b*]' (change of object), 'I did not have sexual relations [. . . *but I did I take a walk on the wild side*]' (idiomatic transformation of verb). Likewise, we can posit substitutions of metaphor and extensions so that instead of 'have sexual relations' we hear 'carefully examined her clothes' (a metonymic extension) or 'made beautiful music together' (a metaphor).

We need also to bear in mind the obvious temporal dimension of speech, the fact that a statement unfolds in time and that the first clause of a sentence cannot properly be understood until we hear what follows. We could ask what effects of meaning are put in play by positing a conjunction ('I did not have sexual relations with that woman . . . *but/although/and then. . .*') or simply by suspending the ending of the sentence, and experimenting with what might emerge: '(I did not have sexual relations with that woman. . . . ' . . . ['*although I certainly tried to!*']). The possibility of an active/passive reversal regards the verb of the statement gives us another humorous way of responding to Clinton: ('*You* did not have sexual relations with that woman . . . but did *she* have sexual relations with *you*?')

We have by no means exhausted the elaborative permutations of Clinton's statement here. My aim has been simply to indicate the profusion of unintended hearings that are latent in a straightforward assertion, to highlight the potential of the signifier to overrun any single trajectory of meaning. To put language into play is to allow for a variety of different substitutions and extensions, substitutions along a metaphoric axis and extensions along a metonymic axis, a fact that in and of itself is enough to supply an unconscious. The site of language, more simply put, is the site of the unconscious.

The repressed as the return of the repressed

We can add a further layer to our developing account of mishearing and an 'external' unconscious by considering Lacan's (1988a) argument that the return of the repressed and the repressed are one and the same. This assertion is strictly correlative to the idea that the unconscious is not an internal space or mentality, an 'intra-psychic' collection of contents and impulses. It is, by contrast, an unconscious that is fashioned from and made possible by language, or, as Lacan would put it, *by the signifier*. This gives us a clue as to how to understand Lacan's statements concerning repression. We need to take seriously the idea that in speaking I create the possibility of a repressed (or, more accurately, of a potential 'return of the repressed').

I once invited a famous actor to a dinner party. I was of course aware that the presence of such a notable person would make a memorable night for my other guests. After the event I felt guilty, because my guest had had to suffer the overbearing attentions of my friends. I resolved to apologize, until I realized that to apologize would alert him to the fact that I had something to be guilty for. 'Why would he apologize?' he might have asked himself. It may never have entered his mind that I had anything to apologize for. The inappropriate behaviours of my friends were not something I was responsible for, *unless* of course I had contrived the situation precisely to entertain those friends. To let him know that I felt guilty would be to indicate my complicity in the situation. This calls to mind the cliché of the guilty husband whose gift of flowers makes his otherwise trusting wife start to suspect that something is amiss.

The beauty of these examples is that my famous guest, like the wife who has received flowers, may not have had *any idea at all* about the 'guilty truth' in question. There was no inner psychology, no 'intra-psychic' repressed material: it was only by virtue of what was said or expressed that a 'repressed' was created. To be clear on this point: in Lacan's understanding of 'the return of the repressed' there needs be no existing 'dirty secret'. All that is required is a signifier – the act of giving flowers – that causes one, in retrospect, to start questioning its broader significance. The act of speaking, the subtleties of communication, following this line of argumentation, are all that is required for a 'repressed' to come into play. Such signifiers are the condition of possibility, they are enough to ignite a thought, a suspicion, a question, and once this is in place (a 'return of the repressed'), then there effectively *will have been* – after the fact – a repressed.

A matrix of latent combinatory meanings

Virtually any communicative instance – any signifier – might form the basis of a 'return of the repressed'. Signifiers provide the 'material', the apparent evidence that brings a repressed possibility to light. Consider the following scene: a woman watching her husband chatting to his secretary at a Christmas party suddenly detects an inappropriate gesture, a giveaway sign that, she thinks, betrays that they are having an affair. One should note again the odd temporality underpinning this logic: the 'repressed' here, the fact of the apparent affair, did not exist as 'repressed' until it came to light. The 'repressed' in effect did not exist, until the observing woman is confronted with the 'return of the repressed'. Although this may seem an unfamiliar conceptualization of the repressed, it of course accords with Freud's (1950) notion of deferred action, that is, with the idea of retrospective causality whereby a current event (typically, for Freud, of a traumatic sort) triggers the latent impact of an earlier incident. What is also notable about Lacan's approach to this question is that he attempts to understand repression not as a psychological quality or function, but as a potentiality within the signifying field. Repression of this order – which is to say secondary repression – is thus contingent upon language, or, more accurately, the reception and production of signifiers, whose meaning is never completely fixed.

This point is worth reiterating: Lacan's notion of the unconscious is not thus 'psychological' – certainly not in any narrow sense of the word – but rather 'linguistic' in its functioning (or, taking Miller's (2011) lead, we may speak simply of the *linguistic* structure of psychology). This is one way of understanding Lacan's 'the unconscious is structured like a language', namely that the unconscious is brought about by – and is hence contingent upon – the productions of language (signifiers). Such an unconscious would be undoubtedly complex, evidently so if we consider the multitude of proliferating interpretations sustained by any instance of linguistic production. It would also, however, be an omnipresent potentiality, by which I mean to stress that it exists as a possibility whenever there is a communicative exchange, or, indeed, the use of language.

Frost/Nixon

Having discussed the idea of an 'external' unconscious, and having established a rudimentary sense of what 'empty speech' is, we now tackle the more difficult task of characterizing 'full speech'. Ron Howard's (2008) film *Frost/Nixon* dramatizes a series of interviews carried out in 1977 between the British journalist David Frost and the former US President. What makes the film so useful a point of reference given our current concerns is that it stages the encounters between the two men as a desperate affair of two egos in crisis, indeed, as a bout – Nixon's aide even likens the interviews to a boxing match – as a 'struggle to the [symbolic] death'. The stakes of such a symbolic demise are real: Frost's career is in free fall; he risks enormous debt and professional humiliation in his attempt to record these interviews with a man who in turn is aggressively intent on using the exchanges as a means of restoring his image, defending himself, potentially returning to public life. Frost's research team, by contrast, want to use the interviews as a means of 'Giving Nixon the trial he never had'.

What accounts for much of dramatic tension present in the run-up to the final interview is that Frost seems completely outclassed. 'Tricky Dicky' has at his disposal all the rhetorical devices of the smooth-talking politician, and is completely at ease at the centre of attention in front of the TV cameras. As soon as filming begins, the beleaguered Frost, by contrast, becomes a virtual irrelevance, his interrogative skills are swept aside, and he is reduced to an ineffectual respondent, a stage prop that allows Nixon (very nearly) to vindicate himself. We have thus an exemplary instance of empty speech: the 'little other' of Frost amounts to no more than a patsy, a means to Nixon's grandiose self-narrativization.

How then does this type of speech tip over into something different? Given his vitriolic assertions of innocence, his declared intent to 'set the record straight', why does Nixon go on to admit error, and culpability in the Watergate scandal? Why the apparent apology for 'letting the American people down' – which, until that point was inconceivable for the recalcitrant Nixon – and the declaration, a perfect instance of the *act* of saying something effectively making it so, that 'My political life is over'? Or, framed more generally: What were the underlying conditions to this dialogue that made it possible for a previously repudiated truth to be spoken, and spoken in such a way that changed not only the life circumstances and role of the speaker, but the socio-political circumstances of the milieu itself?

Nixon's admissions come at a very particular moment in his discussion with Frost over Watergate. After repeated assertions of his innocence ('. . . you're wanting me to say that I . . . participated in an illegal cover-up? No.' (Frost and Zelnick, 2007, p. 244)), Nixon considers the emotive question: 'How do I feel about the American people?', and then changes tack to recall an earlier event:

> I didn't expect this question frankly though so I'm not going to give you that, but I can tell you this . . . I think I said it all in one of those moments when you're not thinking . . . I had a lot of difficult meetings those last days before I resigned and the most difficult one, and the only one where I broke into tears [was when] . . . I met with all my key supporters just a half-hour before going on television . . .

. . . And, at the very end, after saying, 'Well, thank you for all your support during these tough years' . . . And I just, well . . . I sort of cracked-up; started to cry; pushed my chair back and then I blurted it out, I said, 'I'm sorry, I just hope I haven't let you down'.

Well, when I said, 'I just hope I haven't let you down', that said it all.

I had.

I let down my friends.

I let down the country.

I let down our system of government and the dreams of all those young people that ought to get into government but think it's all too corrupt . . .

Yep, I . . . I, I let the American people down, and I have to carry that burden with me for the rest of my life.

My political life is over.

I will never yet, and never again, have an opportunity to serve in any official position . . .

And so I can only say that, in answer to your question, that while technically I did not commit a crime, an impeachable offence – these are legalisms.

As far as the handling of this matter is concerned, it was botched up, I made so many bad judgements.

(Nixon, cited in Frost and Zelnick, 2007, pp. 246–247)

Five aspects of full speech

It is important to maintain some distance from the assumption that truth simply emerges here in the form of an encapsulating statement. If, as Lacan (2007) emphasizes in his later seminars, subjective truth, the truth of desire, *can only ever be half-said*, then moments like that pinpointed above should be treated as a transitory speech event, an event with the potential to open up into something potentially transformative without however ever amounting to 'the full and whole truth'. We have something then more closely resembling a truth trajectory than an absolute truth, a movement towards *a productive saying* rather than exemplified Truth.

We should not forget that for Lacan desire cannot be formulated in propositional form, that it emerges as such instead in the form of formal distortions, contradictions, as instances of the 'real' of what cannot be said. Crucial here also is the distinction between a Lacanian moment of disruption in which the speaker encounters something surprising, leading or disruptive in their speech and a more Habermasian notion of recognition. Clearly my focus here is on the former, and we need to be wary of assimilating the former into the latter. In the former case, given Lacan's emphasis on the 'real' on the ultimate inexpressibility of truth and of the divided subject's desire, no transparent realization of truth through language can ever be expected. In Habermas (1984), by contrast, there is a commitment to deliberative forms of truth and their recognition which may emerge precisely within the context of an 'ideal-speech situation'. For a good rationalist like Habermas, there must a viable transparency of truth; not so for Lacan.

An important clinical implication follows on from the idea of half-said truths: if truth is viewed in this way, not as finalized object, but as movement towards an elusive kind of saying, then the analyst is surely not the person to identify when such a truth-event – an instance of full speech – has occurred. Truth is not thus finally secured by a definitive interpretation of the analyst; it is rather the case that it is the subject who knows that in some or other way they have (half)spoken a truth.[8]

From a Lacanian perspective the answer to why Nixon made such unexpected admissions has little to do with the psychological conditions of an interpersonal two-way dialogue. We should thus bracket a series of banal psychological speculations (such as Nixon's need to 'come clean', ascribing Nixon's outburst merely to the interpersonal skills of the interviewer).[9] A far more feasible explanation, from a Lacanian standpoint, would involve mapping the Frost-Nixon interchange onto the L-Schema introduced in the previous chapter. Nixon's comments might be viewed thus in terms of how the imaginary dimension of empty speech veered into the register of full speech. Now although there are good reasons to question such an assessment – to query whether Nixon's comments really qualified as full speech, as paradigmatically different from empty speech – many of the characterizing features of full speech can be illustrated by means of this example.

We have, first, the factors of error, surprise, the unanticipated (i.e. what Nixon *had not meant to say*), each of which represents a route to a difficult, previously unacceptable disclosure. Put differently, we have a speech moment – as in the case of the typical Freudian slip – in which the subject speaks *beyond him- or herself* (beyond their ego), and ends up saying more than they had meant to (i.e. Nixon's '*I said it all in one of those moments when you're not thinking*'). In such cases there is something *Other* in one's speech, something which seems not to have been said by one's self, or adequately integrated into the field of one's own conscious (ego) identity. This aspect of speaking beyond one's self seems clear in Nixon's words: ('. . . *when I said, "I hope I haven't let you down", that said it all*'). We link back here to our earlier discussion of the speaking *subject* of the unconscious. This is one of the most economical ways of characterizing full speech, and differentiating it from the empty speech of the ego: full speech is speech in which the subject becomes present.

Second, there is the disruption of ego-to-ego speech which occurs when it becomes apparent that it is the *Other* rather than the imaginary respondent of the 'little other' that one is speaking to, and being heard by. That the Other provokes anxiety, upsetting the operations of ego speech, is an important consideration here. When Frost comes fleetingly to occupy the position of this Other – the role of the 'confessional interlocutor' of History, of the expectant American People – *this itself* is a precondition of Nixon's unexpected admissions. Frost himself, as 'little other' could not precipitate such a destabilization. The confessional nature of Nixon's speech is worth considering in this light. Such spoken confessional comments could not have effectively been achieved 'intra-personally' by Nixon; the structure of confessional communication necessitates an Other. Confessing cannot function without this element of symbolic registration, without breaking the intra-subjective circuit of self-narrativization and thus alerting an Other as to what has been done.

We can bring two aspects of full speech to bear as a means of shedding light on Lacan's (1988) puzzling definition of communication, the idea that 'one receives one's own message from the other in an inverted form' (1988, p. 51). How so? Well we can understand the factor of 'inverted form' as the medium of others, that is, one's message reflected via others whose hearing (and potentially, whose responses) participate in its meaning. Lacan's definition implies also a sense of how one's message is relayed via the big Other, a process which entails the elements of surprise and error, involving those facets of my speech that I had not intended but that nonetheless underlie the compromising truth potential of what has been said. Nixon, we might say, receives his own message back from the other in an inverted form: 1) via it being heard by an other to whom it is spoken (an imaginary reflection of contents), 2) by virtue of the presence of a pronounced Other (the symbolic dimension), which emphasizes the conditions of anxiety and unpredictability in the making of the message.[10]

Third, we have the performative dimension of Nixon's comments, the fact of their illocutionary force as speech acts, the consideration, in other words, of the 'what is done' by virtue of what he says. 'Full speech is speech which performs' says Lacan (1988a, p. 107). It is speech that transforms the speaker in the act of speaking. To this we must add the aligned issue of what is changed about the situation, and Nixon's own status, by virtue of what he says and *how* he has said it. This is clear enough in Nixon's declaration that his political career is over, a statement, as noted above, that affects what it says. It is apparent also in Nixon's acknowledgement of wrongdoing, an acknowledgement which confirms the events in question – and his own complicity therein – thus committing these facts to the official historical record. This is, once again, the element of symbolic registration, the event of informing the Other which is likewise apparent whenever someone swears an oath, or puts a contractual relation in place.

Fourth, a different relation to truth has been established. It is not only that something about the structure of the (inter-subjective) situation has been changed by virtue of what Nixon has said. Something *about himself* and his own relation to his past has also changed, has been brought into a different potential relation to truth. So, whereas in empty speech there is a gap between the ego content of what is enunciated and the position of enunciation (what is said does not chime with the truth of the subject's desire), in full speech the subject articulates their position of enunciation (their speaking position of desire) despite its discordance with the ego. This links to another characteristic of full speech: rather than the ego-substantiating function, the imaginary self-making of empty speech that operates to assure and comfort us regards the existence of an ego, full speech resembles more a coming undone of this ego, an experience typically accompanied by anxiety and resistance. Truth here takes the form of that which disturbs, destabilizes; it assumes an almost necessary relation to discomfort, even to pain.

This idea resonates with a theme in Theodor Adorno's (2003) writings, the notion that truth is not attained on its own terms – as a positive assertion or discovery – but rather through the more painful process whereby what had hitherto been considered true is discovered to be false. Lacan spends some time detailing this process whereby full speech runs against the grain of the ego, emphasizing the roles of frustration and aggressivity. Speaking of the patient's empty speech in the analytical session, Lacan (2006) asks the rhetorical question:

> Doesn't the subject become involved here in an ever greater dispossession of himself as a being, concerning which – by dint of sincere portraits which leave the idea of his being no less incoherent, of rectifications that do not succeed in isolating its essence, of stays and defences that do not prevent his statue from tottering, of narcissistic embraces that becomes like a puff of air in animating it – he ends up recognizing that his being has never been anything more than his own construction [*oeuvre*] in the imaginary and that this construction undercuts all certainty in him?
>
> (p. 207)

In such an anxiety-provoking process – a 'hystericization' of the subject – the patient confronts a series of collapsing imaginary self-truths. What Lacan describes is tantamount to a type of negative epiphany in which the subject encounters anew the fundamental alienation underlying the construction of their ego which has been 'construct[ed] *like another*, and that has always been destined . . . to be taken away from him *by another*' (p. 208). This ego, concludes Lacan, is not frustrated merely on the basis of circumstance, but is rather 'frustration in its very essence' (p. 208). The aggressiveness to which such frustration is linked, moreover, is not that of an animal whose desires have been thwarted, it is 'the aggressiveness of a slave who responds to being frustrated in his labour with a death wish' (p. 208).

A fifth consideration includes the role of full speech as a type of founding speech. Indeed, the fact that full speech entails the making of an elementary pact (of speaker and interlocutor), that it implies a contract, the cementing of roles, the acknowledgement of certain reciprocal obligations, is vital. In this respect one should draw attention to the precise conditions immediately preceding Nixon's confession. Surrounded by his most loyal supporters, and about to confront the big Other of the expectant American people, Nixon reaches breaking point at the moment that he is forced to confront not merely his own compromised symbolic position, but the fact of a failed pact, an abused bond, a broken symbolic relation (he has failed his friends, his supporters, the system of government). What is effective and powerful in full speech has much to do with this establishment of a *new order of relationship between myself and my other/Other interlocutors*, a relationship that is 'ratified', confirmed by the very conditions of speaking themselves. Rather than the legal idea of a 'verbal contract' applying only under certain conditions, a Lacanian perspective attunes us to the extent that everyday exchanges of speech continually commit us to types of contracts and roles. Hence the idea that it is speech that locks us into symbolic positions and obligations.

This is partly what Lacan has in mind when invoking the notion of symbolic efficacity – a term he derives from the work of Lévi-Strauss (1974) – namely that the symbolic itself, once set in motion, reproduces a type of symbolic reality above and beyond the requirement of any conscious (which is to say individual, psychological) agency. This self-perpetuating momentum of the symbolic is apparent in the preponderance of certain cultural myths, which despite being subject to multiple variations and elaborations nonetheless persist; it is a function also of the network of interlinked roles and structural relationships that make up a given symbolic community. In both such cases we have a sense of what the 'primacy of the signifier' might mean for Lacan, a sense of how certain structural considerations have an influence on human affairs that is, in effect, unconscious in nature. It is for this reason that when Lacan (1979) engages Freud's famous clinical case of Ernst Lanzer ('the Ratman'), he spends considerable time tracing the complicated cobweb of Lanzer's various real and symbolic debts and obligations, aware of how such responsibilities embody a type of personal symbolic efficacity in the sense that they set in train a series of unconscious compulsions and enactments.[11]

Speech devoid of content

Lacan shares with Austin (1962) at least two vital commitments in his approach to speech. The first of these is a resolutely non-psychological stance which does away with any reference to the conscious intentionality of inner states (which, like the vast majority of appeals to the psychological, are taken to be grounded in the domain of the imaginary). Lacan concurs, second, with the pragmatic imperative of breaking our fixation with the *constative* dimension of language, that is, with the assumption that the functioning of speech is best evaluated with assessments of truth and falsity. In other words, speech should not be viewed as a chiefly expressive vehicle whose primary task is to name, represent and describe the world, and whose efficacy can thus be based on its degree of factual accuracy. Although such properties are vital to language as a communicative modality, they do not best pinpoint its ability to facilitate and convey communicative meaning.

Furthermore, as argued above, this imaginary aspect of meaning-making engenders illusions; it functions to create effects of certainty, stability and ego-coherence, to reify both its speaker and their objects. This is the medium of self-narrative, of the stories we tell ourselves via others, stories which, psychoanalytically, are not to be trusted, even when they do seemingly accord with reality, for the simple fact that their over-riding objective is to sustain ego-affirming images. In this sense they can be said to be fictitious even when they overlap with the truth. It perhaps helps here to recall that for Freud (1927) what defines an illusory belief is not whether it accords with the actual state of affairs – there are illusory beliefs that are, in a strict empirical sense, 'factual' – but whether it is most fundamentally grounded in *a wish for something to be so*.[12]

Empty speech, we could say, has an alienating, inauthentic destination, even if composed of factually true fragments; full speech, by contrast, can be error-ridden, may involve falsities and untruths *en route* to an end point of revelation. The implication of this is that the truth potential of full speech should have little to do with the empirical truth value of its contents. The paradox of this situation is that empty speech is often exceedingly full of non-substantive ego-supporting contents (it is full of shit, we might say); it is heavy on content but light on substance. So, while empty speech is typically loaded with insubstantial materials, symbolic full speech is often stripped of content. This is an idea that resonates with Roman Jakobson's (1960) concept of phatic communication, with the idea of essentially meaningless exchanges that function simply to maintain a social bond, to keep communicative channels open and effective. This is particularly evident in a paragraph in which Lacan draws on Mallarmé, who, he says:

> compares the common use of language to the exchange of a coin whose obverse and reverse no longer bear any but eroded faces, and which people pass from hand to hand 'in silence'. This metaphor suffices to remind us that speech, even when almost worn out, retains its value as a *tessera* [a ticket, password, means of identification]. Even if it communicates nothing, discourse represents the existence of communication; even if it denies the obvious, it affirms that speech constitutes truth; even if it is intended to deceive, the discourse speculates on faith in testimony.
>
> (2006, p. 209)

In how you say it

The above extract is suggestive in a number of respects. Lacan is arguing that how we typically understand the truth function of speech – namely, the correspondence of the content of *what is said* with *how the world is* – needs be revisited. At first this may appear obvious, because how we assess truth is not exclusively about *the content* of what is being said (*who* is saying something, and *how it is said* are of obvious importance in this respect). It is easy enough to imagine an instance of speech which is true by virtue of its *form* rather than by virtue of its content, as in the case of a sincere apology, delivered in a penitent way: minor factual inconsistencies might be less important than how it is enacted.

Another example of how form might trump content: offering an account replete with inaccuracies, omissions and contradictions can, in fact, prove to be an index of truthfulness, as in the testimony of someone who has suffered a traumatic event. If, by contrast, the recollection of the event was crystal clear, a case of full and detailed recall, we would be justified in questioning, as Žižek (2008) emphasizes, whether it had in fact taken place. Likewise, a police detective might be well attuned to identifying a lie, not simply on the basis of its apparent content, but *by how it is delivered* (the 'tells' of the liar), and with reference to the formal features of its construction (its lack of spontaneity; the sense that it is too well rehearsed; the fact of repetitive or overly emphatic denial, etc.).

What are we to conclude from this? First, that the factuality of speech's content is not what qualifies it as 'full' or 'empty'. Full speech involves a type of truth that cannot be reduced to empirical factuality. The truth of full speech is not a truth of content; it is a truth of a more indeterminate variety, a truth not so much of what is said, but of something that has been disrupted, put into question. The parallel to speech-act theory is evident here: one evaluates a speech act not on the basis of its truth or falsity, but according to what it *does*, what it *performs*.

I should be clear here: I do not mean to say that full speech is true simply on the basis of its form, even though the form/content distinction is often of para-mount importance, as intimated above, in psychoanalysis. For Goffman's (1959) theory of impression management and the astute psychoanalyst alike, this remains a crucial consideration: the idea that we may interrogate the content of a given communication *on the basis of its form* (the means in other words through which it is produced and conveyed). (The statement/enunciation distinction introduced above is here being broached in a different theoretical manner.) As listeners, we are for Goffman continually checking *the content* of what is said against *how it is said*, such that even factually true statements can be adjudged to be false if delivered in an unconvincing way by a speaker whose credibility leaves something to be desired. The fact that listeners often intuitively target precisely such formal and performative elements in assessing the truthfulness of what is said opens up new possibilities for dissimulation.

A canny politician, for example, can mime all the expressive aspects of a good apology (appropriate body language, looking aggrieved, miming disappointment in themselves) even while the actual content of their speech falls way short of an actual or self-compromising apology, avoiding thus the legal implications of a more explicit admission. Lying is thus perhaps a little more complicated than what we may have at first thought: dissimulation can occur at the levels of both form and content.

This is a charge we might direct against a number of disgraced celebrities or politicians who pretend contrition, who perform expedient apologies simply to save their careers: you lie not just in what you say, but in how you say it (indeed, *in your relation to what you have said*). One appreciates thus how amnesty hearings – like that of the South African Truth and Reconciliation Commission – take into account not just the degree of disclosure entered into by those seeking amnesty in respect of former wrongdoings, but also their posture of contrition, that is, the extent to which they appear genuinely sorry for what they have done. While this may appear a misguided approach, for reasons noted above (contrition can be mimed), one understands why such a policy is followed: so as to guard against those who offer merely cynical apologies in order to qualify for amnesty.

The contract of communication

Important as the foregoing discussion of the form/content (or statement/enunciation) distinction is, Lacan is aiming at something more radical when it comes to the truth potential of full speech. He has a different order of truth in his sights: the truth of full speech is not simply a truth of verification; it is a truth which relies upon neither the correspondences of form nor of content. In the example of a worn coin passed between people, what matters is neither the detail of its content nor how it is handed over. What is important is that this (essentially meaningless) object is exchanged so as to maintain the *contract of communication itself. The social patterns corroborated and strengthened by communicative behaviour here outweigh the semiotic importance of the content of the message itself.*

The *tessera* that Lacan refers to is a 'dumb element'; the fact of its exchange however confirms a contract, a bond, a pact (denoting that one has paid the price of admission; one knows the password that permits entry). Full speech is thus true not by virtue of its content or its form, but *by means of the symbolic contract that is set in place* between subjects and overseen by the Other. In contrast then to the foregoing examples of contrition, full speech has absolutely nothing to do with sincerity, with the subjective authenticity of the speaker.

What makes an oath legally binding is not that I perform it enthusiastically or with a sense of piety – I can quite easily reel it off like an automaton. More bluntly put: ultimately what seals a contract is not my inner psychological state, but my signature. My word here is indeed my bond, but as *the mark of a contract*, not as an index of a given personal condition. In the case of the mark or utterance that installs a pact – be it a signature, a thumbprint, an oath – what matters is not the representative richness of the signifier in question. It is, after all, *the confirmatory mark* of the promise rather than its deep meaning that counts to confirm a contractual relation, to alter a given symbolic constellation.

This provides an opportune moment to introduce Slavoj Žižek's (2005) critique of a standard misinterpretation of the above concepts. If we view empty speech merely as 'non-authentic prattle' in which the speaker's subjective position of enunciation is not disclosed, he says, and we treat full speech as the expression of the subject's 'authentic existential position of enunciation', then we risk reducing full speech to an expressive modality. More than this, we remain blind to the fact that what enables the pact of full speech is – as in the case of the password – to all intents and purposes 'empty'. It is a token which functions as 'a pure gesture of recognition, of admission into a certain symbolic space whose enunciated content is totally indifferent . . .' (Žižek, 2005, p. 153).

Unexpectedly then, empty speech may be a necessary precondition for the event of full speech, certainly so if it provides the means whereby speech becomes increasingly unmoored from the objectives of truth and sense alike. This would accord with the psychoanalytic conviction that the (relatively) undefended 'nonsense' of free association is a necessary route of access to subjective truth. We need to engage in the nonsense of free association before the truth potential of full speech emerges.[13]

We cannot thus dispense with empty speech; insofar as it can steer us into meaninglessness, it remains an operative ally of the process of full speech. This is a fact which can be lost in the tendency to denigrate empty speech: such talk is not only unavoidable, it is also absolutely necessary. The 'nullity of enunciated content' (the password, the signature, the *tessera*) tells us that human speech [in its most] fundamental dimension functions as a password: prior to its being a means of communication, of transmitting the signified content, speech is the medium of the mutual recognition of the speakers.

(Žižek, 2005, p. 153)

Understandably then, this complicates a neat compartmentalization of the two types of speech. Never fully separable, often coterminous, empty and full speech are thus hopelessly entangled. Just as the truth potential of full speech is always at risk from the disruption of empty speech, so it is that in the midst of the babbling of empty speech a moment of full speech may erupt, a pulse from the Other might break through (the o'–o axis of the L-Schema). For this reason, full and empty speech are best approached as two extremes, the boundaries of a flood-plain across which 'a whole gamut of modes of realization of speech [are] . . . deployed' (Lacan, 1988a, p. 50).[14]

Symbol-as-pact, symbolic-as-law

Grasping this dimension of full speech requires that we add a key qualification to what is meant by the symbolic register. We are not concerned here simply with symbolizations, with representation in its semiotic dimension, but with relations of convention as they install laws, customs and bonds. What becomes apparent here is that the psychoanalytic notion of the symbolic, as Glynos (2000) observes, has been all too easily assimilated into a social constructionist frame that prioritizes a focus on the content and implication of particular objects of knowledge as constructed in discourse.

While this aspect is certainly not absent in Lacan – the 'truths' of symbolic convention can be fictitious as in the case of the referee's 'bad call' discussed above – we do better to approach the symbolic, as does Lacan, via the structural anthropology of Lévi-Strauss (1974), for whom it is a system of exchanges. The symbolic here denotes the effective operation of collective customs and institutions which work not by reference to the intrinsic meaning of symbols, but on the basis of how they locate subjects, and by generating the symbolic co-ordinates that enable such subjects to take up positions in social reality. To use symbols is to be involved in the conferral of symbolic positions. Although afforded a different theoretical inflection, a similar idea is present in Judith Butler's (2000) reflections on the binding power of performative acts ('I pronounce you . . .', 'I sentence you . . .'), and in her assertion that such symbolic assertions occur 'in the context of a chain of binding conventions' (p. 109).

In their commentary on this facet of Lacan's work, Muller and Richardson (1982) remark that the symbolic order 'governs not only the order of language, but the logic of mathematical combination, and . . . the whole pattern of social relatedness that emerges under the guise of marriage ties and kinship relationships' (p. 77). It is in this sense that 'symbol means pact', that exchanged gifts, as in kinship rites, are 'foremost signifiers of the pact that they constitute' (Lacan, 2006, p. 225).

As the recipient of a gift from a figure with criminal connections knows all too well: what matters in accepting such a gift has little to do with its intrinsic qualities, and everything to do with the links and obligations thus established between the parties concerned. Of such a situation we should ask: in what relation of obligation has the recipient been placed; how has their role now been reconfigured relative to the giver; and how exactly has the giver been re-positioned relative to the recipient?

It is unsurprising then that in psychosis, a subjective structure in which the normative values of society are never fully assimilated, problems should arise in connection with such practices symbolic practices of exchange. Two clinical examples suffice. A patient declared to me that he did not believe in the concept of money. He also insisted that he was opposed to any form of capitalist exchange. Ultimately his insistence not to be part of the 'game of capitalism' proved indicative of a broader foreclosure of the symbolic realm. His position – or indeed, one could say, his non-position – was that of not buying into the system of exchanges that make up society. Another and more high-functioning patient spent considerable time avoiding receiving gifts from family members and work colleagues. It was not that he did not understand the implications of such exchanges; to the contrary, he understood the obligations and changed role definitions of such exchanges all too well. The processes of gift giving did not occur in a tacit or subliminal manner for him – the condition under which such obligatory ties are typically most effective – but were, by contrast overbearingly present. The change in symbolic roles – even if seemingly minor – that was conferred by such exchanges, proved unbearable, virtually traumatic, for him.

We would be remiss in not stressing how for Lacan – again here following Lévi-Strauss – the Law underlies all social relations and thus all facets of the symbolic network. As will increasingly become apparent, this is another reason why Lacan's account of the symbolic cannot be equated with the ideas of social constructionism. I have stressed above the importance of reciprocal roles, gift giving, kinship relations and various symbolic exchanges in structuring societal relations, although I have perhaps not done enough to insist on the legalistic quality of such constantly reiterated rules of social exchange. There is an important further dimension of the law to be grasped here, one that is crucial if we are to appreciate Lacan's debt to structuralism, and what this '*Structuralist*' influence means for Lacan's subsequent theorizations of the unconscious.

The Law as it is immanent in forms of social exchange is not something that is present merely via its constant reiteration in instances of communicative interaction (although this is importantly true, also). Lacan has in mind a type of fundamental and indeed 'primordial' Law that is a structural feature of culture *per se*. This Law is present whenever a rudimentary form of symbolic activity is present, whenever – to indulge briefly in more technical terms – a type of combinatory logic is in operation. A key example of such combinatory logic – certainly within Lévi-Strauss's anthropology – concerns elementary kinship structures, that is, the matrix of relations determining what marital relations are possible and which are not.

This example is important inasmuch as it shows that the symbolic is not reducible to the realm of communicative acts and speech (although these are of course crucial realms of symbolic behaviour) but is fundamentally structural. This example demonstrates, in other words, how patterns underlying the arrangement of human societies, like longstanding cultural traditions, are themselves linguistic, 'structured like a language'. Such kinship patterns involve rules of what inter-familial combinations are possible (specifying who may marry whom and under what conditions). These rules are often elaborate, and exceed the subjective level of consciouslty constructed conventions. The insistence of such combinatory rules – which are not reliant on being remembered or on the psychological aptitudes of individuals – continues over generations, and it makes for a case in point of the agency of the symbolic network over and above that of the single subjects who exist within it. It is in this sense that, in *Function and Field of Speech and Language in Psychoanalysis*, Lacan claims that the Law is linguistic:

> The primordial Law is therefore the Law which, in regulating marriage ties, superimposes the reign of culture over the reign of nature . . . This law, then, reveals itself clearly enough as identical to a language order. For without names for kinship relations, no power can institute the order of preferences and taboos that knot and braid the threat of lineage throughout the generations.
>
> (pp. 229–230)

If Lacan seems here to have strayed from the more circumscribed realm of the clinic, his anthropological speculations are soon brought to bear on more obviously Freudian matters, such as the question of the Oedipus complex, and more directly yet, the role of 'the paternal function'. Here, once again, Lacan shows he is a systematic reader of Freud, for whom the father, or more accurately yet, the persistence of the father in various formations of the unconscious, proves a crucial motif. We will pick up this theme, that of the importance of the father (or, more importantly, that of the paternal function) in Chapter 4. For the time being it perhaps suffices to note that for the symbolic to function, it requires a privileged signifier of the Law. We have arrived then at one of Lacan's (2006) most crucial theoretical innovations of his '*Structuralist*' period:

> It is in the name of the father that we must recognize the basis of the symbolic function which . . . has identified his person with the figure of the law. This conception allows us to clearly distinguish . . . the unconscious effects of this function from . . . the person who embodied this function.
>
> (p. 230)

Lacan's theoretical intervention aims not to reify the father – in the sense of the empirical figure of the father in any given household – but to stress instead a function whose structural role far outstrips that of any given 'actual' father. Let us bring this brief discussion of symbolic and unconscious law to a close by noting the intimate relationship between language, the Law and the father in psychical economy for Lacan. Badiou puts it well: 'The human animal . . . is structured by language, assimilated to an immemorial Law whose organizing signifier is the Name-of-the-Father' (Badiou, 2014, p. 26).

The contract of communication

This lengthy expository detour behind us, let us now return though to a focus on communication. For Lacan then the platform established by virtue of a spoken exchange installs a code of sorts, 'rules of the game', consensual parameters that characterize the implicit contract of communication itself. The first extra-linguistic facet of this agreement concerns the fact that *there can be communication*, that a communicative attempt is possible, and that, presumably, some understanding can in principle be achieved, even if misunderstanding and miscommunication are, oddly enough, the condition of possibility for this to happen. The second facet concerns the fact that speech does indeed represent a viable route to truth, a means of attaining (even, for Lacan potentially *constituting*) unexpected truths that may not have otherwise come to light, despite that this route involves the contradiction of what has been accepted, what seems to be so. Third, despite the fact that deception is a constant possibility of all human speech engagements, a given communicative exchange nonetheless entails an aspect of 'good faith' (*bona fides*), apparent in both the elementary trust one exhibits towards what one is told (there is always the potential that something genuine, authentic is being said), and in the implicit pledge one makes in speaking (that I have committed this act of saying something to you).[15]

These then are the meta-communications underlying any speech situation. Lacan is directing our attention to what is communicated by the fact of communication itself. Such meta-communications are not dependent on the content of what is said, on how it is said, or the psychological conditions under which the speaking occurs. They nonetheless install a rudimentary social bond, a 'kinship of com-munication' that ties both participants into their shared symbolic-societal world. Communication is thus involved in the constant renewal, the re-instantiation of the social bond itself. What this means in turn is that empty gestures ('Can I get you anything?' when the expected answer is no), despite seeming to be lacking in real purpose, are important communicative acts. The same holds for rhetorical questions that ask after what *they know not to be the case* ('Are you OK?' when someone clearly is not). Despite being redundant at the most literal level, such questions, like empty gestures, nonetheless add something to the communicative exchange. They move a social bond along, they strengthen an interpersonal tie; more than just fostering a relation, they secure and reiterate certain roles.

The case of politeness is likewise of interest in explicating the notion of meta-communication. Consider the extreme indirectness exemplified in certain forms of politeness. What, we might ask, is polite about the oddly roundabout request: 'Could I ask if you would you mind passing me that book?' Taken at a purely literal level, this appeal misses the mark twice: it is a request as to whether the recipient objects to being asked something and, furthermore, a query as to whether they mind passing a book. What makes the request polite is its indirectness. By couching the request in these terms I make apparent the fact of *my relation to the content*, that is that I am not really in a position to make such a request; that I am not issuing a command; that I respect their prerogative to turn down my appeal, and so on. Indirectness, in other words, itself communicates something. It signals to the hearer, as Pinker (2006) stresses, that an effort has been made, that their feelings, their situation – and in the case of the bribe or come-on, their ability to save face – has been taken into account. 'The mere perception that the speaker has gone to this effort makes the hearer appreciative of his considerateness' (2006, p. 416).

Naming you, naming me

The above discussion sheds further light on an aspect of full speech that we have touched upon only briefly, namely the fact that it affirms and registers interlocking dialogical speaking-positions. Full speech instantiates reciprocal roles and subject categories, symbolic designations supported by the contract established by the event of communication itself. This mutual role-designation function will be important in distinguishing full speech from something with which it is frequently conflated, namely, the theory of speech acts.

The reciprocal dimension of speech is minimally present even in the basically collaborative nature of a conversational speech exchange: if a question is posed by my interlocutor, then what I say in return is framed as a response; if a demand is made, then my answer supports either a concession to, or refusal of this demand, and so on. This role-designation functions at its most compelling when types of explicit naming or role categorization are involved. Lacan puts it this way:

> Speech commits its author by investing the person to whom it is addressed with a new reality . . . if I call the person to whom I am speaking by whatever name I choose to give him, I intimate to him the subjective function that he will take on again in order to reply to me, even if it is to repudiate this function.
>
> (1977, pp. 85–87)

The best way of grasping what Lacan has in mind here with what he calls 'founding speech' is to return to a notion introduced above, the idea that each instance of speech involves an interlocutor. We need now take a second step: this interlocutor will in many instances be named, their position relative to me declared – you are my sister, you are my boss, my child, my parent, my colleague, my client, my friend and so on. Such a definitional declaration, this allocation of role, does not of course end there. It is not merely a descriptive task, it implies a position for the speaking subject also, the role of the sister's brother, the boss's worker, the child's parent, the parent's child and so on. To define the position, the role of the other is also thus to locate one's self in an act of symbolic positioning that ties one into the socio-historical network of roles. One such spoken role designation (even if only implicit) implies another; a chain of roles is thus continually affirmed in the practice of speaking. This for Lacan is the highest function of speech, a modality of spoken language that defines symbolic subjectivity:

> In as much as speech commits its author by investing the person to whom it is addressed with a new reality, as for example, when by a 'You are my wife', a subject marks himself with the seal of wedlock.
>
> (2006, p. 246)

What is indicated here is nothing less than the ongoing maintenance of the network of interlinked and jointly affirming symbolic relationships. We contribute daily to the labour of maintaining particular symbolic 'relation domains'; in addressing an interlocutor, we as speakers invest them, and thereby ourselves, not only with a general role, but with a more finely configured or readjusted symbolic location. We have thus an exemplary instance of receiving one's own message (or one's own symbolic position) back from the other in an inverted form. This is, we might say, a mode of *self-interpellation*, an answer to the ongoing unconscious question of how one fits into the social network. We should not under-estimate the force or complexity of founding speech – or indeed its historical dimension – especially given that this function of symbolic positioning is refreshed each time one enters into role-designating forms of dialogue:

> Founding speech, which envelops the subject, is everything that has constituted him, his parents, his neighbours, the whole structure of the community, and not only constituted him as a symbol, but constituted him in his being.
>
> (Lacan, 1988a, p. 20)

Founding speech is thus a specific variant of full speech, a naming of the other that transforms *both involved parties* in the act of saying. It is an invocation, following Forrester (1990), 'in which the *I* and the *you* are simultaneously modulated' (p. 159). Forrester adds a vital observation here: although such utterances are speech acts in Austin's sense 'they go beyond those acts he studied most closely, in *necessarily* implicating both subject and the other' (p. 153). Now, to avoid the obvious over-sight, Austin (1962) does of course discuss the effect of speech acts on others: 'perlocutionary force' is the term he uses to designate the effects – behavioural impacts, resulting actions and so on – that speech acts have on those to whom they are uttered. Nonetheless, Austin does not discuss in any detail the complex binding effects of this form of speech in the conferring of symbolic relations, in view of the generation and maintenance of roles. The notion of founding speech takes into account this *pairing effect*, aware that it is not simply the declarative role of speech acts that is crucial in the location of subjectivity, but *the inter-dependence of the speech acts of two participants*. What counts thus is not merely the 'I do' of the marriage vow, but the fact that the first 'I do' 'receives its ratification as a solemn pledge from the other "I do"' (p. 159); after all 'you need two people, both saying "I do" [to one another] for the marriage to come off' (Forrester, p. 158).

A Lacanian analysis of speech would as such prioritize this question: how are types of contract activated in verbal exchanges? Furthermore, what is set in place by virtue of the communicative bridge thus established? If each communicative engagement instantiates a relationship bounded by conventional roles and implicit rules, then what reciprocal role-positions are cemented by virtue of this pact?

Historical reflexivity

By way of emphasizing one final aspect of full speech, let us refer to a passage in which Lacan reflects on what might have been learnt from pre-psychoanalytic attempts to affect a cure via hypnosis. A question before doing so: what is meant by the criterion whereby full speech 'is defined by its identity with that which it speaks about' (Lacan, 2006, p. 319)? How are we to understand full speech as speech within which 'the subject can articulate their position of enunciation' (Žižek, 2005, p.193)? This is our challenge in what follows: to understand the *enacted reflexivity* that in full speech the subject demonstrates towards their own subjective truth.

In the hypnotic state 'verbalization is dissociated from conscious realization', previous (and presumably difficult) events, furthermore, are forced into words, 'into the *epos* [the tale, the song, the narrative] by which [the hypnotized subject] relates . . . the origins of her person' (Lacan, 2006, p. 212). The question of symbolic co-ordinates is crucial here, as is the juxtaposition of an earlier mode of speaking – the vernacular of an 'archaic, even foreign tongue' (p. 212) – against the present discourse of the subject's contemporaries. Such a spoken representation of the past brings with it not only a degree of distance from what is being spoken of, but a performative dimension also, given that this is 'speech . . . performed . . . on a stage' before an audience (p. 212). As in the epic dramas of antiquity, which rendered the myths of the state in such a way that 'a nation . . . learn[ed] to read the symbols of [its] destiny', (p. 212), so here too a new relationship to history is made possible. There is, it would seem, an opening up of contingency, not only the return of historical events, but their relativization, a reshuffling of historical elements that neither takes them for granted nor assumes the sequence and meaning of an apparently fixed destiny. The interrogation of the present by means of history, the factor of 'conjectures about the past' with the ability to make 'promises about the future oscillate' (p. 213) is key here. This 'assumption by the subject of his history, insofar as it constituted by speech addressed to another' (p. 213), is the basis of psychoanalytic method once it has dispensed with hypnosis. This alerts us to the dimension of historical reflexivity, crucial to the effect of full speech [which] is to reorder past contingencies, by conferring on them the sense of necessities to come, such as they are constituted by the . . . [limited] freedom through which the subject makes them present.

(Lacan, 2006, p. 213)

The bond resulting from a full-speech speech act is not only a tie of reciprocal roles to my interlocutor, or a tie to the Other grounding the structure of speaking. It is a bond also to my own declarative position and the history it entails. This returns us to the question of how full speech goes beyond the speech act, to which Žižek (2006) responds by evoking the 'twofold movement' of the symbolic. In other words, it is not just a question of how a form of speech performs an act, but of how this act itself is reintegrated by the subject. There is a subjective after-effect to the speech act, the prospect whereby a subjective 'truth change' can be effected by virtue of it having been uttered. This is not just an issue of what I *do* by means of saying something, but of what is *done to me* by my saying – I can after all be surprised by virtue of what is thus done, by what I have committed myself to – of what subjective 'truth change' has been instantiated.

That is to say, the perlocutionary effect of a speech act contains a reflexive impact, so much so that what I enact in saying provides the basis for a different order of subjective truth. Let us imagine that I am attending the trial of a man who is about to be found guilty of a crime that I in fact committed. If, at the right moment, I stand up, declare my guilt and provide telling evidence, such a declaration not only effects a change in proceedings, and a re-ordering of symbolic positions (the accused now assumes a different role, the official record of the crime will now need be re-written). It affects also my own subjective position: by saying what I have said I perform an acknowledgement of what I have done, a declarative instance from which a series of subsequent acts and psychological changes may well follow. Such a symbolic act is pre-emptive: my speaking itself becomes a condition of possibility for a series of subsequent subjective dispositions: a broader acknowledgement of my crime; a sense, perhaps, of remorse; a readiness to accept the consequences of my actions, etc., now can begin to take hold. The symbolic gesture of an apology often works in the same way. Even in circumstances where I feel a degree of lingering resentment, where I feel in some ways that I might still be the aggrieved subject, to make an apology and have it received and reciprocated by the person with whom I am in conflict can clear the air and change my attitude towards them.

We might take up a related example that links back to the idea of appealing for amnesty as discussed above. It is perfectly conceivable that I, an offender, a man who abused human rights under the rule of a former oppressive political regime, might plan to testify before a truth commission, to cynically pretend contrition not because I feel it, but simply to claim amnesty from prosecution. I may feel only a belated sense of guilt, and have no intention of assuming any real remorse in respect of my actions. It is only when, assuming the stand, beginning to speak, seeing the cameras and the assembled families of my victims, upon hearing my own mimed apology ('I am sorry for my actions'), that the full weight of my previous actions, the full weight of the words that I have just uttered, hits me. The point, once again, is that certain symbolic utterances themselves function as acts necessary for transforming the dispositions of the speaking subject.

Here then is the twofold movement of the symbolic which entails the possibility of subjective communicative change:

> One does something, one counts oneself as (declares oneself) the one who did it, and on the base of this declaration, one does something new – the proper moment of subjective transformation occurs at the [initial] moment of the declaration, not at the [subsequent] moment of the act. This reflexive moment of declaration means that every utterance not only transmits some content, but simultaneously, *conveys the way the subject relates to this content*.
>
> (Žižek, 2006, p. 16)

Without the enacted reflexivity that, in full speech, the speaker demonstrates towards their position of enunciation, there would be no psychoanalytic cure. The performative dimension of speech rebounds on the speaker and their receiver alike: the fact of what is done by being said installs a relation, a relation in the sense of both how I am linked into my socio-symbolic network, and, in the terms of how I myself have assumed my own subjective truth (the truth of my desire). This is a vital consideration in how the impact of full speech might be said to exceed what is theorized by way of speech acts: full speech implements an extra reflexive turn by means of which the performative act is *subjectivized*. The subject can be changed, in short, by virtue of how its enunciations, its Other utterances and acts *effect a different relation to the symbolic*, a relation which in turn impacts subjectivity.

Between a theory of the signifier and a materialist 'psychology'

What then can we conclude from the foregoing chapters about the relation between Lacanian psychoanalysis and psychology? One initial response would be simply to state that Lacanian theory often appears tantamount to a systematic refutation of the psychological. Where, for example, we may have presumed a basic dyadic schema of interpersonal communication, Lacan insists that such two-way psychological models will not suffice. He disputes such dialogical conceptualizations, and subverts any priority placed upon the communicative productions of *the ego* insisting instead upon the role of the Other and the disruptive potential of full speech. The same holds true in respect of psychological presumptions regards an 'intra-psychic' realm prior to, or beyond, the remit of the symbolic – such assumptions are summarily rejected by Lacan. As we will see in subsequent chapters, he radically externalizes – or more appropriately perhaps, *flattens* – such presumptions of psychological depth.[16]

One implication of this is that the unconscious can no longer be viewed as an internal capacity; it must instead be approached as an external function of language.

Such an unconscious does not exist beyond the range of words (beyond, that is, the operation of signifiers) but is instead wholly contingent on symbolic functioning, contingent also, importantly, on the *materiality* of the signifier, that is, it's formal features, as *spoken*. Why the particular importance of the materiality of the signifier? Well, in spite of a great deal of theoretical attention being devoted to the role and structure of language in Lacan's thought (particularly the operations of metaphor and metonymy) the crucial role of *actually enunciated* speech is sometimes neglected by scholars, particularly by those who are more interested in the formalization of Lacanian ideas for use in other disciplinary fields than in the clinical practice of psychoanalysis.[17]

It is precisely by prioritizing speech, by paying attention to the particularities and idiosyncrasies of an individual's spoken language that we grasp the link between the unconscious and materiality. Fink (2004) discusses Lacan's idea of the materiality of the signifier by referring to Saussure's qualification of the material aspect of the signifier as the *image acoustique*, the 'sound-image' or acoustic trace which is not to be understood as 'pure phenomenon of physics' but rather along the lines of 'the impression or stamp of the sound' as it is heard (p. 77). What follows on from this is decidedly *not* an attention to what is assumed to lie behind speech – the conscious meanings or intentions that we mistakenly assume speech simply expresses – but rather a refined attention to the vicissitudes of *what might be conveyed* by the multiple dimensions (the materiality) of speech as it is *actually spoken*. Hence the idea that the analyst should play up the ambiguity of a patient's discourse, and call attention to homophony and effects of equivocation in their speech. Fink (2014a) thus reiterates the importance of listening attentively to 'all the slips, stumblings, double *entendres*, and compromise formations endemic to speech' (2014a, p. 21) before citing Lacan's insistence that analysts should listen to 'sounds and phonemes, words, locutions . . . not forgetting pauses, scansions, cuts, periods and parallelisms' (Lacan, cited in Fink, p. 21). The materiality of the signifier indeed!

Why then am I drawing such attention to the materiality of speech in the context of Lacan's anti-psychology stance? To set it against an idealist form of psychological conceptualization. Attention to the systems of signifiers that comprise the symbolic, says Parker, brings Lacanian psychoanalysis

> closer to a 'materialist' account of mental processes than an idealist one which attempts to ground its account in invisible meanings inside the heads of individuals.
>
> (2015b, p. 45)

Parker augments this description elsewhere, likewise stressing both the materialism of Lacanian psychoanalysis and the materiality of the signifier. The analyst, he observes, avoids appeal to any 'more real' psychological qualities (such as feelings) that apparently lie hidden beneath signifiers. Lacanian psychoanalysis is materialist insofar as it attends only to the actual signifiers and their position in relation to the system of signifiers in the analysis, materialist insofar as it is a 'concrete psychology' that does not treat the unconscious or other phenomena as hidden spectres that guide human activity.

(Parker, 2015c, p. 48)

It is for this reason that we would be remiss if we did not underline the constituting role of *speech* within the realm of human 'psychology' and if, further-more, we did not reiterate the multiple aspects of the symbolic functionality of speech precisely *as a condition of possibility for 'the psychological'* (or, differently put, for symbolic capacities of subjectivity).

So while we need to avoid the imaginary lure of getting caught up in the meanings, the *thematic contents* of speech which resonate with the preoccupations of the listener's own ego, we nonetheless need to think of speech in its symbolic dimension. We need to consider speech as: instantiating a subject; producing their unconscious; as enacting and reiterating symbolic positions, roles, obligations, debts; and as locating the subject within a trans-subjective symbolic network. The point is worth reiterating: we should focus on the symbolic roles and operations of speech above its (imaginary) meaning, attune ourselves thus to what speech incarnates as *an act*. Jamieson Webster extends this line of argument, by stressing that: '[w]hen speech functions as an act, when it deploys meaning by summoning the symbolic, it brings a subject into being' (2017, p. 25). Subjectivity per se then, is, in an important sense, contingent on speech, on the subject enacting itself in language.

(Full) speech eclipsing the psychological, or: a materialist unconscious

For Lacan, as we are often told, the unconscious is 'structured like a language'. This means, in effect, that there is no subject beyond the horizon of the symbolic and no subjectivity beyond of the remit of language (that is, beyond the operations or structures of language, language both approached diachronically, as unfolding in time, and synchronically as system).[18] We can take this argument a step further, by stressing once again the factor of what might variously be referred to as enacted, 'live', performative, enunciated or indeed, simply *spoken* language, and asserting that there is very little if any human 'psychological' capacity that is not in some way structured by the symbolic activities of *speech*. More bluntly put: there is no distinctively human 'psychology' that is not structured by symbolic interactions most concretely instantiated in the linguistic exchange of signifiers.

Speech practices are not thus of secondary importance in the making of subjectivity. They do not represent merely the *expression* of a series of preceding and primary psychological operations. Such an order or priority is repeatedly challenged and reversed by Lacan: it is the symbolic and *material* activities of *speech and symbolic activity* that are in an important sense 'more primary' than the stuff of internal cognitions. If this seems a radical or counter-intuitive claim to make – namely, that there is no distinctively human psychology without speech or its communicative equivalent – then it helps to stress that Lacan is not alone in advancing such a thesis.

Readers familiar with the history of developmental and cognitive psychology may recall the work of Marxist (Soviet, Belorussian) psychologist Lev Vygotsky. Vygotsky insisted that the domain of uniquely human psychological operations – the realm of higher order mental functions that sets humans apart from mammals – is not only fundamentally linguistic in nature, but is contingent upon *material* symbolic practices, speech being afforded here the primary role. In Vygotsky's approach, says Wertsch (1985), psychological tools (such as speech, the use of symbols)

> are not viewed as auxiliary means that simply facilitate an existing mental function while leaving it qualitatively unaltered . . . the emphasis [rather] is on their capacity to transform mental functioning.
>
> (p. 79)

We can pinpoint several expressions of this idea in Vygotsky's work. In his article 'Sign operations and organization of mental processes', for example, Vygotsky observes that 'symbolic forms of activity . . . speech, reading, writing, counting . . . are usually considered as something peripheral and accessory with respect to internal mental processes' (2004, p. 552), before strongly disputing such a view and stressing instead how crucial such functions are to the system of higher mental functions (that is, the properly symbolic domain of cognitive functioning). All such higher mental functions were originally practical forms of social (symbolic) cooperation, Vygotsky argues, which, upon being transferred 'into the psychological systems of the child', retain 'the basic traits of symbolic structure, changing only its situation' (2004, p. 553).

Now while Lacan, of course, is not concerned with cognitive processing or developmental psychology, and while we must remain aware of the epistemological and disciplinary chasm separating the work of these two men, it is nonetheless true than an important aspect of Vygotsky's socio-genetic approach applies also to Lacan. For Lacan, the signifier is not an auxiliary means that simply facilitates existing mental functions, leaving them unaltered; rather the space of the psyche becomes a theatre for the operations of the signifier. For both theorists then, the human organism is fundamentally altered by the operation of symbolic processes, which, furthermore, retains not only a material origin, but an agency and history irreducible to the parameters of individual consciousness.[19]

There is, of course, at best a provisional overlap in the respective theorizations of Lacan and Vygotsky. Given my objective here, of introducing key facets of Lacanian theory in terms of its apparent intersection with elements of psychological conceptualization, Vygotsky can be identified as something of a distant ally, certainly so in his insistency on the primary role of symbolic and linguistic systems in the fashioning of subjectivity. This being said, Lacan is no doubt the more radical theorist. Not only does he prioritize the unconscious in a way which would be foreign to Vygotsky, his conceptualization of agency is also fundamentally different. For Vygotsky, the focus is very much with how the field of individual cognitive functioning and thereby conscious agency can be increased by attending to how symbolic processes are gradually internalized. For Lacan, by contrast, the stress is more on how such symbolic functions operate below the level of consciousness and take on, in an almost parasitic fashion, a type of autonomous functioning which hitherto determines the subject as such.[20] Another way of making much the same point is to reiterate that Lacan dispenses with the category of the psychological subject (although some facets of this notion are, admittedly, retained in his theorization of the ego). In fact one can say that Lacan's true focus in his '*Structuralist*' period of the 1950s is not human subjectivity as such, but rather the operations of the signifier, the field of the Other, as this impacts – as this in many instances *is* – the unconscious.

In light of the foregoing discussion, we appreciate better what is at stake in Lacan's theorization of full speech. Full speech is not so much an isolated concept as an architectural framework within which a whole series of symbolic psychical functions can be conceptualized in a 'non-psychologistic' way.[21] More simply put: the various practices and operations of speech constitute an elaborate type of external scaffolding; these are all 'extra-psychological' functions. The list of such functions developed in Lacan's conceptualizations of full speech is impressive, it includes attention to, among others: the role of declarative or performative speech; the importance of the *marking* function of signifiers that operate as oaths or pledges; the production of pacts and laws via even rudimentary forms of symbolic exchange; the reciprocal dimension of founding speech; and the reflexive subjective impact of declarative acts. In each of the foregoing ideas we see how for Lacan the domain of symbolic acts of exchange and the associated materiality of such practices, necessarily take precedence over psychological explanations.

If there is a single concept in Lacan's conceptual *oeuvre* which concretizes both the externality and the fundamentally symbolic nature of the processes which shape the subject, it is the notion of the Other. This is a concept deserving of further explanation, particularly so in view of the *trans-subjective* register it brings into play. It is to a more detailed consideration of this theme that we now turn.

Notes

1 There is, admittedly, some excellent work within the field of psychoanalytically-informed narrative analysis (Emerson and Frosh, 2009; Frosh, Phoenix and Pattman, 2000) that takes seriously the need to disrupt 'ego narrativization'. Stephen Frosh (2008) for example, points to the role of narrative interpretation in consolidating wholeness, in integrating fragmentary experience into the unity of narrative. For Frosh (2008) such fantasies of resolution are necessarily illusory. The objectives of interruption might thus be preferred to those of interpretation such that what is effectively offered 'is not a sense of holistic closure, but rather a set of provoking questions' (Frosh, p. 11).

2 One might however suspect an intuition of such a mis-knowing, ego-substantiating function in Frankfurt's conclusion. There is, he suggests, nothing to support the judgment that truths about ourselves are the easiest to know:

> Our natures are, indeed, elusively insubstantial . . . less stable and inherent than the nature of other things. And insofar as this is the case, sincerity itself . . . is bullshit.
>
> (2005, p. 67).

3 As we press on, the parallels between Heidegger's commitment to *Rede* as enabling truth (making the intelligibility of Being-in-the-world possible), and Lacan's adherence to the subjective truth potential of full speech, will become apparent. Despite this resonance, we should be aware that these thinkers differ when it comes to the possibility of the subject's assumption of their own truth in discourse. As Borch-Jacobsen (1991) emphasizes: '. . . in Heidegger's eyes nothing is more foreign to the original essence of truth than truth thought of as the certainty of a subject assuring himself in his representation or discourse' (p. 107).

4 As Lacan puts it in *The Function and Field of Speech and Language in Psychoanalysis*: '[in psychoanalysis] speech is driven out of the concrete discourse that orders consciousness' (2006, p. 232).

5 Leader expresses this adroitly: 'This imaginary matrix will give the measure of the objects within the narcissistic field, and any addressee of the subject's speech will be caught up in this' (2000, p. 179).

6 The repeated refrain: 'What do you (the Other) want of me?' can never be finally answered. Any momentary hypothesis earned in this way (via guesses made of the Other) is impermanent; the resultant uncertainty de-stabilizes the position of the subject.

7 Psychology is charged then not only with the prioritization of the ego and consciousness, but also with an over-reliance on a type of realism. In respect of his discussion of anxiety, Lacan notes: 'I have opposed the psychologizing tradition that distinguishes fear from anxiety by virtue of its correlates in reality. In this I have changed things, maintaining of anxiety – *it is not without an object*. What is that object? The object *petit a*' (Lacan, cited in Eyers, 2012, p. 31).

8 I owe this point of clarification to Ian Parker.

9 The film's representation of these events is already saturated with quasi-psychoanalytic notions of Nixon being trapped up by the truth, of somehow needing to confess. Indicative here is the scene in the film that most stretches the credibility of its rendering of actual events: the drunk Nixon's late-night phone call to Frost in which he rants about those who have unfairly opposed him in his career. This event, later forgotten by Nixon, sets up the premise that he does want (however 'unconsciously') to confess.

10 A nice feature of this reading of Lacan's definition is that it foregrounds how the same figure – in this case Frost – can alternate between the role of other and Other.

11 For a more detailed commentary on this facet of Lacan's teaching particularly in respect of obsessional neurosis, see Leader (1992) who offers an informative account of Lacan's project in his 1953 paper 'The neurotic's individual myth'.

12 For a lively exposition of this notion apropos the functioning of ideology, see Pfaller (2005).

13 If one aims at attaining full speech within the analytic setting, says Lacan (1988a), one

> starts off on a path leading in the diametrically opposed direction, in so far as it instructs the subject to delineate a speech as devoid as possible of any assumption of responsibility and that . . . frees him of any expectation of authenticity . . . It is through these very means that it facilitates . . . his return on to the path which, in speech, is below the level of recognition and concerns the third party.
>
> (1988a, p. 108)

14 Jacqueline Rose adds a note of caution in respect of the idea of full speech. In the 1950s, during the period of Lacan's *Function and Field of Speech and Language*, language was conceived of 'as a (potentially full) speech which breaks the impasse of imaginary relation

(hostility, rivalry, etc.)' (Rose, 2005, p. 176), yet in subsequent years this conceptualization undergoes a crucial change. 'At the point where language ceases to be a potentially full speech and is seen as a structure or set of differences based on a primary absence, there can no longer be a simple progression from the Imaginary (misrecognition) to the Symbolic (mediation, recognition), since the emphasis is on the "splitting" which is constitutive of language itself' (Rose, 2005, p. 176).

While Rose's (2005) point is no doubt apt, her comment should not be read as invalidating the clinical utility of the concepts of full and empty speech, which, I would argue, remain crucial in sensitizing clinicians to the deadlocks of the 'wall of language' and the truth potential of the slippages, enactments and mis-pronouncements of full-speech.

15 In Seminar III Lacan (1993) reflects on two fundamental aspects of full speech. There is, first, the factor of faith (*fides*), '*the certainty of what I pledge*' (p. 37) to the person I am speaking with. 'This speech is speech that commits you', says Lacan, '[t]he unity of speech insofar as it founds the position of the two subjects is made apparent here' (p. 37). The second facet is the reverse of the good faith promise activated by the fact of speaking itself, and it can be discerned by way of a comparison.

What is it though that enables us to distinguish a subject-to-subject relation as opposed to a subject-to-object relation? The first immediate test of the difference between a subject and an object for Lacan concerns the fact that a subject can *deceive* you by means of what they say and do, and, moreover, that they can deceive you *by way of a truth*. 'What the subject tells me is always fundamentally related to a possible feint, in which he sends me, and I receive, the message in an inverted form' (1993, p. 37).

16 The obvious drawback with the idea of 'externalizing' ostensibly 'internal' psychological operations is that this term re-entrenches the external/internal binary. The category of the internal is thus preserved, even if, at first, it seems to have been left behind, and the internal/external distinction thus remains in place as the basic categorical basis for making sense of psychical operations. Lacan's later (1960s) turn to topological models is an attempt to avoid the pitfalls of such conceptualizations, to collapse such binary oppositions with which we have become so used to thinking the psychological.

17 This, incidentally, is one of the problems that attempts to apply Lacanian theory as a type of critical reading practice, or mode of discourse analysis (Hook, 2013b; Neill, 2013; Parker, 2005; Parker and Pavón-Cuéllar, 2012; Pavón-Cuéllar, 2010), necessarily confronts: the analysis of written language lack something of the performative spontaneity of speech as it is spoken 'in the moment'.

18 Even the extra-discursive charge of *jouissance*, i.e. that of libidinal enjoyments that cannot be encapsulated by words, remain in a relation of sorts to the world of symbolic values. How else to account for the particular thrills of transgressive enjoyments that are constituted precisely in terms of deviation from a given law or moral boundary?

19 This concurrence of views takes us to an unexpected conclusion. We might say that the Lacanian notion that the unconscious is structured like a language, is also, in a qualified sense, a Vygostkian postulate. I do not mean by this to say that Vygotsky was concerned with the notion of the unconscious. The point is rather to stress that for Vygotsky, with his insistence on the social origins of higher mental functions and his concern with external symbolic tools as the basis for subsequent internalized psychological operations, it would most likely not have been a radical thesis to suggest that the domain of 'unconscious thought' was itself structured by the operations of language.

20 To this we should add that for Lacan what remains a crucial conceptual idea for Vygotsky, namely the idea of a time before the internalization of symbolic functions, is at best a relative and contested category; the symbolic is for Lacan always-already in place, and any appeal to the pre-linguistic risks under-estimating the extent and influence of language.

21 That is to say: in a way which does not prioritize 'internal' mental processes over the social, symbolic and material exchanges that are their necessary condition of possibility.

3

THE PRISONER'S DILEMMA
AND THE TRANS-SUBJECTIVE

Subjectivity, inter-subjectivity, *trans*-subjectivity

This chapter explores the logical puzzle of the prisoner's dilemma as analysed in Lacan's March 1945 article 'Logical time and the assertion of anticipated certainty'. While several excellent commentaries on this intriguing paper already exist[1] my concerns here are somewhat different, and not only by virtue of what I hope to be a more basic expository style. My over-arching objective here is to utilize Lacan's discussion of the prisoner's dilemma as a means of grounding a theory of the *trans-subjective*. More specifically, I use the dilemma, and Lacan's associated three-fold schema of logical time, to make two general arguments. First, I argue that we need to grasp a logical succession of modes of subjectivity – from subjectivity to inter-subjectivity, and from inter-subjectivity to a form of *trans-subjective social logic*. Second, I assert that various symbolic gestures – acts of a performative or declarative sort – are important *non-psychological* bases for imaginary (or what we might loosely call 'psychological') identifications. These two arguments are interlinked: the distinction between the *trans-subjective* and the *inter-subjective* proves crucial in understanding the difference between forms of identification based on linguistic functioning and symbolic processes of exchange, on the one hand, and those of a more overtly imaginary or psychological (which is to say, ego-based) nature, on the other.

In turning to Lacan's (1945) 'Logical time' essay we are focusing on a period of his work prior to the height of his 1950s '*Structuralist*' period. The reason for this is simple enough. It is crucial, in a book concerned with Lacan and the psychological to invoke certain of the phenomenological qualities apparent in Lacan's pre-1950s work, precisely such as the notion of inter-subjectivity.[2] While Lacan will increasingly move away from this concept – eventually abandoning it altogether, no doubt largely because of its psychological resonances – this facet of his work should not be minimized or completely 'over-written' by subsequent developments. To the contrary, this period, where rudimentary features of both structuralism (time as logical structure) and phenomenology (the prioritization of inter-subjectivity) are combined, is of considerable interest in appreciating how Lacanian theory draws aspects from a phenomenological tradition that will subsequently disappear as explanations of structure and the signifier take precedence.[3] Accordingly, by the end of this chapter we will have a sense of Lacan's intellectual development away from a phenomenological (and psychological/imaginary) domain of conceptualization towards a more robust theorization of structural and symbolic relations. We will also be better placed to understand what Lacan calls the 'subject of the signifier', and to appreciate why, for Lacan, the level of collective or societal functioning is only attained at a symbolic level (that of the trans-subjective) that exceds *a mere aggregation of subjectivities*. I should add here an important caveat: although Lacan himself does not utilize the term 'trans-subjective' (preferring instead, in characterizations of the unconscious, the term 'trans-individual') – the imposition of this term is my own – I maintain that it remains faithful to a reading of his early work, and that it provides a means of linking his ideas to more current debates.

Although I focus most directly on the topic of identification in the chapters that follow (Chapters 4 and 5), it proves useful to provide a few definitional comments here. Laplanche and Pontalis (1978) define the psychoanalytic notion of identification as the (largely) unconscious process 'whereby the subject assimilates an aspect, property or attribute of the other and is transformed, wholly or partially, after the model the other provides' (p. 206). To this we should add the necessary Lacanian qualification: with *imaginary* identifications we are primarily concerned with the domain of interpersonal ego-other (or 'psychological') identifications, with how subjects take on *images* that provide the basis for the formation of their ideal-ego. As can be anticipated from the foregoing chapters, there is an idealizing and narcissistic quality to such imaginary schemas which prioritizes visual markers of difference and/or similarity. This imaginary register of identification should be differentiated from that of the symbolic, which is best grasped via anthropology's emphasis on social convention and the codification of social relations (bonds, exchanges, kinship structures) that structure experience. The symbolic order is the 'extra-psychological' realm of differential systems, language, law and prohibition. It is an a-subjective social grid in which subjects must necessarily assume a position, a role, a place which, despite the ego's imaginary reassurances, is never merely spontaneous, 'natural'.

One last preliminary question: surely, given the sophistication of recent work on the topic of inter-subjectivity, this concept, rather than the idea of the trans-subjective, should suffice?[4] As perspicacious as much of this scholarship has been, I follow Moghaddam (1997, 2003) in arguing that there are important limitations characterizing the psychological literature on inter-subjectivity. Most pressing here perhaps is the charge of reductionism, the claim that studies of inter-subjectivity examine intra-personal and interpersonal experience at the cost of collective or structural perspectives. That is to say: psychological approaches to inter-subjectivity often lack an adequate examination of the logical relations and symbolic structures underlying such interactions. It is precisely the latter that I prioritize in the discussion that follows.

The chiming + 1

Before turning to Lacan's discussion of the prisoner's dilemma, let us consider a similar logical puzzle which will set the scene. I have in mind Steven Pinker's (2007) 'Barbeque Sauce Problem', which, like the prisoner's dilemma, necessitates the dimension of the trans-subjective in its solution. Here then follows the basic scenario as sketched by Pinker.

A chef at a Sunday barbeque becomes aware of a potentially embarrassing situation: a number of distinguished guests have sauce on their faces. The chef quickly devises a plan by means of which the messy eaters – all of whom, fortunately enough, are professors of logic – will clean their faces without the need for him to approach them one by one. 'At least one of you has sauce on your face' he announces to the party. 'I will give you a minute to consider this situation, and then ring a bell. If someone still has sauce on their face, then I will wait a minute and ring it again, and continue to do so, until you all have clean faces.'

How then does the logic of the situation unfold? Well (to adopt for the moment the perspective of one of the participants): if I look around and see no one with sauce on their faces, I immediately realize *I* must be the culprit. When the bell rings, I wipe my face. The logic here is straightforward and immediate. In a second variation of this situation, I look about after the chef's announcement, and see one colleague with sauce on his face. I know that at least one of us has sauce on our faces, so there is no need to assume that it is me. However, if by the close of the first period – the first chiming of the bell – the colleague has not cleaned his or her face, there can only be one reason: they have seen *someone else* with a messy face. Given that I see no one aside from this colleague with a messy face, I realize that this someone else is in fact *me*. So, when the bell chimes a second time, I wipe my face, as does my colleague; we have both worked our way through the same logic.

The crucial factor here concerns the realization that after the first (or second, or third) ring of the bell there must be at least *one additional messy face* to what I see before me. What is particularly interesting about this example is that the number of messy-faced eaters can be indefinitely extended, and the same logic will hold: if there are four messy eaters, it will require four rings of the bell before the logicians simultaneously clean themselves, in the case of five messy faces, five rings, and so on. There is a theme here that we will return to: the fact of a universal logic that – bearing in mind a minimal degree of inter-subjective awareness – bypasses the requirements of interpersonal exchange and yields a trans-subjective solution.

This brief overture enables me to add a further qualification to the arguments that follow. The treatment of inter-subjectivity and trans-subjectivity I develop here may seem to supersede the stuff of subjective personal reactions by prioritizing the role of logical relations.[5] Let me concede as much: I am not addressing the most obvious 'psychological' aspects of behaviour in the prisoner's dilemma. In this respect I am staying true to Lacan's abiding concern with symbolic operations which play a structuring role above (or perhaps, better yet, *before*) the level of subjectivity. This much is evident in the Barbeque Sauce Problem: the subjective stance of the participants is here all but irrelevant. What co-ordinates their behaviour and structures the solution is something external and impersonal: the ringing of a bell.

Time pressure

There is one further stop we need to make before proceeding on to a discussion of the prisoner's dilemma. The BBQ sauce problem foregrounded the dimension of logical structure in a collective situation. We do well here also to include an instance of compressed or hurried time, indeed, of *hastening*, as it appears in Freud's work, as this factor of temporality will feature in Lacan's elaborations on the prisoner's dilemma.

Advocates of a non-pressurizing ('containing') modality of psychoanalytic time often overlook, or underplay, an instance of unorthodox time management in Freud. In his work with the Wolf-Man, Freud felt that he had arrived at something of an impasse. The patient, says Freud,

> remained for a long time unassailably entrenched behind an attitude of obliging apathy. He listened, he understood, and remained unapproachable . . . [He] gave up working in order to avoid any further changes, and in order to remain in the situation which had been thus established. His shrinking from a self-sufficient existence was so great as to outweigh all the vexations of his illness. Only one way was to be found of overcoming it . . . I determined . . . that the treatment must be brought to an end at a particular fixed date, no matter how far it had advanced. I was resolved to keep to the date . . . Under the inexorable pressure of this fixed limit his resistance and his fixation to the illness gave away, and now in a disproportionately short time the analysis produced all the material which made it possible to clear up his inhibitions and remove his symptoms.
>
> (SE, 17, p. 11)

What is so intriguing about Freud's direction of the treatment in the above case is that it is markedly anxiety provoking. It relies on a compression of time, indeed, upon the pressure of an advancing termination date as an ally in the overcoming of resistances and in the production of new material. It is only by means of the ticking clock, we might say, that the analytical subject is effectively brought about. Perhaps contrary to commonplace presumptions, the argument can be made that there is something fundamentally ethical about this mode of time management, inasmuch as it calls upon the subject to act, to become an agent, even indeed, to *subjectivize* the conditions of their own treatment. Let us now turn to Lacan's account of the prisoner's dilemma.

Three times of subjectivity

In a key section of his 1945 paper on logical time, Lacan asserts that each of us is reliant not only upon others, but upon hypotheses concerning the rigor (or logical reasoning) of those others:

> Only the slightest disparity need appear in the logical term 'others' for it to become clear how much the truth for all depends upon the rigor of each; that truth can engender . . . error in the others; and [that] . . . in this race to the truth . . . no one can get there but by means of the others.
>
> (2006, p. 171)

With this emphasis upon our dependence on the logic of the other, let us take up the challenge of the prisoner's dilemma. Place yourself in the following position: you are one of three prisoners who have been given the opportunity of wining their freedom, provided that you are able to give the correct response to a simple question, namely: 'What is the disk that has been affixed to your clothing?' You cannot see the colour of the disk, and each of the other two prisoners facing you is likewise unaware of the colour of the disk that has been pinned to them. A series of basic rules apply to the challenge. First, only one prisoner will win their freedom in this way, and this will be the first prisoner to stand up and correctly tell the warden the colour of the disk they are wearing, along with the logical reason underlying their deduction. Second, no verbal communication will be allowed between the prisoners. Furthermore, the parameters of the game state that there are two black disks and three white. There is thus a limit to the possible combinations of disks.

Here then is the first of the possible scenarios you might be faced with: each of the two prisoners facing you is wearing a black disk. Little calculation is required here. Given that there are only two black disks that can be put into play, a single glance is enough to confirm that you must be wearing a white disk. All that is required here is an instantaneous deduction – no significant period of time needs to pass. This is what Lacan refers to as 'the instance of the glance'. We might call this a time of singular subjectivity; no inter-subjective dialectic is involved. I depict this situation in Figure 3.1.

The second possible situation is more challenging. Of the prisoners before you, one is wearing a white disk, the other a black. In contrast to the first scenario you

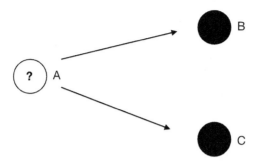

FIGURE 3.1 The first moment of logical time: the instance of the glance

Prisoner 1 (A) sees before him prisoners 2 and 3 (B and C), both of whom are wearing black disks. A is immediately able to deduce what colour disk he is wearing: there are only two black disks that can be put in play, therefore his disk must be white.

will make no headway here unless you make recourse to the inter-subjective dialectic of *how another sees you*. So, following this direction, and extending the logic already utilized, you would need to ask yourself: what are the other prisoners seeing? More particularly, you would need to ask yourself what the prisoner *with the white disk* sees. Why is it so important to imagine what the white disk prisoner is seeing? Well, if this prisoner were to see two black disks, they would stand up and leave, having arrived at the conclusion that they must be white. If the white disk prisoner does not stand up to leave, it can only be because you are wearing a white disk rather than a black (see Figure 3.2). Clearly, a form of inter-subjectivity is involved; the subject needs to reason from the place of the other. It is also necessary that a certain time elapse; this is not an instantaneous moment of recognition but rather what Lacan refers to as 'the time of understanding', which varies in length. There is thus a shift in the modality of time involved. We have moved from the time of the instant realization to the slowed yet no less anxious time of guess–work, calculation and waiting. This is the inter-subjectivity of the indefinite reciprocal subject, as Lacan puts it, a phrase which points to an important reliance on the action (or inaction) of the other.

The most difficult variation of the dilemma occurs when the prisoners before you are both wearing white disks. Once again, it becomes necessary to refer to the reasoning of others. Given that your own disk could be white or black, it helps to work through both possible options. Assuming then for the moment that your disk is black, then each of the other prisoners would see one black disk, and one white. They would each hypothesize that if their own disk were black, then one of the remaining prisoners would stand up and leave. This has

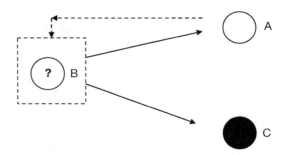

FIGURE 3.2 The second moment of logical time: the time for comprehending

A sees before him one white disk (B) and one black disk (C). This is not enough information to draw a conclusion regards the colour of his own disk. A thus needs to see the situation from the perspective of B. B sees one black disk (C) and A, who could be wearing either white or black. Here it becomes necessary for A to hypothesize. If B were to see two black disks, he would conclude that he is white, and get up and leave. B does not do this – therefore he cannot be seeing two black disks. Given that A knows C is black, he concludes that he must be white.

not happened. You are thus in a position to disconfirm your hypothesis: if you were wearing a black disk one of your rivals would have left by now – having worked their way through the logical steps detailed in the second situation above. They have not done so. Therefore you must be wearing a white disk (see Figure 3.3).

The logical reasoning in this third situation requires not merely reasoning from the position of a second (the inter-subjectivity of how I imagine the other sees me). It requires my hypothesis of what a second subject hypothesizes *about a third*. This is not just a case then of what I think (the subjectivity of 'the instant of the glance'). Nor is it simply a case of the inter-subjectivity of what is deduced by virtue of how the subject imagines he is seen by a second (the 'time for comprehending'). A three-fold structure is in operation whereby I imagine myself via the position of a second *who makes a guess at and responds to a third party*. A twofold mediation is at work: who I am is not simply mediated by a second, but by what this second hypothesizes about me via a third. Part of what makes this such an anxious experience is that my identity cannot be fixed simply by capturing the perspective of one other; I am dependent here on the *other's Other*. This three-fold structure is vital: it is only at this third moment of logical time, Lacan's 'moment of concluding', that a type of *trans-subjective social logic* is activated; it is only at this point, as Žižek (1996) asserts, that the big Other starts to function (as what I have called 'the other's Other'). This three-fold structure is required before an elementary form of 'social objectivity' becomes possible.

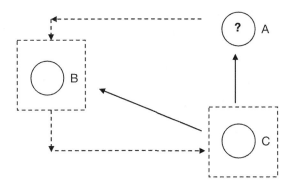

FIGURE 3.3 The third moment of logical time: the moment of concluding

A sees before him two white disks (B) and (C). He puts himself into the position of B. B sees one white disk (C) and A (who could be either black or white). This in itself is not enough information to go on, a further step is required. A is obliged to hypothesize, to play through the options of being either black or white. In the first of these options, of A wearing black, B would see one black (A) and one white (C). Unable to conclude the colour of their own disk on this basis, B would wait to see *how C acts*, because, after all, if A is (hypothetically) black, then C should stand up to leave if B were also black. C does not stand up to leave. Therefore, assuming that A is black, and given the fact that C does not leave, B must be white. On the basis of this conclusion, B is in a position to stand up and leave, but he fails to do so. Neither does C. This means that A cannot be black, for if he were black one of the other prisoners would have made a move to leave.

The emergence of the Other can thus be seen as a structural necessity as borne out of the hopelessness of the subject's failed attempt to ascertain meaning in themselves, a failure which obliges them to look for it in an other, who is likewise contingent on yet another and so on and on *ad infinitum*. In order to halt this infinite regress, to find some centre of meaning, some means of choreographing social activity, one presumes the existence of an already existing Other. We may hence think of the Other as 'a constellation of postulates, a series of propositions' embodying what others are thought to believe.[6] The big Other is thus a necessary working hypothesis, a principle of co-ordination via which human actions can be structured and tentatively understood, even if ultimately it proves to be inconsistent, a repository thus of both truths and fictions.

The interpersonal beyond

A few brief examples may help affirm the distinction between the inter-subjective and the trans-subjective. Consider the idea of signifiers of special significance, that a given individual or couple may utilize as private code words. In Alan Hollinghurst's novel *The Stranger's Child*, for example, the two young lovers Peter and Paul use the name 'Cecil' to refer to one of their planned romantic trysts. As functional as such words might be within the (inter)subjective exchanges of their 'private' usage, they remain separated from the properly trans-subjective value of accepted linguistic terms – they would not be understood by others who stand outside of the (inter)subjective frame of their private significance.

For members of a given language community, accepted words have a conventionalized meaning that necessarily takes precedence over idiosyncratic personal significance. Bluntly put: communicative use value outstrips the particularity of subjective nuance. There is, as such, something tantamount to a shift of paradigm when we move from the psychological frame of (inter)subjectivity to that of the objectivity conferred by the use of symbolic/logical processes or by types of social convention. A brief qualification follows on from this: despite the objectivity of conventionalized meaning we are discussing – namely, that of the signifier to which the signified is, in Saussure's (1974) classic formulation, arbitrarily attached – the question of its final meaning is always potentially deferred. Deferred, that is, by the question of what this signified meaning may 'really mean' for an Other. One may have a clear enough understanding of what a given word means, for example, yet if it is used in a way at odds with its typical meaning (as in the case of slang), or in different pragmatic contexts (used to do a different kind of performative work), this ostensibly objective meaning is very quickly undermined and meaning is again deferred.

Kotso (2008) provides a valuable link here, noting that the deferral apparent in inter-subjective processes works in parallel to the endless chain of signifiers whereby one signifier refers to another and so on.[7] This sliding movement is inevitably halted by a master signifier which is essentially empty, self-referential and that functions as a mooring point, a basis upon which meaning can be stabilized. Paraphrasing Žižek, Kotso makes a further illuminating comment on the necessity of the Other:

> If human subjects were transparent to themselves and to each other, then the virtual order of the big Other would not be necessary: we would automatically know how to interact with each other. It is because subjects are opaque to themselves and to each other that they must posit the big Other.
>
> (p. 56)

For a second example of the inter-/trans-subjective distinction we may return to the parental exclamation 'Look at you!' that I introduced in Chapter 1. This comment seems already to suppose an understanding of the trans-subjective. How so? Well, the comment is not simply equivalent to 'I am looking at you', a descriptive statement which – in its non-reciprocal form at least – connotes a subjective standpoint. Neither is it merely 'Yes, I am looking at you', the reciprocal – and thereby seemingly inter-subjective – response to the imperative 'Look at me!'

(Importantly, part of what qualifies the inter-subjectivity of this order of response is that the remark conveys the possibility that the child might look at themselves not only *with* the parent, but *from their perspective*.)[8] 'Look at you!' then occurs at a level beyond that of (inter)subjectivity. It combines the subjectivity of '*I* am looking at you' with the inter-subjectivity of the response [Yes] 'I *am* looking at you', with a more open-ended invitation that is not circumscribed to 'I', 'we' or 'you'. It opens up to a broader and more 'objective' trans-subjective field. It facilitates something beyond the interpersonal domain; it places the ostensibly universal 'they' within the situation. We might draw here on the terms of literary theory. 'Look at you' transcends the level of a *first-person point of view* ('I', 'we') for it implies the form '*I* am looking at you' but is not limited to it. It also transcends the *second-person point of view* because it implies '*You* are being looked at', without, once again, being reduced to it. It attains the third-person point of view ('They' or 'It'). The latter, in its impersonal neutrality and universality necessarily extends beyond the confines of the first two forms to address the Other.

A third example concerns the phenomenon of anxiety. Anxiety is a common enough response when one is introduced to a group of unfamiliar people. Interestingly, the degree of anxiety is often proportionate to the number of people, and the difficulty one has in reading their prospective intentions. One way of domesticating this anxiety is to gravitate to someone similar to one's self within the group and establish a degree of common ground. Although this person may be a stranger, a brief interaction with them will provide clues as to who they are, and, more importantly, as to *what they might think of you*. This minimal inter-subjectivity provides a frame of sorts, the elementary (and hopefully reassuring) co-ordinates of how you are understood within the perspective of this other. Such assumptions are of course continually being revised, and are subject to errors of interpersonal judgement, and by the deliberately misleading cues of other social actors. Nonetheless, they provide navigational cues for how to conduct one's self and to assess and predict the reactions of others. They are, in this sense, a means of counter-acting anxiety. What is far more anxiety provoking – presumably because it is more difficult to control – is the question of how an unfamiliar group *as a whole* sees one, a group that one confronts without any (inter-subjective) recourse to one isolated member. What is in question is not simply an aggregate of inter-subjectivities (the sum total of possible one-to-one relationships you may have with each member). One confronts here rather an unstable group consensus which emerges through the *double mediation* of what members in the group think not simply of you *per se* (that is, inter-subjectively) but what group members think *other group members think of you* more generally (that is via the Other of the others). It is on this basis that a type of consensual 'social objectivity' becomes operative.

This is not to deny that there is a collection of subjective views. Each single member of a group *does* no doubt have a view of you, a view which can count as an important variable in any emerging group dynamic. Nonetheless, one should not under-estimate the degree to which such forms of inter-subjectivity are always mediated by (what is taken to be) the 'crude objectivity' of a group consensus. As ardently as one may stick to one's subjective views, these will always be contextualized, evaluated and made coherent in reference to an imagined bench-mark of value, the hypothesized sum total evaluation of the group in question. The prevailing norm, whether we refer here to it as a discourse, a type of hege-mony, or a condition of trans-subjectivity, has a different order of agency, an agency with the ability to potentially eclipse an amassed collection of inter-subjective reactions.

One should avoid a potential error here. The decisive factor in differentiating between (inter)subjective and trans-subjective is not simply the factor of double mediation. This in itself – the inter-subjectivity of imagining being a position of a second or third other – need not necessarily attain the level of the trans-subjective. Much as is the case in the distinction social psychologists make between perspectives, meta-perspectives and meta-meta-perspectives (what I think; what I think you think; what I think you think I think), this could represent simply a more complicated version of inter-subjectivity. So while it remains helpful to emphasize the distinction between *what I think an other thinks*, and *what an other thinks and does via the actions of a third party*, this in itself is not enough to guarantee that we have moved beyond the level of inter-subjective speculation. One may conclude on this basis that the decisive element is not simply an extrapolated inter-subjectivity (being able to imagine what a second subject might do and think in respect of a third party). What is crucial is rather the fact that a type of social objectivity is attained, be it in the 'crude objectivity' of a social con-sensus or via the universality of a deductive mathematical solution. An important clarification follows: by 'double mediation' I mean to refer to different *formal* levels of mediation (of little others and the big Other; the inter-subjective and the crude objectivity of the Other), not merely to the numerical extension of inter-subjectivities. In this respect, the solution to the Barbeque Sauce problem could be said to more clearly exemplify the trans-subjective; what is involved is an over-arching logical deduction that occurs above the level of extended inter-subjective reasoning.

What then are some of the implications of what I have described as double mediation? There are many. The canny politician, to give one example, realizes that their destiny depends not on the amassed subjective opinions of voters, but on the less predictable 'collective gestalt' engendered by public opinion. Such a trans-subjective consensus can never be reduced to the aggregated (inter)subjectivity of those who make up society. We have cause here to reflect on suddenness and unpredictability of change in public opinion. As the eponymous character in Stephen Frears' (2006) film *The Queen* suggests to the character of then Prime Minister: Tony Blair: enjoy your popularity while it lasts, because how the public sees you may all too abruptly shift and be transformed into an altogether more negative disposition.

We can easily enough imagine the situation of a political constituency in which each member thinks positively of a given political candidate – and plans in fact to vote for them – but which, nevertheless, as a whole, ends up voting for a rival candidate. The difficulty of gauging such a political situation is made apparent by a simple fact: no *subjective* opinion needs in fact to change before a broader trans-subjective tipping-point is reached. What matters is not so much what *individuals think*, or even the debates and exchanges at the *inter-subjective level*; more important by far is apprehension of what the Other of the group thinks.

One might consider here the case of Hollywood stars or so-called super-models. What matters is not whether agents or promoters of such figures personally experience them as uniquely charismatic, alluring, beautiful, etc. What matters rather is that such promoters are in a position to make people believe *that the majority of other people believe* their stars are talented in such ways. We can, in short, imagine the case of movie stars or models that no one in particular likes, but that maintain their position of distinction simply because enough people believe that the Other finds them charismatic, alluring, beautiful, etc.[9]

We might take up a similar argument in reference to racism. It is quite possible to find a community where no one – quite honestly – feels themselves to be subjectively racist. This may in fact be an accurate psychological portrayal of the individuals within this group. Nevertheless such a community may well retain deeply racist assumptions embedded within its de-subjectified symbolic and institutional practices, or – crucially – within the anonymized trans-subjective framework of *what others are considered to believe*. What I am pointing to here is rather a case of distributed or delegated racism which can quite adequately persist in ostensibly de-personalized institutional forms, without any obvious need for psychological agents – an instance thus of what Eduardo Bonilla-Silva (2003) calls 'racism without racists'.[10]

Such a thesis calls to mind Žižek's (1989) analysis of inter-passivity in ideological belief. Žižek contends that believing often occurs in an *extra-psychological* manner via the role of external objects or others. This is the idea, in short, that I need not personally believe, for there nonetheless to be a believing of which I am effectively a part. Thus, in line with the above argument, we might contend that I need not be 'psychologically' racist, that is, in any way subjectively invested in or consciously identified with racist values, *for there nonetheless to be a racism of which I am a part.* One should be attentive to the nuance of Žižek's point, he is not simply eliding the category of subjectivity: the believing subject *does* effectively (indeed, for Žižek, *objectively*) believe, just not in an overtly personalized or subjective manner. They believe instead at one step's remove, with the comfort of cynical distance from their belief. The 'believing' is effectively delegated to a series of institutional operations, symbolic actions or, crucially, to the trans-subjective network of the beliefs of others.[11]

Discursive versus structural positioning

We can shed further light on the distinction between the (inter)subjective and the trans-subjective by referring to an important notion within social psychology, that of positioning (Davies and Harré, 2001; Harré and van Langenhove, 1999; Wetherell, 1998), and by contrasting *discursive* as opposed to *structural* forms of positioning. The influential notion of positioning described by Davies and Harré (2001) is 'the discursive process whereby selves are located in conversations as observably and subjectively coherent participants in jointly produced story-lines' (p. 264). Davies and Harré speak of positions as 'cumulative fragments of a lived autobiography' (p. 265).

What is immediately apparent is that this notion of positioning is contingent upon discourse. It is a discursive practice and it is content-rich, which is to say that it is stories, narratives, conversations, interactional content that substantiates or 'fills out' the positions in question. Discursive positioning is also a sense-making procedure: 'We take on the discursive practices and story lines as if they were our own and make sense of them' (Davies and Harré, 2001, p. 271). This type of positioning thus entails an interpretive aspect. It is, likewise, a process of negotiation in which subjects respond to different or contradictory social demands, weaving together a variety of cultural, social and political values available within a number of different discourses.

Now while initially this account may seem to overlap to some degree with the positioning dilemma proposed by Lacan, it is important to stress how different the two approaches in fact are. Lacan (1988a, 1988b) is constantly wary of subjective meaning as a questionable ego-construction designed to substantiate effects of knowledge and stability. He will approach a discourse not as a set of thematic or narrative contents, but rather in view of the set of relations, in terms of the particular social links, the *structural positions between people* that it holds together (Lacan, 2007). His attention is not drawn by the 'descriptive materials' of a discourse, i.e. its narratives, meanings, stories, etc., which for the most part he discards as imaginary lures, but *by the relations established between participants*. Hence Lacan's (2007) model of four fundamental social bonds (the discourses of the master, university, analyst and hysteric) in which the thematic contents may vary widely despite that the structural positions remain intact (master and subject; doctor and patient; teacher and pupil, etc.). Verhaeghe's (2001) distinction between the approaches of Foucault and Lacan is instructive here:

> In his discourse theory, Foucault . . . puts the accent on the *content* of a discourse. Lacan . . . works beyond the content and places the accent on the formal relationships that each discourse draws through the act of speaking . . . Lacanian discourse theory has to be understood primarily as formal system, i.e. independent of any spoken word as such. A discourse exists before any concretely spoken word.
>
> (p. 21)

Grigg (2001a) makes much the same point in relating the Lacanian conceptualization of discourse to speech. Discourse is not speech itself; it is the structure of the speech exchange that accounts for the complexity of such an exchange more broadly conceived.[12] Lacan is thus interested in structural positions that are not simply 'secured' by meaning or by the contents of discursive practices, but which remain in question, uncertain, reliant upon the views of others which are themselves contingent on the presumption of given social norms and values.

Lacan's attempt then is precisely to circumvent the psychological ('imaginary') concerns of subjective sense-making and meaning by looking to an *underlying grid of interlinked symbolic positions*. These positions are both more precarious and opaque than those afforded by subjective attempts at making meaning. They are, furthermore, always linked, as in the prisoner's dilemma, to other positions (indeed, to a chain of interlinked positions). Furthermore, each of these related positions remains uncertainly related to a key signifier – in the prisoner's dilemma, the black disk – which remains both conventional (it embodies a certain consensus) and yet uncertain (in the pragmatic sense of what it may mean here and now). Lacan's focus on the trans-subjective, certainly inasmuch as it prioritizes structural positions and the contingency of symbolic values, exists always at a step's remove from the (inter)subjectivity of discursive positioning that focuses on subjective forms of meaning, narrative and sense-making.

Two suspended gestures

There is a further facet of the prisoner's dilemma that demands our attention. As noted above, the second period in Lacan's sequence of logical time, the 'time for understanding', varies in length because each of the prisoners is reliant in their reasoning upon the (in)action of the others. This introduces a problem because this inaction – precisely what the logical deduction is dependent upon – will evaporate the moment one of the prisoners stands up.

The instability of this logical reasoning is compounded by a further consideration: the impetus to act *first*. It is no surprise that Lacan comments that 'the ontological form of anxiety' manifests at this stage of dilemma. Why so? Well, each of the prisoners realizes that their rivals are capable of reaching the same conclusion that they have, if they have not in fact already done so. The brief triumph accompanying the realization that there is an apparently objective solution to the puzzle is thus undercut by the anxious recognition that *it may be one of the others who acts first*. There is a switch-over here between a time of suspension (in which one ensures that one's fellow prisoners are not standing to leave) to the sudden rush to *pre-empt* the action of departure of the others that would then invalidate the basis for one's own conclusion. This is the 'temporal pulsation' as Forrester (1990) puts it, 'whereby the time for understanding is transformed into the moment for concluding' (p. 181). Or, as Pluth and Hoens (2004) sketch the situation:

> A realizes . . . that he urgently has to end his thinking process and head for the door. So, he jumps to a conclusion that closes the time for comprehending, and makes time retroactively meaningful . . . he can and has to end his thinking by an act. Is A sure of his act? He is sure that it is necessary to act, but cannot be sure of the soundness of his reasoning. This is the moment [of] . . . anticipatory certitude. . . . A leaps to a conclusion whose ground or reason can only be verified after the act.
>
> (p. 184)

In other words, the logical solution to the dilemma proposed above is all well and good, but it must be reached and acted upon within a context of *inter-subjective* reliance. The grounds of this decision *may themselves* be put in question. As in the above reference to what the broader meaning of a given signifier might be, we are dealing here with oscillations between ostensible objectivity and the attenuated question of what that objectivity *might pragmatically mean*. We can say then that this scenario represents an intersection of logical and anxious 'psychological' considerations. In this respect the prisoner's dilemma can be interestingly contrasted with the Barbeque Sauce Problem in which there are no 'stand out' subjective acts; the acts in this scene remain trans-subjective in the sense that they are fully choreographed by the Other.

So, if the three prisoners are all of a similar intelligence, they will all, when each wearing a white disk, finally arrive at the same conclusion: 'None of the other prisoners is making a move, hence I must be wearing a white disk.' The delay preceding this point is followed by a moment of indecision. If each of the three rises at the same time, how are they to interpret the reactions of the other prisoners? They will each need to ask themselves whether the other prisoners has arrived at the same logical conclusion as they have, or whether they stood up simply because they saw a black disk. Lacan (2006) describes this situation in the following terms:

> If A, seeing B and C set off . . . wonders again whether they have not in fact seen that he is black, it suffices for him to stop and newly pose the question . . . For he sees that they too stop: since each of them is really in the same situation as him . . . each encounters the same doubt at the same moment as him. Regardless of the reasoning A now imputes to B and C, he will legitimately conclude again that he is white. For he posits anew that, had he been a black, B and C would have had to continue.
>
> (p. 164)

The awkwardness of the shared indecision does not last long. It is the fact of the hesitation which gives the game away: if one of the other prisoners had seen a black disk, he would have no reason to stop and question the gestures of his fellow prisoners. The mutual hesitation can only mean that they're each in the exact same position, that each is wearing a white disk. The solution to the dilemma relies then on a halting sequence whereby inter-subjectivity and trans-subjectivity come to be transposed. An initial suspension in which the subject is reliant on the actions of their fellow prisoners to stand up (or not) leads to a logical conclusion ('I am white'), but this is followed by another moment of inter-subjective hesitation ('We have all three stood up. . . . why?') which again gives way to a trans-subjective solution ('None would have hesitated if they saw a black disk, thus we are all white'). As Pluth and Hoens (2004) explain: 'During the halts, what was subjective about the line of reasoning gets de-subjectified, and becomes a shared . . . truth. Beginning with an uncertain, singular decision A reaches a certain and "universal" truth' (p. 184).

The ambiguous act

It is worthwhile pausing here to stress the paradoxical nature of the decisive act which plays such a prominent role in the prisoner's dilemma. This act, in which the prisoner makes for the door in 'the time of concluding', remains in an important sense *ambiguous*. The anxious conditions of the competition mean that the reasoning process is rushed; the prisoner is forced to reach a conclusion at the fear of being left behind. As such their act is not simply the result of a rational process of calculation; it cannot be seen as the outcome of pure, abstracted reasoning. Yet, on the other hand, as we have seen, such an act may equally not be reduced to the purely subjective. It helps here to stress the *anticipatory* nature of the act. An anticipatory act

> is neither an act that simply follows from a line of reasoning, nor is it an act that is purely spontaneous and *ex nihilo*. The act contains aspects of both. There is a line of reasoning, and there is spontaneity.
>
> (Pluth and Hoens, p. 186)

We can say then that the *objective* (the factor of rational calculation) and the *subjective* (the individual's impetus to act) here coincide. Differently put: the objectivity of the symbolic reasoning passes through the subject and is given form in *their* anticipatory act. This subjectivized action then plays its part in making that which is objective, namely the decisive action which effectively ends the 'time of understanding'. As Pluth and Hoens emphasize: the act is both something which interrupts the line of reasoning, and yet it is equally *an element of that reasoning itself* (by acting, the prisoner retrospectively gives his reasoning a sense). That is, *the subjective act that the subject performs becomes part of the objectivity of their reasoning.*

It is worth dwelling a little longer on the role and status of the act inasmuch as it pertains directly to our understanding of the *subject* of psychoanalysis (as opposed to what we might call 'the egoic subject' of psychology). A wonderful description of the act is provided by Butler (2014), which highlights not only the mutual imbrication of subject and symbolic, but the role of the subject in making the symbolic that then in turn determines them:

> In the act, we do not follow a pre-existing symbolic mandate . . . The act neither simply breaks with the symbolic nor merely returns us to the symbolic . . . It forces us to (re)experience the introduction of the symbolic and thus to confront its contingency. What is realized in the act is the fact that, against the idea that the subject is a creation of the symbolic, the symbolic depends on the subject. In the act, there is no relying on the authority of a subject or any transparent self-reflection by the subject in a non-alienated fashion. On the contrary, it dispenses with the illusion that there is a subject, or at least a self-conscious and self-possessed subject that knows the effects of its actions in advance. We return to that 'primordial' experience of the subject as empty, as a moment of doubt and uncertainty. Or the act *is* the subject in Lacan's sense that 'I am not where I think' and 'I am where I do not think'.
>
> (p. 241)

The act is not thus to be understood within the parameters of the psychological, that is, as performed by a 'self-conscious . . . self-possessed subject' (p. 241) – an illusion dispensed with by the act itself. It stems from and is grounded in the subject-as-split, as that which is incommensurate with itself.

An example suffices to affirm the performative non-psychological dimension of such an act. In J.M. Coetzee's (2013) *The Childhood of Jesus*, a central character, Simone, implores a young woman, Innes, to adopt the young boy that he, Simone, has been caring for. After multiple requests to take on the child and treat him as her own, Simone presses further, insisting that to say yes, to agree, to offer such a symbolic gesture would make everything clear to Innes. It would, in effect, initiate the psychological change that would make such a role 'natural', inevitable. This of course is less an act than an attempt to induce an act.[13] Nonetheless, the logic is clear: if Innes were to announce something like 'I take this child to be my son', she would not only have made a subjective statement, an enunciation of personal intent. She would also have made a symbolic declaration, a commitment to assuming an appropriately parental relationship to the boy. Such an act, while executed in the form of a symbolic utterance, is the necessary precondition for a change in the symbolic. We have here, as in the examples discussed in Chapter 2, a declarative event which – insofar as it is performed under the appropriate conditions – not only describes the world, but introduces a change into it. And just as this act of the (uncertain, split) subject forms the basis of a new objective state of affairs, so the state of affairs thus affirmed – a symbolic pact of parenthood – proves the platform for a series of subjective dispositions that might well follow (a sense of maternal obligation, an increased sense of love for the boy, and so on).[14]

Hastening to identity

What then does the foregoing analysis have to tell us about identification? Let us briefly consider again the decisive act that the prisoner confronted by the two white disks in the suspended 'time of understanding' is forced to make. The retroactive impact of this act, whose grounds can only be subsequently verified, directs us to a discussion of the pre-emptive quality of symbolic identifications. As Žižek (1996) emphasizes in his discussion of Lacan's 'Logical Time', symbolic identification – one's assumption of a given social role, of a structural location in a socio-symbolic realm – always maintains something of an anticipatory character. Succinctly put: there is a psychological time lag in taking on a symbolic mandate. Or, differently put: there is no psychological pre-adaptation to what at basis amounts to an anonymous subject-position ('grand-mother', 'brother', 'doctor', 'justice of the peace', 'commander', etc.) in the symbolic network. One might take as a case in point here the 'rehearsals' – and I use the word in view of its full theatrical significance – of recently married couples, whose repeated reference to the nominations 'my husband', 'my wife', form part of their attempt to symbolically 'play themselves into' their new roles. This is likewise the case in respect of the gap between the empirical event of a child's actually being born (or, perhaps, conceived) and the active assumption of the roles of mother and father which come to be tirelessly reiterated and – eventually by the child themselves – within the family ('Daddy will pick you up from school', 'Your mother said no!', etc.).

In respect of this time lag between event and its (lack of) subjective integration, one might consider the response of athletes in the seconds after a great victory. The sense they often exhibit in interviews immediately after the event is that 'It hasn't quite sunk in', 'I can't quite believe it', etc. A line of analysis attuned to the importance of symbolic factors in supporting and making various imaginary identifications possible, would point to the trans-subjective framework of such events. Great national sporting victories require multiple symbolic and historical markers: not just the events on the pitch, but the souvenirs, newspaper headlines and the assembled crowd of supporters through whom affective responses are both heightened and made somehow more (symbolically) real.

It is important to bear in mind again here that the '*Structuralist*' thrust of Lévi-Strauss's (1974) conceptualization of the symbolic – to which Lacan is obviously indebted – advances a form of *symbolic* agency over and above notions of subjective agency. The symbolic order thus conceptualized is, to reiterate, a matrix of spaces, an a-psychological network of relational positions. There is no intrinsic psychological essence to these subject-positions, no relation of innate belongingness between the subject and their social mandate. Much the same point can be made via the clinical psychoanalytic cautioning to attend carefully to moments of abrupt symbolic change in the lives of patients. Such shifts in status are, not incidentally, often considered to be potential triggering-events in the case of psychosis. That is to say, no hand-to-glove relationship exists between imaginary and symbolic facets of identification. The 'who' I think I am, my experiential and *imaginary* sense of identity, on the one hand, as opposed to *what I am called to be*, how I am socially recognized, my social or symbolic identity, on the other, is always qualified by a minimal gap.

The fact of (trans-subjective) symbolic performance as condition of (subjective) belief can be illustrated via the social rituals that need to be adhered to in the public lives of people of historical or political importance. In fact, the more illustrious or elevated the symbolic position, the more elaborate the performative rituals tend to become. We may go back to the example of *The Queen*, which playfully invokes all the extraordinary rules of conduct one is expected to abide by when meeting the Monarch: one does not touch the Queen, or turn one's back on her, one does not address her ('Your Majesty') without first being addressed, etc.

One might likewise cite the ceremonial activities accompanying the inauguration of a new president. Such symbolic activities need to be performed correctly, and to be publically witnessed, if they are to be registered within the trans-subjective network of a given social mass. It is as if without these seemingly redundant and slightly ridiculous rules of conduct the involved subjects might effectively cease to believe in, or credit, the elevated social rank in question. One might jokingly remark that this was the reason Barak Obama had to be sworn in twice as part of his presidential inauguration in 2008. The problem was not so much that his hand had not touched the Bible, as had been suggested. It was rather the case, given the 8 years of Conservative Republicanism of George W Bush and the obvious fact that Obama was the first African-American president, that he had to be sworn in twice so that a global audience could actually *believe* that it had really happened.

Interesting here also is the curious title – 'President Elect' – given to the winner of a presidential election before their inauguration. This temporary sobriquet reflects the time lag between these two events (election victory and inauguration), and functions presumably to prepare the country (and the new President him- or herself) for the transition in authority which may otherwise be too abrupt. Staying with the presidential theme one might cite the final episode of the television drama *The West Wing* which comes to a close with the fictional President Jed Bartlett leaving office. A memorable sequence shows how at the same moment, all across the country, portraits of the former president are taken down and replaced by the image of the new commander-in-chief. The suddenness of the gesture helps make the point that symbolic change inevitably occurs ahead of the pace of the psychical adaptation of individuals – or indeed of the national community itself – to such changes.[15]

Precipitate identification

The reason for this lack of congruence, for the fact that there is no spontaneous or natural assumption of symbolic roles – and here I borrow from Žižek's (1996) gloss on these issues – is that they can always be questioned with 'But why *me*?' At the level of rational discourse answers can be always be provided: 'I am a prince because my father is the king'. Answers of this sort can themselves be put into question: 'But what is it about *me* that justifies this symbolic destiny?' The situation is akin to the communicative dilemma alluded to above: 'Yes, I understand that you have told me something, I can interpret the meaning of your words; what eludes me is the broader implication of why you're telling me this now, to what further ends?' Symbolic roles, in other words, are not groundless; reasons can be given for them, it's just that the 'grounds for the grounds', so to speak, remain open to question.

One way of negotiating this gap between imaginary and symbolic identifications, of avoiding the unease of this disjuncture, is to vigorously grasp one's symbolic mandate, to pronounce myself as the thing I am taken to – or might – be. I must, in other words, pronounce myself as the role I might be, declare myself *as that* and recognize myself as such. What this means is that there is necessarily something which precedes the psychological activation of a role, namely the symbolic conferral – and more importantly yet, the declarative event, *the act of the subject* – that provides the symbolic basis to make the latter possible. As in the declarations of speech-act theory, we have thus an extra-psychological element that forms the basis for imaginary identification. Hence the idea of precipitate identification and the anticipatory, hastening character of my symbolic identifications that come prior to their actual psychological subjectivization. In his discussion of the 'genesis' of objective socio-symbolic identity Žižek claims that

> if we simply wait for a symbolic place to be allotted to us, we will never live to see it. That is, in the case of a symbolic mandate, we never simply ascertain what we are; we 'become what we are' by means of a precipitous subjective gesture. This precipitous identification involves the shift from object to signifier.
>
> (p. 76)

In the case of the prisoner's dilemma, this is the shift from the *object* of the disk – which remains inaccessible to me, an indication that I can have no full understanding of what I 'objectively' am – to the assumption of *the operation of the signifier*, an understanding that my role is effectively what I am in the negotiated network of trans-subjective meanings. In the first case, at the level of objects and their apparent meanings we are in the imaginary register; in the second, we are in the domain of symbolic identification. In order not to be left behind in the prisoner's dilemma, I actively declare myself; I nominate myself as, and act in accordance with, the symbolic identity of 'white'. In so doing

> I assume a symbolic identity which fills out the void of the uncertainty as to my being. What accounts for this anticipatory overtaking is the *inconclu-sive* character of the causal chain . . . [W]ithin the space of symbolic inter-

subjectivity, I can never simply ascertain what I am, which is why my 'objective' social identity is established by means of 'subjective anticipation'.

(Žižek, p. 76)

One may think of this as a type of self-interpellation motivated by the anxiety of a primary state of non-inclusion. The subject hopes, via a peremptory self-inclusion, to forestall the possibility of social non-belonging. It helps here to cite the stark 'syllogism' with which Lacan closes his paper. This syllogism is notable both for the blunt formula of human belonging it offers – the zero-level, we might speculate, of such a self-nominating declarative event – and for the fact that the first-person pronoun (indicative of the fact of *subjectivization*) only appears in the last line:

A man knows what is not a man;

Men recognize themselves among themselves as men;

I declare myself as a man for fear of being convinced by men that I am not a man.

(Lacan, 2006, p. 174)

Indeterminate objectivity

As we have seen, the prisoner's dilemma is structured by three 'times' or periods – the modalities each of the instant, the suspended time of understanding and the rushed moment of concluding. These are neither purely subjective in nature nor wholly objective, but somehow between these two modalities. Such a logical time, so Lacan (2006d) claims, plays its part in organizing and structuring human action. Logical time, as Evans (1996) stresses, is neither objective (the chronological 'time of the clock') nor simply a matter of subjective feeling. We are dealing with 'a precise dialectical structure', an unfolding sequence of types of inter/trans-subjective logic 'based on a tension between waiting and haste, between hesitation and urgency' (Evans, p. 206).[16]

This movement between inter- and trans-subjective logic casts a light on the three instances in this chapter where I have reflected on types of trans-subjective objectivity, namely those of: deductive logic (the universal/mathematical solutions to the two puzzles discussed above); the conventional nature of signifiers; the 'crude objectivity' of forms of social consensus. In each case a form of trans-subjective objectivity is evinced that exceeds the level of subjective or inter-subjective interpretation. In each case there is thus a 'ground'. Importantly however, and as already stressed – a crucial reason why Lacan's work is never simply an extension of Lévi-Strauss's Structuralism – the grounds in question can always be subjected to the 'psychological' articulations of questioning, doubt, anxiety. Hence the idea that while there is an order of trans-subjective objectivity (of logical reasoning, convention, general consensus) underwriting social life, the 'ground for the grounds' can always be scrutinized, brought into question.

What becomes evident then is that neither the notion of the subjective nor that of the objective emerges unaltered in the course of Lacan's musings on the prisoner's dilemma. True enough, I have stressed above the categorical difference between the (inter)subjective and the trans-subjective on the one hand, and the process of psychological/imaginary as opposed to symbolic identification on the other. Then again, as the oscillation between interpretative inter-subjectivity and trans-subjectivity in the prisoner's dilemma makes clear, these two respective dimensions can never be fully separated. We need, as such, to insist on the over-lapping, inter-penetrating quality of these two aspects of social and psychical life.[17] Even ostensibly objective social facts are still filtered through the prism of what given individuals (subjectively) think of them, just as these subjectivities are never (save perhaps in extreme cases of psychosis) completely cut adrift from a modicum of social convention implied by the functioning of the Other. Hence the apparent disjunction in Evans's (1996) previously cited definition of the big Other as simultaneously the radical alterity of the trans-subjective symbolic order on the one hand, and the 'the symbolic order . . . [as] *particularized for each subject*' (p. 133, my emphasis), on the other. This two-way problematization is crucial for psychoanalytic practice, which, as Lacan insisted, cannot be reduced to either the subjective or the objective.[18] That is to say, an analyst must remain attentive both to how subjects subjectively interpret and make sense of given (trans-subjective) forms of social objectivity, just as they need attend to the dimension of the trans-subjective (or, the symbolic) in the individual utterances and speech of the patient.

Subject of the Other

The above qualifications being noted, it is crucial that we not lose sight of the correct level of intervention for Lacanian psychoanalysis. Crucially, the point is most certainly *not* to collapse the trans-subjective into (inter)subjectivity. The psychoanalytic priority lies firmly on the trans-subjective, the domain of the Other, as it enters into and seemingly over-writes the subjectivity of individual social actors. Why so? Well, it is at this level that the unconscious speaks. It is as a trans-subjective formation that the unconscious – as precisely 'the discourse of the Other' – breaks through the enunciations of individual speech. Here we need to permit the apparent paradox according to which it is in the guise of the Other, in the public tongue of trans-subjectivity, that the individual's unconscious emerges.

We have the opportunity then to assert the fundamentally non-psychological status of Lacanian psychoanalysis. The point made previously can be restated: Lacanian theory avoids reduction to the frame of psychological (inter)subjectivity by time and again prioritizing the role of the Other. A Lacanian approach grapples with how the (inter)subjective is always profoundly moulded by the trans-subjective. Johnston provides an adroit sketch of the irreducibly trans-subjective dimension of subjectivity:

> Lacan goes to great lengths to undermine ... the apparent clarity and firmness sometimes attributed to the distinction between individual and collective levels of human existence ... [F]rom a Lacanian perspective, there is no such thing as strictly individual psychology per se. The singular person scrutinized by psychoanalysis, in all the richness of his/her memories, identifications, fantasies, and patterns of comportment, is inherently intertwined with larger, enveloping matrices of mediation. That is to say, the individual is always trans-individual ... Lacan maintain[s] that each individual ... is a bundle of numerous inter-subjective relations (i.e. bonds with 'little-o' others) and trans-subjective structures (i.e. ties to the 'big O' Other).
>
> (2004, p. 260)

Johnston's description helps us understand how the particularities and eccentricities of individual psychical functioning are always more than merely subjective. This in turn helps us to characterize the Lacanian unconscious which can be reduced to neither its unique instantiations in the lives of singular subjects nor the anonymous structural network of signifiers (the field of the Other) which forms the necessary backdrop for such productions.

If this seems a difficult notion to grasp, we might propose essentially the same conceptual challenge in the form of a question about language. That is to ask: what is *the location* of a given language? Is a language located at a performative level (of *parole*), in the everyday utterances of the extended community of its speakers, or is to be found at the level of structure (or synchrony), in the conventions of usage, rules of grammar and syntax that govern that make up a language in its irreducibly social nature? The answer of course is that this is a badly posed question; language is necessarily spread between both such locations, and cannot be exclusively situated at either such site. The same holds for the Lacanian unconscious which manifests in distinctive forms in the enunciative acts of individuals, but that can never be separated from structural trans-subjective matrix that makes such acts possible. In both cases we have the prospect of infinite possible articulations within a finite system (of linguistic rules and signifiers).

Before concluding this section, let us make the case for the prioritization of the trans-subjective via a brief discussion of the subject of the Other. Perhaps the most economic overview of this topic is to be found in Chiesa (2007), who prefaces his discussion of the relation between these concepts with a succinct definition of the Other (which, incidentally, usefully consolidates a variety of such perspectives introduced in Chapter 1). The big Other:

> may be equated with (a) *language* as a structure (as in structural linguistics); (b) *the symbolic order* as the legal fabric of human culture (in accordance with Levi-Strauss's anthropology); (c) *the Freudian unconscious* as reformulated by Lacan in his ... return to its original, subversive signification.
>
> (Chiesa, 2007, p. 35)

This is a helpful typology; it proves useful when navigating the confusion which can result when the concept is deployed in a loose, unqualified fashion (all too typically the case in Lacan's own use of the term). And it comes with an equally useful qualification. Chiesa warns that despite the 'mutual superimpositions' possible in the varying applications of the concept 'it would be misleading to immediately assume that these notions perfectly overlap' (p. 35). Furthermore: 'The subject of the Other can appropriately be grasped only by clearly defining these three vertices' (p. 35).

Lacan's growing attention to the notion of the Other in the mid-1950s had direct bearing on the development of his (decidedly non-psychological) theorization of the subject:

> With particular reference to the notion of subjectivity Lacan's new interest in the big Other corresponds to a shift in emphasis from the formula 'The ego is an other' to the formula 'I is an Other'. Having almost exclusively concentrated on what the subject was *not* (the ego), Lacan's theory becomes more constructive: first and foremost, the subject is now positively identified with the subject of the Other.
>
> (Chiesa, 2007, p. 35)

Chiesa extrapolates from this, arguing that the Lacanian subject as precisely the subject *of the Other* should thus be understood equally as:

> the subject of language; (b) the subject of the Symbolic; and (c) the subject of the unconscious.
>
> (p. 35)[19]

This discussion of the subject's relation to the Other enables us to advance upon this topic as we have broached it in earlier chapters, as a type of 'extimacy', that is, as the presence of a kind of intimate otherness.[20] What is required now is a further step in this logic, one which is wary of the apparent divisibility implied by earlier treatments of these respective concepts. That is to say: what is inassimilable in the Other (as radical alterity, etc.) must not be figured as a type of alien quantity simultaneously 'within' yet nevertheless cut-off from the subject. This would be to imply that the Other exists somehow apart from the subject, and, worse yet, that the subject persists as a minimally unified entity, unified particularly perhaps by virtue of its difference from the Other.

The further step that we are compelled to make here, to resist two untenable conceptualizations (the Other as somehow divisible from the subject, the subject as unified) is to realize that this inassimilable quality to the Other is also, as it were, *folded into the subject itself*. The subject, we can say, is the outcome of the fact that this never-to-be-integrated component always-already was a constituent element of what they are (and what they will be). It is by virtue of the factor of 'that which cannot be integrated' that there is a subject in the first place. This then is not merely a barred or split subject – such characterizations inevitably imply an earlier undivided subject – it is rather the subject as incommensurability-to-itself. Or, in Chiesa's (2007) elegant phrase: we are not concerned here merely with the *lacking* subject, but with *subjectivized* lack.

On the significance of objects

Before closing, it is tempting to juxtapose the type of trans-subjective 'objectivity' which has emerged in the foregoing discussion with the notion of inter-objectivity developed within French sociology. I have in mind here particularly Bruno Latour's (1996) influential discussion of the notion, which explores how the 'affordances' of various objects condition and shape the relationships between social actors. The role of such objects in shaping such relations occurs, importantly, in ways which allegedly bypass symbolic considerations. Latour (1996) makes reference to the organized behaviour of simian societies, explicitly thus seeking to avoid any recourse to the 'role of the signifier', to any structuring function of the symbolic, which he feels are frequently inadequate and typically over-used theoretical notions. Now while it is beyond our scope here to enter into any detailed consideration of Latour's theorization of inter-objectivity, it perhaps suffices for me to close with a question drawn from a comparison between the notions of inter-objectivity and trans-subjectivity.

What is path-breaking about Latour's sociological re-conceptualization of social objects is that it substitutes considerations of *material affordances* for the analysis of inter-subjective or associated symbolic and structural factors. By affordances he has in mind the material properties of given objects which enable forms of action while inhibiting others (an elementary example: the speed bumps which slow and minimize traffic in one part of town thereby maximizing the use of other routes). Objects in this sense are actors of sorts – they are possessed of a type of facilitating/ inhibiting agency. They must, as such, be credited with a crucial role in under-standing the patterns or outcomes of social relations (hence the term 'inter-objectivity').[21]

How might we complicate this view? Well, a Lacanian approach warns that objects in a world of signification cannot be severed from signifiers; within the social domain there are never merely material objects (or affordances) separated off from the dimension of *what they might be thought to mean for others*. In what is perhaps Latour's most direct critique of the prioritization of the symbolic over the material in sociological analysis, he questions what it is that symbolism presupposes:

> We often appeal to symbols and the tricky notion of symbolism . . . we need, it is said, to supplement primate social links with human symbolic links. However this hypothesis does not hold . . . for what do symbols hold on to? If the social is not solid enough to make interactions last . . . how could signs do the job?

(1996, p. 234)

From a Lacanian perspective we might reverse this argument, retorting thus that the materiality of objects is never merely material if human actors are present. Objects themselves may operate as signifiers and can come to play a significant role in the complex field of the overlapping desires and intentions of others. Indeed, the affordances of such objects itself implies signification, assumptions and questions of what the objects in question might be used for, of what they – like the disks in the prisoner's dilemma – might mean to both others and the big Other.

The contrast with Latour's theory enables us to emphasize how the 'objectivity' in the Lacanian account discussed above is *always symbolic*, always to be understood in reference to the role of language, to 'the operation of the signifier' in the production of a symbolic universe. This suggests that the role of signifier is apparent even where we might not expect to find it, even within – to draw on Latour's (1996) example – the social negotiations of simian actors. To insist then that an object is never merely an object within human relations, but an element in a distributed and never fully resolved signifying game, means that it becomes necessary to question whether the notion of a type of non-symbolic inter-objectivity is plausible. The question then is this: can a notion of ostensibly 'non-symbolic' inter-objectivity be considered tenable, if inter-objectivity always entails a minimal degree of signification? We should, in short, be cautious of assuming that inter-objectivity, in Latour's sense of 'the materiality of object-relations', ever occurs in a vacuum of signification.

Notes

1 See for example: Badiou, 2009; Fink, 1996; Johnston, 2005; Pluth and Hoens, 2004.

2 There is another reason for tackling this paper only after a discussion of the 1950s work. I deemed it better to first introduce as clearly as possible a series of important Lacanian concepts – the Other, the symbolic order, the subject, the imaginary – that exist in a far less definitive form in the Logical time essay.

3 Phenomenological conceptualizations thus could be said to play the part of a 'vanishing mediator' (to use Žižek's (1996) phrase) in the development of Lacanian theory. For an assessment of various claims regards the influence of phenomenology upon Lacan, see Eyers (2012).

4 Within the field of social psychology Gillespie and Cornish (2009) have for example illuminated the concept from the perspective of dialogical analysis. Gillespie and Richardson (2011), similarly, have explored the topic via discussions of position exchange, perspective taking and actor-observer communication. Coelho and Figueiredo (2003), furthermore, have brought philosophical and psychoanalytic insights to bear in their categorization of four basic forms of inter-subjectivity, each of which is based on a matrix of otherness. They distinguish a phenomenological type of inter-subjectivity from *traumatic*, *interpersonal* and *intra-psychic* forms (Coelho and Figueiredo, 2003).

5 This certainly appears to be the case in the above scenario, to which we might respond by posing the obvious question: surely most individuals would repeatedly wipe their faces before the necessary number of chimes, just to be sure that their faces are clean? It is perhaps for this reason that Pinker so emphatically frames the puzzle as that of *logicians* attending a barbeque.

6 I have indulged in a little inter-textuality here: the phrase is Frantz Fanon's (1968, p. 78). Although originally deployed as part of his analysis of colonial racism, the phrase perfectly encapsulated this aspect of the Other.

7 The lateral level of this seemingly endless chain of deferrals is one way of approaching the functioning of human desire; it provides one means of approaching Lacan's repeated insistence that 'desire is the desire of the Other' as discussed in Chapter 1.

8 It is surely the emerging prospect of doing so – of seeing themselves from their parents' perspective – that makes such forms of interchange so appealing and important for children.

9 This is not to say that there are never instances where the Emperor is shown to have no clothes: i.e. where the collective gestalt concerning a given much-touted actor or model's apparent star-status is called into question and refuted. An instructive case was the meteoric rise to the 'A-list' of the actor Shia LaBeouf, much debated and questioned in the entertainment pages at the time, presumably because many – myself included – were immune to his apparent charms. The subsequent downturn in LaBeouf's acting fortunes indicates that despite the attempts of various agents and studios the big Other was not ultimately charmed.

10 The laterality of this mode of knowing (or believing or desiring) is crucial for another reason. It demonstrates the metonymic quality of these functions which can as such be achieved via types of displacement or extension. This observation in turn enables us to highlight an important element of the Lacanian unconscious, namely the fact that it is a distributed, *external* unconscious which functions not only via the 'vertical' or metaphoric operation of repression, but via displacements onto a variety of proxy elements existing on the very surface of social and symbolic life.

11 What holds for the Other, we might note, holds for the unconscious also. That is to say, the extended chain of postulates that we have been discussing holds also for *the split subject* of the unconscious. That is to say, trans-subjective structures (like the unconscious itself) can, as we are beginning to see, accommodate apparent contradictions, inconsistencies, simultaneous modes of belief and disbelief. We have then in such an understanding of the trans-subjective, an original and distinctive perspective on Freud's primary process thinking, which famously does not abide by the law of non-contradiction.

12 This is a notion of discourse, furthermore, which asserts that the outcome of a speech-exchange is separate – and in some respects incommensurable with – the truth acting upon speaker and recipient alike.

13 A further qualification: an act shouldn't be understood simply within the terms of personal pressure: as a non-egoic event, an act occurs as part of the agency of the subject not of the ego.

14 The role of the speaking subject in the (re)making of symbolic is of course an ethical necessity if psychoanalytic practice is to be able to produce change.

15 We have an interesting basis then to question the extent to which certain unsymbolized yet actual events remain insufficiently registered psychically (indeed, at the level of the unconscious). How many of us have not experienced an extended sense of disbelief at a change – whether welcome or unwelcome – in the status of a key relationship, a professional or social position? We can appreciate then how a lack of symbolic declaration enables us to continue to believe, unconsciously, that a prior state has continued such that we never quite come to terms with the end of a job, the death of a loved one, a radically altered social position, etc.

16 Lacan's fascination with an inter-subjective triad that structures a series of relationships and dispositions can be seen in his *Seminar on the Purloined Letter*, in which he muses on a situation from Edgar Allan Poe's novel. While the triads of that situation and the prisoner's dilemma are obviously distinct, they can be interestingly juxtaposed. In the crucial scene from *The Purloined Letter* the character of the Queen finds herself in a difficult position: she is found with a compromising letter in the presence of the King and several ministers. The King's disinterested gaze fails to notice the incriminating document,

and the Queen breathes a sigh of relief. However, an unscrupulous minister, who has observed the Queen's nervousness and intuited the importance of the letter, is bold enough to snatch it away. He correctly guesses that the Queen cannot object without attention being called to the secret contents of the letter.

Felman's (1987) description of the dilemmatic scene in *The Purloined Letter* stresses that what is in question is not 'the individual psychology of a character, but three functional positions in a structure which, determining the three viewpoints, embody three relations to the act of seeing' (pp. 40–41). We have then, first, the naïve subjectivity of the King's glance which sees nothing, followed by the inter-subjectivity of the Queen's glance which sees that the first sees nothing and deludes itself to the secrecy of what it hides. Then there is the third glance which sees 'that the first two glances leave what should be hidden exposed to whomever would seize it' (Felman, 1987, pp. 40–41). While this third glance does not qualify as trans-subjective, it does represent a step up in a progression from the singular subjective glance and the moment of two-person inter-subjectivity that precedes it. It involves a triadic sensibility, an awareness of the conjoined sensibilities of both the King and the Queen. From this we may conclude that a more complex sequence of inter-subjectivities is not in and of itself sufficient to attain the trans-subjective (as argued above), even if such a structure of inter-related positions does exercise a determining influence on the 'psychological' dispositions of each of the actors in the dilemma. We see here yet another example in Lacan where structure trumps psychology: it is not the individual disposition of the actors within Poe's scenario that counts, but their position in a triadic set of interlinked roles.

17 In response then to the foreseeable criticism that the prisoner's dilemma is not structurally or logically pure enough an instance of the trans-subjective (say, as by contrast to the Barbeque Sauce problem), we should instead insist that Lacan's choice of the dilemma was apt not in spite of but precisely *because* it involves both (inter)subjective anxiety and a universal solution.

18 I take up and elaborate this point in the book's concluding chapter.

19 Chiesa adds to this a further clarification: the subject of the unconscious 'is both the *unconscious* subject, a psychic agency that is opposed to the agency of consciousness (or, better, self-consciousness), and the subject *of* the unconscious, the subject *subjected* to the unconscious' (2007, p. 35).

20 In previous chapters I have stressed the inextricability of the Other to the subject. Verhaeghe's (2001) discussion of the dialectical exchange between drive, subject and Other allows us to add a further layer to this characterization, characterization by exploring how 'primordial' this enmeshment with the Other is. In the earliest months of life, Verhaeghe remarks, following Freud, the experience of pain can be compared to a trauma. The reaction of the infant to this unpleasurable situation is prototypical, constitutive for future inter-subjective relationships:

> The helpless infant turns to the Other by crying, and it is the Other who has to take a 'specific action' through which the inner pressure is relieved . . . [T]his proto-typical situation causes a connection between the originally internal tension and the Other. The link between the two, i.e. between inner drive and the Other, is the crying or shouting [that is] . . . the expression or representation of the drive. In other words, the original bodily drive acquires right from the start an intersubjective dimension.
>
> (2001, pp. 150–151)

Internal drive thus becomes 'indissolubly connected with the external Other'; the subject's relationship to their own bodily impulses is thus refracted through the symbolic, through an agency of appeal. The Other, in this qualified sense, can be understood as a bodily element.

21 Using the example of conducting a transaction at a post office, Latour asks:

> How could you conceive of a counter without a speaking grill, a surface, the door, the walls, a chair? Do not these, literally, shape the frame of the interaction. . . . Are sociologists barking up the wrong tree when patching [up explanations of social events] . . . with the symbolic, while objects are omnipresent in all the situations in which they are looking for meaning?
>
> (Latour, 1996, p. 235).

4

LOVE, ARTIFICIALITY AND (MASS) IDENTIFICATION

Over-extension of the ego

What does Freud have in mind with his idea of 'the libidinal constitution of the mass'? As a prelude to answering this question, let us picture a familiar scene. A die-hard sports fan is glued to the screen, watching the final minutes of a crucial game (of soccer, football, hockey, etc). Suddenly, a member of his team steals possession, evades the members of the opposing team, and scores to win the game. In the ensuing moments of elation, the supporter feels that the goal is in some ways *theirs* also; he or she feels that 'we' scored, 'we' won, etc. For a few minutes – or, in cases of more historic wins, even for a few *weeks* – there is a giddy sense of narcissistic unity among the team's supporters.[1] Such a phenomenon of group narcissism is also often in evidence when countries successfully host mass-scale sporting events (such as the Olympics, the soccer World Cup, etc.).

While this example may seem to touch only on a limited aspect of the broader topic of identification and mass identification, it nevertheless dramatizes the central question of this chapter, namely: how might we account for such an over-extension of identity, this apparent short-circuit between the 'I' and the 'we'? Differently put: how does one come to experience oneself as part of a given group whose membership could always be said to be circumstantial, contingent, less than essential? Answering this question will provide the opportunity to explore a variety of conceptualizations of identification and affect, as they occur in the work of both Freud and Lacan.[2]

Two further issues will prove to be crucial in considering the above questions. The first concerns love, or, as is more befitting of psychoanalytic conceptualization, the fact of *libidinal ties* underlying a mass identification. The second concerns what we might refer to as *the detour through others* that qualifies many of our most powerful affective experiences. This brings to mind the (not infrequent) paradox whereby many people can claim that a sporting victory – an event in which they had no integral role to play and which in no way necessitated their presence – *was one of the greatest moments in their lives.* The same holds of the 'identification power' of large-scale collective events – the death of a loved national icon, for example – that prove such striking historical markers in the lives of their participants. Such affects need to be routed through an Other, afforded a minimal degree of externality. The consideration of such externality will also prompt discussion of the symbolic paraphernalia – the flags, songs and insignia associated with popular sports teams and political parties – that so frequently accompany and support the expression of collective emotion. This in turn poses questions concerning the apparent necessity of a degree of artificiality as – paradoxically – a condition of the 'authenticity' of emotion.

I begin the chapter by taking up many of the key tenets of Freud's 'mass psychology'[3] which I extend via a series of Lacanian conceptualizations. This Freudian basis in place, I turn more directly to a set of Lacan ideas – the symbolic basis of affect, for example, and, in the ensuing chapter, the notions of the master signifier and the unary trait. I aim thus to supplement Freud's idea of the libidinal basis of the mass with a Lacanian attention to the roles of the signifier and the Other in anchoring such processes of affect and identification.

Psychoanalytic *identification* versus psychological *identity*

Before embarking on this discussion of identification, it is important to note how the notion of identity is typically broached in psychological theory. Doing so will help us appreciate the nature of the challenge confronting us in thinking through psychoanalytic notions of *identification*. The task at hand is to view identification less as set of psychological contents or as a normative psychological state than as *the process* whereby the subject is positioned, 'constituted' even, in relation to the play of the signifier.

In an informative overview, Frosh (2010) highlights a number of crucial themes associated with the notion of identity. Identity, approached as a 'primarily psychological phenomenon', typically refers to 'the feelings and actively chosen self-definitions of individuals' (p. 99). The idea of 'personal identity' focuses

> on how people construct their sense of themselves, the basis being an assumption of the normativeness and stability of individuality as a developmental achievement. A central task of life is to find an identity within which one can live, which organizes one's experiences and allows one to become a 'person'. Identity is *agentic* when thought of this way: it is centred on the human subject as an individual and enables that subject to integrate experience in. . . . a 'personal project' . . . [S]ubjects are seen as. . . . possessing the capacity for self-actualization and the potential to change their social position.
>
> (Frosh, 2010, p. 100)

As Frosh well appreciates, the psychoanalytic idea of identification can be distinguished from the above approach virtually on a point-by-point basis. Identification, approached psychoanalytically, is largely an unconscious as opposed to a 'self-willed' or agentic process; it is less a normative psychological achievement than the result of those contingent images and signifiers that have exerted a determining role on the subject; rather than a stabilizing or integrating 'personal project', identification (certainly in its imaginary forms) is, furthermore, an alienating process in which the subject takes an external form as the basis of their 'identity'.

As Vanheule and Verhaeghe (2009) reiterate, the concept of 'identity' as it is typically deployed in academic psychology, with its presumptions of an undivided and integrated personality, is hopelessly at odds with psychoanalytic conceptualizations. The starting point of psychoanalysis lies, in their estimation, precisely with the realization of the inner division – the constitutive split – that marks the subject. One of Vanheule and Verhaeghe's (2009) conclusions in their comparison of psychoanalytic and psychological conceptualizations is that 'identity must not be restricted to its content . . . but must be understood in terms of functioning' (p. 406). This is not to say that identification approached psychoanalytically has no content – 'identity', they insist, 'comes down to representations, understood by Freud as thing and word representations, by Lacan as imagos and signifiers' (pp. 406–407). That being said, the emphasis on psychoanalytic approaches to identification remains on the *functional* aspect, on the bindings of images by signifiers and on *operations* of identification rather than identification as a somehow finalized (and hence *imaginary*) product or 'substance'.

To this we can add two further qualifying considerations, remarking that identification is not merely an instance of copied behaviours, first, and that it entails a structural and anticipatory component, second. Lacan puts it this way:

> *identification* . . . is quite different from the process of *imitation*, which is distinguished by its partial . . . form of approximation; *identification* contrasts with imitation not simply as the *global* assimilation of a structure but as the *virtual assimilation of development* implied by that structure in a still undifferentiated state.
>
> (2006, p. 71)

The power of the pageant

We can animate many of our theoretical concerns here with a textual example, a description offered by a South African journalist of his euphoric – yet initially guarded – sense of being caught up in the patriotic celebrations of the 2010 Soccer World Cup.

> Sixteen years after experiencing the unforgettable rush of belonging and relief at Nelson Mandela's inauguration in 1994, I felt it again last month

> . . . watching the South African national team play their last World Cup game . . . although the victory was insufficient to qualify us into the next round, the consensus across the country following the game was that 'we won!' Why? . . . because we proved to a skeptical world – and thus ourselves – that we could host a World Cup . . . But 'we won' most of all, because we could finally say 'we' . . . something shifted during the World Cup . . . we found ourselves all on the same side . . . South Africans were waving flags, and supporting their team out of a sense of joy and belonging.
>
> (Gevisser, 2010)

Gevisser adds a further remark, describing how his own ebullient behaviour took him by surprise:

> At the beginning of the match, I had found myself – to my astonishment – singing the South African national anthem. In the spirit of the reconciliatory Mandela era, the anthem is an amalgam of the liberation hymn, *Nkosi Sikelel 'iAfrika* and the apartheid-era *Die Stem*. I have not been able to bring myself to sing the latter, but as I watched the Afrikaners around me trying to twist their mouths around *Nkosi Sikelel* and black South Africans in turn belting out *Die Stem* with unfettered delight, my stand seemed ridiculously churlish.
>
> (2010)

This account contains several key themes that feature in what follows: the experience of being swept up in a contagious mass emotion that potentially supersedes one's own feelings; the formation of transitory collective 'we' able to span existing social divisions; the narcissistic high of securing the approving gaze of the Other; and the key role of visual markers and insignia of mass identity which play their part in the performance of ritualized symbolic acts. How then are we to understand the phenomena of mass identification as epitomized in such exhibitions of national feeling?[4]

On libido

In thinking of World Cup enthusiasms and passions such as those described above, it is tempting to say that it is precisely a kind of love that we are observing. In the language of psychoanalysis we speak of love in terms of an attachment, as a libidinal tie. It is worthwhile directly citing Freud here, so as to ground from the outset what may otherwise seem an anomalous term:

> Libido is an expression from affectivity theory. It is how we refer to the energy . . . of those drives having to do with everything that can be brought together under the heading of love. The core of what we call love is . . . sexual love . . . However we do not separate off from that the other things that share the name of love: self-love . . . parental and infant love, friendship,

general love of humanity, and even dedication to concrete objects as well as abstract ideas.

(2004, p. 41)

Freud adds to this list a few pages later, noting, hypothetically, that 'we shall try adopting the premise that love relationships . . . also form part of the essence of the mass mind' (2004, p. 43). This modest formulation eventually gives away to a bolder proclamation: 'The essence of the mass . . . consists in the libidinal attachments present within it' (2004, p. 53). As Ernesto Laclau would reflect some 80 years after Freud published those words: 'Freud already knew it: the social link is a libidinal link' (2004, p. 326).

We should not neglect this opportunity to remark on the breadth of what might be included in the notion of 'libido'. This psychoanalytic concept refers to a huge variety of affective bonds and attachments. It is the 'glue' through which subjects, in their own varying ways, become affixed to an array of practices, objects and experiences. Leader and Corfield (2007) draw attention both to how widely the concept may be applied and to the particularity of each subject's distinctive libidinal preferences. The presence of libido, they note

> can be inferred in a wide range of individual and social activities: falling in love, sexual preferences, hobbies, drug addictions, sports enthusiasm, and all the drives and interests that make up our daily life. Libido may attach itself to almost any aspect of our existence. This allows us to channel and shape the experiences of excitation, unease, distress and passion that make up our early life. They become set into particular patterns that will be unique to each of us.
>
> (Leader and Corfield, 2007, p. 203) [5]

We can refer here to two colloquial phrases in order to link the Freudian concept of libido to everyday speech, and so as to invoke the associated Lacanian notion of *jouissance*. The query 'What are you *into?*' is essentially a question regards one's *libidinal investments*. The not-dissimilar 'What do you *get off on?*' is a question about libidinal enjoyment, about one's *jouissance*.

The love of the mass

Freud's mass psychology proves a useful starting point for many of the arguments I want to develop here. For a start, it involves a series of questions on the nature and form of identification, and, indeed, posits two crucial interlinked modalities of identification, both of which will be crucial in maintaining the 'libidinal economy of the mass'.[6] Rather than rehearse the details of Freud's broader arguments in his 1921 text, something which has been done by numerous scholars (Adorno, 1991; Ahmed, 2004; Billig, 1976; Laclau, 2004), I want to extract a few central points, and overlay them with a series of Lacanian perspectives.

As is well known, Freud (1921) begins his analysis of mass psychology with a lengthy discussion of Gustav Le Bon's study of crowd behaviour. There is much there which appeals to him, notably the postulate that crowd membership leads to a lowering of intellect, an inflated sense of invulnerability and to the contagious spread of irrational ideas. These features resemble the functioning of the unconscious. Le Bon's conceptualization is however found wanting by Freud inasmuch as it is lacking in psychological complexity. It fails to understand the bonding component of the mass, to grasp the positive motivation underlying such groupings, indeed, to appreciate exactly the facet of shared *identification*. This is Freud's cue. He wishes to contribute this missing psychological component, and to do so by pinpointing the bonding passion that centres a mass and proves able to over-ride the tensions and differences within its members by means of a shared affective commitment. It is the role of the leader, argues Freud (1921), that Le Bon's account lacks, and it is precisely this, the question of the relation to – or love of – the leader that Freud goes on to develop. This libidinal focus, which Freud will repeatedly associate with love of the father, will provide the much needed factor of a shared interest, of group cohesion, indeed, of mass identification.

'Who's your daddy?'

Without wasting further ink on a feature of Freud's account that has been much criticized, namely the ostensibly reductive and patriarchal emphasis on the paternal, we might simply add a basic Lacanian qualification. Within Lacanian theory 'father' typically designates the role of a symbolic operator, never reducible to actual (human) fathers, through which social law and cultural norms are conveyed into the life of the subject.

We can speak of the father not as a real or imaginary person, but as a symbolic function, an internalized compass of culturally and socially viable principles (Vanheule, 2011). As such we are concerned with a factor of *symbolic law* rather than with any series of acts or interventions that could be entirely circumscribed within the actions of an actual physical father. Furthermore, whatever figure seems – however temporarily – to embody this role need not be a literal father or even a man. Roudinesco emphasizes this: the '*symbolic* function of the father can be assumed as much by a woman as by a man, and in a homosexual couple, by one or the other partner' (Badiou and Roudinesco, 2014, p. 25). We are here approaching the concept of the Name-of-the-Father, with which Lacan hoped both to draw attention to the role of the father in the unconscious, and to stress the inscription of cultural law which installs prohibitions and locates the subject within the symbolic realm.

As is well known, Lacan's (1993) play on words in referring to the Name-of-the-Father (*le nom du père*) refers both to the 'no!' and the *name* of the father, both of which play their part in conferring symbolic identity.[7] The Name-of-the-Father instates an order of prohibitions (most fundamentally, the prohibition against incest) at the same time that it inscribes the subject in a generational order (the son/daughter of a given father and mother) and places them within a given socio-cultural milieu. Badiou nicely invokes the function of the concept when he notes that subjects are for Lacan structured by language and 'assimilated to an immemorial Law whose organizing signifier is the Name-of-the-Father' (in Badiou and Roudinesco, 2014, p. 26). Or, to draw on Lacan's own words: 'It is in the *name of the father* that we must recognize the basis of the symbolic function which, since the dawn of historical time, has identified his person with the figure of the law' (2006, p. 230).

This provides us with a way of interpreting the father-leader equation that appears so frequently within Freud's discussion. The leader here is a father in the foregoing (Lacanian) sense: they represent a focal point through which cultural norms, symbolic ideals and social proscriptions are condensed and relayed. This reference to social laws and ideals provides a clue regards how we will respond to two contentions levelled at Freud: surely not all groups have evident leaders, first; and the role of the leader – even if not of an obvious sort – is surely not a precondition of collective belonging, second? My argument, of course, is that by focusing on the *symbolic place* rather than the *figure of* the leader we can still utilize elements of Freud's account in respect of a variety of ostensibly 'leader-less' mass identifications. Freud concedes relatively early on in his mass psychology that there is '[t]he possibility of the leader being replaced by a guiding idea' (2004, pp. 46–47).

We should not be too quick in dismissing the role of actual leaders/father in phenomena of mass identification. Here it is worth remarking how frequently the name of Nelson Mandela – undoubtedly the father of the post-apartheid nation – was evoked in relation to South Africa's hosting of the FIFA event. We could put it this way: when a set of social and symbolic ideals are powerfully animated, then a leader is never far away. Much by the same token: when a social contract is put in place, when a foundational gesture confers (social, historical, subjective) identity, then a symbolic father is likewise never distant. We have a nice instance here of a Lacanian amendment to Freudian theory: it is not simply the case that charismatic leaders embody social and symbolic ideals; a surge of such ideals also engenders leaders and – by extension – symbolic fathers. This perhaps sheds some light on a colloquial quip. *Apropos* any symbolic identification (or any collective or mass bond) we can ask: '*Who's your daddy?*'

From love to identification

It is worth pausing over a further conceptual clarification here, so as to consider whether the love in question is not a more nuanced category than we may have at first assumed. That is to say, we need to think of this love as a *libidinal tie* which exhibits a variety of vicissitudes. Not the least of these concerns the oscillations of ambivalence (loving and hating) and the movement between the positions of wanting *to have* and wanting *to be like*. In this respect it is worth recalling Freud's distinction between three types of identification in his *Massenpsychologie*, particularly his characterization of a first mode, 'identification [as] the most natural form of an emotional attachment to an object' (2004, p. 59).[8]

A further qualification regards the love of the leader should be added here. The love in question may be a love we don't know we have, a disavowed or displaced love. Such a love might be managed precisely via attributions made of *the affective ties of others*, vicariously enjoyed by myself yet not admitted to. This would be love at a distance, love enabled via the loving relations of others, which serve to channel my own love in an ostensibly external manner. This poses an interesting line of enquiry in respect of the phenomenon of being swept up in the contagion of group affect. The enthusiasm and excitement of others is enough to activate my own, which may seem – like Gevisser's (2010) singing of the South African national anthem – to spring into life despite one's own contrary views. That is to say: we may love where we don't realize we love, just as we may identify with figures we purport to hate.

This love is, in a significant sense, premised on an impossibility. The difference signalled above between wanting *to have* and wanting *to be like* comes into play here. The leader, or, the symbolic place the leader comes to occupy, does not typically represent a realistically viable love object; they cannot be possessed as a love partner. Given that such a libidinal tie cannot be realized as a romantic relationship, it must take a different form. This mode of love – which will also become the basis of a formative symbolic identification – is not just a failed romantic love. It is love taken to a higher level, a love of – and a belonging to – a series of abstract ideals.

When this love cannot be realized as a romantic relation, it undergoes a transformation. Identification – a psychical operation distinct from the relation of 'being in love with' – takes its place.[9] A crucial distinguishing factor here is loss. The impossibility of possessing the leader means that this figure has to be given up. This leads to a compromise: aspects of the lost loved object can be retained, reinstated in the ego, with 'the ego undergoing a partial change, modelling itself on this lost object' (Freud, 2004, p. 67).

This pattern of identification premised on a mode of loss or failure is what Freud calls regressive identification. The wish to *have* (an erotic object-choice) has been transformed, via introjection, to *being like*. This process enables the internalization of an ego-ideal. This, in turn, provides the basis for what Freud refers to as 'the libidinal constitution of the mass'. In his words: '[a] primary mass is the number of individuals who have put one and the same object in the place of their ego-ideal and who have consequently identified themselves with one another in terms of their egos' (Freud, 2004, p. 69).

Divisions of loss

It is easy enough, following the above discussion, to remain focused on the role of shared *conscious* ideals. However, the factor of loss ensures that the bond in question is more complex than it first appears. We could say that symbolic identification always entails a death, the painful giving up of a loved or hoped for object. It is then not the mere mutuality of shared positive values that bonds a group; a profound sense of likeness is also fostered by the fact of (an often traumatic) loss, by the consideration of what members in a given community have each had to forego. This is one of the lessons of Freud's (1912) *Totem and Taboo* concerning the killing of the primal father, namely, that a traumatic event precedes the formation of the social bond and the ideals associated with it.

This has a direct bearing on the empirical example we are considering in this chapter. The celebratory mood of South Africa's World Cup, that is to say, needs to be situated as a definitely post-apartheid phenomenon, as following after the historical trauma of apartheid. We should thus pause to interrogate presumptions of unity; despite the euphoric sentiments of 'inter-racial' unity described above, we must be wary of assuming that shared symbolic ideals and shared bonds of loss do actually bond South Africans. This speculation prompts a further consideration. Pride, it seems, is the affect realized in the attainment of given ego-ideals; it is the emotion we experience as we approach the ego-ideals we have come to cherish in relation to a loss. If this is so, then pride is always more than a simply positive emotion – it is an affect that occurs on the horizon of an earlier loss, in response, most typically, to something that we were unable to possess.[10] This is not to deny that a wave of exuberant national feeling did occur. It is however, in a properly psychoanalytic way, to question what underlies an apparent preponderance of affect, to ask what *loss* underlies the celebration of given ego-ideals. It is also to question whether what really bonds diverse (and historically divided) groups is not ideals as such but *what these ideals mask*, what they enable subjects to forget, to *repress*.

What comes into view then is the possibility of an alliance of repressed losses which, paradoxically, comes to the fore precisely in shared moments of jubilant national togetherness. This follows on from the Lacanian imperative not to accept affects at face value. More simply put: in exulting in such national sporting pageants, 'we' do not all exult at the same thing, even though in exulting we do share a certain commonality – that of the very fact of repressing (potentially very different) senses of loss. This line of discussion perhaps helps circumvent the assumption that Freud's model entails the commonality of *conscious contents*. As is by now evident, it is not so much a focus on (shared, conscious) contents that serves us in Lacanian theory as an attention to *signifiers*. And the apparent meaning of signifiers remains circumstantial inasmuch as their meaning is refracted through the Other and open to the specificity of individual libidinal investment. More simply put: what is in question in our example is not 'South Africa' taken as an objective entity that can be wholly enumerated, but the *signifier* 'South Africa' whose meaning is always subject to what we think Others mean by it.

'Hysterical' identification

Having discussed two types of identification discussed by Freud (ties of affection-ate attachment and regressive identification), it seems appropriate to briefly introduce a third mode. I have in mind here a type of identification which 'wholly disregards the object-relationship to the person copied' (Freud, p. 59). This type of identification – hysterical identification, or identification via the symptom – is important to note precisely because it runs counter to our commonplace notions of identification as affectionate link, as the loving assimilation of qualities of the other. Freud (1994) provides the example of a girl at a boarding school whose jealousy is provoked upon receiving a letter from her secret lover. Her subsequent hysterical fit might easily then spread to other girls – not because they have any affectionate attachments to the first girl, but rather because they want to be *in her position* (of having a secret lover). This is not about sympathy or 'fellow feeling', stresses Freud – quite the contrary, no love is lost between the parties concerned – it is identification with *the place that the other occupies*. One ego here has perceived 'a significant analogy in one point' (p. 59) with another. Clearly then, this is a very different situation from a more encompassing identification with the image of the other in which a variety of the other's traits are assumed. Identification here 'is partial and highly restricted, borrowing only a single feature' (p. 59) from the other. This idea of a single (or 'unary') trait is one we will return to in the following chapter.

Freud (2004) adds to the complexity of our understanding of identification by adding a further example, that of a daughter who takes on her resented mother's painful cough. One can conceive thus of an identification precisely *with a hated object*, that is an identification – no doubt effected under Oedipal conditions of resentment and rivalry – which gives voice to a hostile desire to replace the mother. The triangular structure of this identification is notable: this is (a partial) identification with someone *in order to be desired by a third*. Likewise significant is the wholly contingent nature of the symptomatic feature that has been mimed. The feature in question is very much of a means-to-an-end sort, it has no intrinsic meaning; it is a vehicle through which an identification with the place of the other may be effected.[11]

One should not neglect an additional facet of this account: the girl's identifications 'will on one occasion copy the unloved person, on another the loved person' (p. 59). So, contrary to the assumption that identification functions as an all-or-nothing process that maintains a fidelity to an object of over-riding importance (a 'whole object' identification), Freud's account could once again be said to prioritize identification with *signifiers* rather than clear-cut objects or contents. There is a proto-Lacanian dimension to this argument. Hysterical identifications, identifications by way of a symptomatic element, are identifications of just such a partial and indeed *symbolic* sort. They differ as such from more encompassing imaginary types of identification which take the (whole) image of another as their basis.

The (symbolic) place of love

There is a further amendment to Freud's 'love of the leader' thesis that follows on from the above emphasis on structural positions and signifiers. In grasping the libidinal 'aura' of the leader we should avoid falling prey to a type of psychological reasoning. From a Lacanian perspective it is not the individual person of the *leader themselves* that we should focus on – their charismatic charms, their personal features, etc. – but the position, *the symbolic place* a leader comes to occupy as a signifier.[12] Within Lacanian theory such personal attributes only really start *to function* – as hallmarks of integrity, intelligence, leadership, etc. – once viewed from a very particular and historically located set of symbolic co-ordinates. Such perceived qualities are always-*already* mediated by the Other. A given set of features is never in and of itself lovable, desirable; any such set of features presupposes a gaze, a symbolic standpoint which sets the parameters of what counts as attractive, successful, praiseworthy, etc.

The example of the political leader adds a further dimension to our discussion of signifiers and identification. As any pundit knows, the success of political campaigns depends very much on what we might call 'signifier management'. The candidate's full 'personality' – who they 'really' are – cannot be conveyed in any real depth to the electorate. We are not able to enter into some kind of direct apprehension of the personal qualities of such figures (even though we tend to believe we can – a type of imaginary illusion). What is occurring here is that a potential series of signifiers come to be associated with the politician, signifiers (flighty, tempestuous, haughty, etc.) which are then arranged by a master signifier of sorts (arrogant, out of touch). Political campaigns are won and lost on such a basis: the single acts which allow a given candidate to be encapsulated as 'immature', 'unpresidential', 'crooked', etc. In such cases – to paraphrase Lacan's definition of the signifier – the signifier represents a subject not directly to another subject but *to another signifier.*

The symbolic place of the leader corresponds to what Freud calls the 'ego-ideal', that is, the collection of the cherished and respected societal ideals which mean more than the ego itself.[13] This is the 'to live and die for' element underlying the affective substance of the mass. It is by virtue of ego-ideals that subjects can move beyond their own egoistic concerns. Importantly, while social ideals are in some sense conscious, that is, open to the prospect of verbal articulation, it is nevertheless true that once installed in the form of ego-ideals they also maintain a powerfully unconscious aspect.

It is useful to turn directly to Freud's own description of the ego-ideal which clearly resonates with aspects of Lacan's notion of the Name-of-the-Father as outlined above:

> the ego-ideal answers to everything that is expected of the higher nature of man. As a substitute for a longing for the father . . . the ego-ideal contains the germ from which all religions have evolved. As a child grows up, the role of the father is carried on by teachers and others in authority; their injunctions and prohibitions remain powerful in the ego-ideal and continue, in the form of conscience, to exercise the moral censorship.
>
> (1923, V. 19, p. 37)

Ego-ideal, ideal-ego, super-ego

Freud's above description brings with it a prospective problem, namely that of adequately differentiating the notion of the ego-ideal from the subsequent conceptualization of the super-ego in *The Ego and the Id* (1923). The ego-ideal, says Sharpe and Boucher (2010), responding to this issue, is the result of the desexualization and idealization of the parental images, and it is developed

> through identification with the noble social ideals promoted by the parents, and repression of the Oedipal desires the individual experienced during infancy. The super-ego is where the sexuality went, when the ego-ideal was . . . idealized.
>
> (p. 153)

This is not the place to elaborate in any detail upon the Lacanian notion of the super-ego as obscene and ferocious, possessed of a 'senseless, blind character, of pure imperativeness and tyranny' (Lacan, 1988a, p. 102). That being said, Lacan does contrast the two agencies – 'The super-ego is constraining and the ego-ideal exalting' (p. 102), noting also how the super-ego entails a certain *jouissance* imperative, which is to say that it pushes the subject to libidinal enjoyments, to gratifications of excess. Such libidinal excesses do not necessarily occur beyond the parameters of symbolic law, but typically take the form of 'subterranean' reinforcements of codified rules and proscriptions (the thrills and excess-enjoyments, for example, of imposing laws on others, of dispensing judgement or enacting punishments). One appreciates thus Lacan's characterization of the super-ego as possessed of 'a senseless, destructive, purely oppressive, almost always anti-legal morality' (p. 102). Suffice then to say that the super-ego is neither desexualized nor 'moral' in any uncomplicated sense.[14]

i(o) and I(O): Imaginary and symbolic identification

Freud's theory of mass identification entails two different lines of attachment. Group members are 'bound in two directions by an intense emotional tie' (2004, p. 74), that is, by attachments to the leader and to fellow group members who can be identified with – and indeed, loved – by virtue of such a set of shared ideals. Intragroup tensions, although never completely eliminated, are thus significantly minimized: 'through bestowing equal love upon the same object . . . [potential rivals] come to identify with one another' (Freud, 2004, p. 74).[15] It is thus through the figure of the leader, or extrapolating somewhat, through an associated set of ego-ideal values, that we transcend the anarchic state of every subject against every other subject and experience an elementary sense of community. In this way it becomes apparent that brotherly or communal love is only possible via the mediation of symbolic ideals. The Lacanian priority on the symbolic over the psychological is again here evident. A whole series of psychological attributes

– phenomena of imitation, sympathy and suggestibility – are aroused by such symbolic values being stressed and reiterated.

The two types of libidinal bond described by Freud (2004) are effectively illustrated in his example of the 'artificial mass' of the military. The soldier, to paraphrase Freud, thus takes the superior figure of the general as their *ideal*, whereas they *identify with* their peers and thereby derive the obligations and benefits of comradeship. Adopting the habits of one's peers – the particular jargon, mode of dress and behaviour, etc. – makes an individual increasingly part of the group, one of the 'band of brothers' who live and undergo shared hardships together. However, notes Freud, if a soldier were to imitate the general, to adopt the general's behavioural traits, then he, the soldier, would look a fool. In other words, this anchoring type of symbolic identification does not operate on the basis of imaginary likeness.

If we were to try and plot the vectors of Freud's mass identification we could think of symbolic (ego-ideal) identifications as of a vertical sort (see Figure 4.1). Such identifications would necessarily entail a hierarchical dimension; they constitute a relationship with values and ideals of a higher level than that of the ego itself. Symbolic identifications, to reiterate, involve identifications not with another subject but with values (signifiers) experienced as (at least minimally) external to the subject. Ego-ideals are the means through which these values are 'folded into' the psychical make-up of the subject:

> the Ego-Ideal holds the place of the Symbolic Order in the psychic economy of the subject. It allocates the subject a position in society, a symbolic mandate with social authority that is defined as deriving from a socio-cultural totality: I(O).
>
> (Sharpe and Boucher, 2010, p. 49)

That is to say, ego-ideals entail an attachment to the entirety of the socio-cultural network as embodied in the big Other.

By contrast, ideal-ego identifications would be of a horizontal sort (Figure 4.1), between 'like others', who represent my own possible mirror image (alter egos, we might say). The distinction between these two modes of identification can be further developed along Lacanian lines. On the one hand we have an *imaginary* type of identification (*i(o)* in Lacanian algebra) which unfolds along the lines of likeable images that have a self-valorizing, affirming quality. These are the grandiose or idealized, indeed, narcissistically gratifying, images of ourselves – or our group – that we hold dear; our preferred self-images.

This imaginary dimension prioritizes visual markers, the dimension of the image and the factor of resemblance.[16] It comprises the field of mirror-images through which the inter-subjective dialectic of *seeing others as one's self* and *one's self as others* plays out. This theoretical point is nicely illustrated by the World Cup behaviours mentioned above: fans dressing in the jerseys or colours of the national team, flying flags, painting their faces, etc. From a Lacanian perspective, this is not merely

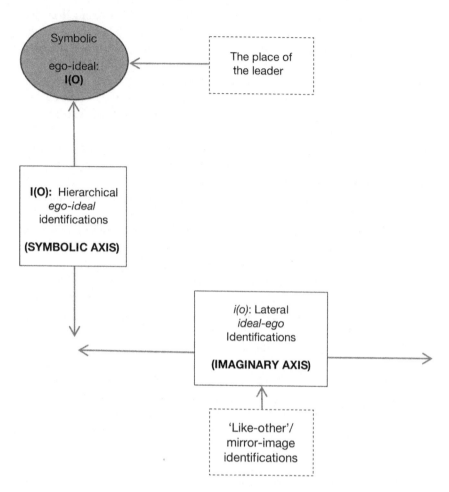

FIGURE 4.1 Ego-ideal [I(O)] and ideal-ego [*i(o)*] lines of identification

decorative or cosmetic behaviour, it is quite literally a case of 'identity within the visual field', an instance of how such visual insignia provide a basis for the ongoing process of imaginary identification. A related point: if one is to fully assume a symbolic identification with one's team, it is not enough to dress in the colours of the players, or to adopt the characteristic gesture and behaviours of the team's supporters. A symbolic identification cannot be limited to such imaginary facets alone – important as they in capturing and intensifying libidinal investments – it will necessarily involve a structural dimension. It will, in short, require the taking on of signifiers from the field of the Other, not merely the adoption of mirrored images. A symbolic identification means being rooted in a field of signifiers; it is always more than a performance of resemblance.[17] We can draw on an important moment in Lacan's Seminar XI (the session of 24 June 1964) to reiterate this distinction:

the identification in question is not specular, immediate identification. It is its support. It supports the perspective chosen by the subject in the field of the Other, from which specular identification may be seen . . . The point of the ego-ideal is that from which the subject will see himself . . . *as others see him* . . . [A] specular image . . . is situated in the field . . . centered on the ideal point . . . placed in the Other, from which the Other sees me.

(1979, p. 268)

History versus likeness; speech of the Other versus *Gestalt*

We may contrast the domain of imaginary identification with the 'structural' or historical dimension of *symbolic* identifications (I(O) in Lacanian algebra). This is the regime of identification which corresponds to one's symbolic co-ordinates, to the historical location, societal ideals and ideological values that importantly *delimit and condition* the imaginary field of imaginary identifications. A schematic difference comes to the fore here: whereas the imaginary register emphasizes the dimension of resemblance and likeness, the symbolic dimension prioritizes *history*, along with a set of associated socio-symbolic roles, inter-subjective positions and mandates. The factors of lineage, inheritance, historical continuity, of symbolic debts and unfilled promises all come to be prioritized in a symbolic register of analysis.

We may extend the above comparison via a consideration of how the imaginary/ symbolic registers of identification are operative in individual names. A nickname ('Speedy') clearly has an imaginary quality; it encapsulates an image of the person in question, typically exaggerating a physical characteristic or aspect of their personality. The function of a surname ('Gonzales') is less effective in capturing an image, an imaginary identification, and is more strongly related to the dimension of history, linking the subject to a family name; it provides as such a point of symbolic identification.

Rose adds to this distinction between (imaginary) ideal-ego and the (symbolic) ego-ideal identifications by identifying the psychical processes underlying each:

The ideal ego would . . . be a *projected image* with which the subject [identifies] . . . [T]he ego-ideal would be a[n]. . . . *introjection* whereby the image returns to the subject invested with . . . new properties [developed via] the 'admonition of others'. . . . The distinction here is that between projection as related to *Gestalt*, and introjection as invariably accompanied by the speech of the Other, that is, to introjection as a symbolic moment.

(1986, p. 177, *added emphasis*)[18]

The projected *image* (or *Gestalt*) and the symbolic instantiation of *speech* (of the Other) each thus lend themselves to respective processes of imaginary and symbolic identification. This distinction can be further developed in terms of the temporal relation implied by each. Drawing on Freud, Rose (1986) suggests that the ideal-ego corresponds to that loved image for the subject of what '*he himself was*', while the ego-ideal corresponds to what '*he himself would like to be*'. The backwards-looking trajectory of the ideal-ego corresponds to the fixity of imaginary. The future-bound orientation of the ego-ideal brings with it not only the aspirational quality of such ideals, but also – as we will go on to see – the factor of symbolic destiny.[19]

Imaginary built on symbolic

Although imaginary identification typically feels primary, it must in fact be considered *secondary* relative to the particular socio-historical co-ordinates of symbolic identification. This Lacanian stress on symbolic identifications over and above imaginary identification seems at first counter-intuitive. After all, it is imaginary ego identifications, that is, the stuff of mirror-image, 'like-other' reflections – what we may think of as the psychological facet of identification – which we experience as more immediately relevant. The prioritization of symbolic identification is, however, axiomatic for Lacanian theory. We may thus describe the ideal-ego as *constituted*, that is, as assembled or fabricated with available imaginary materials, whereas the ego-ideal, by contrast is properly *constitutive*, which is to say that it is foundational; it provides the underlying structural basis which anchors and holds in place imaginary identifications.[20] It is for this reason that Lacan (2016) speaks of the ego-ideal as 'the place of the determinant' in Seminar VIII.

If the above account sounds overly theoretical, consider the example of the British TV show, *How to Look Good Naked*. Participants in the make-over show are people who are clearly not happy with their own body image. Through the course of the show and the attentions of the show's flamboyant host, participants undergo a series of wardrobe, dietary and lifestyle changes that enable them 'to look good naked'. The climax of the show involves the unveiling of an image of the show's guest in some or other highly public place – in a storefront window on a busy street, on a billboard poster, etc. It is only in this final moment (which, not incidentally, is televised to a mass audience) that it can be confirmed that they do in fact 'look good naked'. The point of this example is, I hope, clear: contentedness with one's own naked body image – an ostensibly private, personal (and *imaginary*) relationship – is never merely subjective. It is always conditioned by the attending gaze of the Other, filtered, as such, through the lens of a broader set of *symbolic* values, upon which it is ultimately shown to be contingent. The ideal-ego, in other words, is always reliant upon the mediating factor of the ego-ideal, itself located in the field of the Other. Hence Lacan's description of symbolic identification in Seminar XI as

> not specular, immediate identification . . . [but] its support. It supports the perspective chosen by the subject in the field of the Other, from which specular identification may be seen . . . The point of the ego-ideal is that from which the subject will see himself . . . as others see him.
>
> (1979, p. 268)

So, by the time an imaginary identification is in place, a more substantive symbolic identification is already in operation as its founding condition. This is a logical necessity: unless there was some delimitation and prioritization of what particular imaginary features are most lovable, how would I even know what images, and as importantly, *what facets of those images*, to love? What delimits the particular features that I find lovable in my own (ideal-ego) image – 'I'm a pretty girl', 'I'm a big strong boy' – is reliant upon a particular set of values, in this case that of patriarchal norms of femininity/masculinity. In the absence of any symbolic co-ordinates, no imaginary identity is possible. Similarly, if a given set of symbolic co-ordinates were to be summarily erased, then the contingent imaginary identification would disappear. So, in the various scenarios – in fiction, in clinical case material – in which a subject has no reflection, no clear mirror image, we need to assume that the symbolic co-ordinates of their world have fallen apart.[21] Two questions can then be posed of any identification: what is the lovable image it attempts to embody; and in terms of what symbolic values, or, for whose gaze – for what Other – is this image being enacted?

The case of shame proves interesting here. The South African political commentator Eusebius McKaiser (2012) recently provided a poignant account of his shame at his 'coloured' (mixed-race) identity which, in his view, is inevitably associated with the social problems of poverty and drug-abuse. Initially, such an affective relation seems difficult to understand within the Freudian theorization of the libidinal ties that bond a mass. While the lateral, intra-communal ties bonding group members yield a variety of affects – most notably the ambivalences of aggression and narcissistic love – shame doesn't easily manifest at this level. However, when one imagines oneself as viewed from the position of symbolic ideals existing outside the internal identifications within the community itself, shame certainly becomes operative. It should be clear then, in returning to the South African World Cup example, that the narcissistic enjoyment of hosting the event – which itself exemplifies the imaginary jubilation of an ideal mirror image being reflected back at one – was ultimately contingent on a gaze located beyond the immediate level of the South African community itself.[22]

Identification in the field of the Other

Two themes are crucial in how Lacan revisits and develops the Freudian notion of the ego-ideal. The first is the role of desire. The second is the relation between the ego-ideal and the Other. Fantasy similarly becomes a crucial element here, unavoidably so given that the question of the Other's desire is – as noted in Chapter 1 – elusive, enigmatic, impossible to pin down. We might illustrate the centrality of desire in the role of identification by sketching the dilemma faced by the young subject – an adolescent, say – in making sense of the competing symbolic values that make up their immediate social environment.

There are, for such a youngster, a great many signals from their social and peer networks indicating what they could or should aspire to. This cluster of signifiers is, typically, vague, less than clear-cut. Even when clearly articulated imperatives are present, they tend to be complicated by contrary directives. The Other that encapsulates the values of their social world is not just lacking but also *inconsistent*. Complicating this still further is the fact that the field of social injunctions is comprised of signifiers which are themselves open to speculation.

This anxiety-provoking situation of needing to respond to the questions '*What am I for the Other?*', '*What does the Other want of me?*', is managed via the creation of a hypothesis that provides tentative answers to these vexing questions. This, I should stress, is not a predominant cognitive or conscious operation (concerning concrete 'answers' and 'hypotheses'); it is rather an 'existential' dilemma, an unconscious operation of fantasy. The repeated need for the subject to provide an answer *about themselves* that responds to the desire of the Other is what sets fantasy in motion. This ongoing unconscious interchange of conjectured desires and wishes for recognition is, for the vast majority of us, never-ending. This unconscious conjecturing is never definitively resolved: the subject's guesses as to what makes them valuable in the eyes of the Other are contingent on shifting constellations of symbolic values. Some signifiers, we might say, 'count more than others'. There are signifiers that enjoy a privileged relation to the Other (that regularly emerge in the discourse of persons that are influential for the subject), or that represent nodal points in fantasy (that are disproportionately invested with *jouissance*).

We can appreciate then that at this (ego-ideal) level, the process of identification goes beyond 'the creation of a self-image in relation to other perceived images' as Vanheule and Verhaege (2009) insist, 'it exceeds the process of bringing the ego to perfection by . . . turning it into [mirrored] ideal egos' (p. 397). We leave the realm of imaginary (or we might say, psychological) ego-to-ego identifications behind here:

> Directly in line with his development of a theory on the role of the signifier in mental functioning, Lacan claims that the process of identification is symbolically mediated . . . The symbolic elements that fulfill this function are the ego-ideals.
>
> (Vanheule and Verhaeghe, 2009, p. 397)

This is an excellent clarification of the role of signifiers in the making of ego-ideals. Furthermore:

> In Lacan's interpretation, ego-ideals are symbolic elements that subject takes from the discourse of the [O]ther. This means that they are nothing but privileged discursive elements: specific traits and characteristics of others that arrest a subject's attention, and are unconsciously adopted to the extent that they are considered to imply an answer to the riddle of the [O]ther's desire.
>
> (p. 397)

So, extending the example supplied by Vanheule and Verhaeghe: a small boy may take up a characteristic – an isolated gesture or habit perhaps – from his father or his grandfather, but will do so 'to the extent that these characteristics don't leave his beloved mother unaffected' (p. 397). That is to say – a point typically overlooked in thinking of identification as occurring between two people – the identified characteristic in question has an effect also *on a third party's desire*. Identification then involves not simply the 'taking on' of somehow likeable signifiers from various important or influential others. It involves the assumption of signifiers from a second party (a 'little other') that puts the identifying subject into the position of *being desired by a third* (the Other). A minimal form of triangulation is thus necessarily involved in any situation of symbolic identification.

The pattern here as it exceeds the merely (inter)subjective calls to mind the trans-subjective structure discussed in Chapter 3 and anticipated in Chapter 1's gloss on the notion of 'the desire of the Other'. This helps in emphasizing a further aspect of symbolic identification: the signifier that the identifying subject takes on also sets in play a relation to desire *in the identifying subject themselves*. This identification operates as a support of the subject's desire; it is a type of compass for what *the subject* wants, for what *they* might become in the future. *Apropos* a symbolic identification then, we can ask: what new horizons of desire does it open up for the subject?

Žižek provides a wonderfully apt example of the triangular structure underlying symbolic identification (and fantasy). In his discussion of Freud's daughter's fantasy about eating a strawberry cake, Žižek stipulates that what is in question is not merely the simple case 'of the direct hallucinatory satisfaction of a desire (she wanted a cake, she didn't get it, so she fantasized about it)' (1997, p. 10). The crucial feature in the formation of the fantasy involved the fact that

> while she was voraciously eating a strawberry cake, the little girl noticed how her parents were deeply satisfied by this spectacle, by seeing her fully enjoy it – so what the fantasy of eating a strawberry cake is really about is her attempt to form an identity (of the one who fully enjoys eating a cake given by the parents) that would satisfy her parents, would make her the object of their desire.
>
> (Žižek, 1997, p. 10)

We might say then, bearing in mind the permutations of Lacan's notion that 'desire is the desire of the Other', that there are three intersecting levels of desire that are operative in symbolic identification. There is, first, desire as it occurs in the initial identification with a signifier (the signifier is taken from a place of love and/or authority, or from a structural position the subject would like to assume). This signifier, second, makes the subject desirable both to others and from the perspective of a third party (the Other). Third, in taking on such a signifier, the parameters of the subject's own desire are refined (in terms, for example of fantasmatic hopes of what they might become).[23]

The inheritance of desire

What then is the practical or clinical importance of all this attention to symbolic identifications? Why this repeated emphasis on those ego-ideal identifications that both structure the subject's life and yet remain largely beyond the remit of consciousness? Has this been merely an academic exercise, differentiating imaginary and symbolic identifications? The most direct answer to this question is already implicit in the differentiation offered above: it is typically those *unconscious* structural (which is to say *symbolic*) identifications which exercise the most determining influence on the subject.

We have seen how ego-ideals relate to desire, and how symbolic identifications can be understood as a response to the Other's desire. This means – to put things in more concrete terms – that crucial aspects of one's life might be devoted to pursuing *an Other's desire* as opposed to what we might consider to be our own 'individual' desires. Allow me a personal example. Some 10 years after moving from Johannesburg to London I had a conversation on the phone with my father, who despite having lived most of his life in Southern Africa – where I was born – was a native Londoner. Towards the end of our conversation, he casually asked how I was finding my work, and my university teaching in particular. I told him that I was enjoying it much as I always did. There was a pause, and he said, much to my surprise: 'I always wanted to teach.'

This was a wish that I had not – at least not consciously – realized that he harboured. It was only some time later, reflecting on the conversation that it occurred to me that I was, in effect, living out crucial aspects of my father's desire. I found myself in England, a place he spoke of with great nostalgia, in a job that, apparently, he had always wanted. This is not to suggest that I didn't really desire these things – my career, my choice of city – I did, I was proud of them (they were as such components of my ideal-ego, conditioned by broader ego-ideals), and yet they were not exclusively my own. They did not begin with me.

The point is not to dispute that these were 'my' desires, but simply to observe that such desires cannot be thought of as purely subjective, cut off the inter- and trans-subjective symbolic nexus which sustains the production of desiring as such.[24] Leader and Groves (1995) provide a similar example, of the philosopher Bertrand Russell, who, upon reading through his father's diaries is stupefied to realize that the details of his parents' courtship were virtually identical to his own. In response to the foreseeable contention, 'How can such identifications have taken place when there was no conscious knowledge of the desire that was identified with?' one can reply that the more the subject didn't (consciously) know, the better. That is to say, there was presumably some unconscious knowledge at work, even if the 'knowledge' in question took the form of a *hypothesis regards the desire of the Other*. As such no direct or conscious transmission of knowledge would be required. The Other's desires are, in such cases, correctly intuited *at the level of fantasy*. We have a case in point then in which the unconscious knowledge of the subject far outstrips that which they consciously know. Psychoanalytically then, we must not under-estimate the role of the unconscious as a type of thinking, a means of responding to what is enigmatic or difficult to process. As far back in the history of psycho-analysis as *The Interpretation of Dreams*, Freud had already maintained that 'dreams are nothing other than a particular form of thinking made possible by the conditions of the state of sleep' (1900, p. 650).

An inversion comes into play in psychoanalytic clinical practice – and this is of course a crucial element of psychoanalytic epistemology – whereby fantasmatic postulates are elevated above objective empirical facts. This is not without its humorous side: I recall a clinical supervision session where I complained to my supervisor that asking a patient *ad nauseum* about the historical details of their grand-parents and great-grand-parents was surely pointless given that they had never known these people and had access to very little – if any – information about them. 'All the better!' was the response of my supervisor.

Such a transmission of desires represents a crucial area of psychoanalytic explora-tion. Many of us are presumably living our lives, our desires, in the wake of some or Other foregoing desire which we take to be our own (if we have even registered it as such). If this seems unlikely, it helps perhaps to stress the fundamental import-ance of desiring relations within ego-ideals, noting in turn the indispensable role of ego-ideals in situating the subject in a given social-cultural milieu. Rather than it being an extraordinary circumstance that a subject has taken on the unconscious agenda of furthering some Other's desire, we could ask: how could it be otherwise, given that the co-ordinates of desire are, certainly within Lacanian theory, always trans-subjective, necessarily shaped and informed by the desires of Others? Hence the importance in clinical practice of exploring in extensive detail the questions of symbolic inheritance, indeed, of structural ego-ideal identifications in the lives of patients, such that the subject might thus have the opportunity of disengaging themselves from the unconscious project of completing an Other's desire.

This discussion connects back to Lacan's qualification of identification as entailing the facet of *undifferentiated structure*. Identification in the examples discussed above is not simply about exhibiting an affinity to someone one, or reflecting overt or conscious relations of similarity (although this aspect may of course be present). Identification, certainly in its symbolic forms, is to inherit something more structural in nature, namely, something of a *desiring position* as such.[25]

Delegated beliefs/affects

Before proceeding, we should pause to ask a question about the foregoing discussion of ego-ideals. Surely, in thinking about ego-ideals, we are dealing with something more substantial and significant than the 'artificial' instances of sporting spectacle and national feeling that I cited at the beginning of this chapter? Such feelings and their related activities are, after all, relatively transient; they seem insubstantial, 'shallow', relative to the depths of affective belonging outlined in Freud's model. It pays here to stress a Lacanian approach that grasps the unconscious not in 'depth' but rather in *surface* phenomena. This, after all, is a model concerned with an external (trans-subjective, symbolic) rather than an internal ('intra-psychic') unconscious.

A Lacanian perspective consequently points to the importance of the socio-symbolic frame and underlines the factor of *artificiality* as a platform, a basis, for certain types of affect.

I am thus making the claim, perhaps unusual for psychoanalysis, that some of our most powerful emotions require not only a degree of exteriority to be effectively realized – reference to others, the field of the trans-subjective (the Other) – but also recourse to the anonymous 'fictional' framework of available symbolic forms. There are at least two component strands to this line of argument. The first stresses the role *of others* as intermediaries in the effective expression of a given affect. The second entails the notion that without symbolic activity, that is, the mediation of popular cultural forms and fictions, certain affects would not be effectively realized as such.

Apropos certain 'detached' forms of ideological belief, Slavoj Žižek (1989) observes:

> the most intimate beliefs, even the most intimate emotions such as compassion, crying, sorrow, laughter, can be transferred, delegated to others without losing their sincerity.
>
> (p. 34)

For Žižek, the idea of a degree of detachment is important, for both ideological belief and powerful affect. He draws here on Lacan (1992) who provides a series of historical examples of affective exteriorization, in which our most intimate feelings are transferred to others. Professional mourners ('weepers') paid to attend and express despair at funerals of those they didn't know makes for one historical example, as does the chorus in Greek tragedy who effectively feel for, *emote* on behalf of, an audience who is thus permitted a degree of detachment from the dramatic proceedings. It would be a misunderstanding of Žižek's Lacanian assertion to conclude that the subject who delegates their feelings or belief in this way is not effectively *experiencing* such affects. They most certainly are feeling/believing, all the more effectively so, one might argue, but *via the medium of the other*.

Žižek's argument – which neatly demonstrates how the unconscious may operate in external, social forms – is that, via the medium of others, we may *believe* without consciously knowing we do so.[26] We have thus a case of believing – or feeling – *by extension*, in the guise of the other. By the same token – and here the phenomena of cynical detachment is for Žižek the most striking contemporary example – we may believe, in, say, nationalism, even racism, without any (apparent) participation in the belief in question via the mediation of others who *do* actively participate in such beliefs. As Dolar (2008) puts it:

> One can believe by proxy – it is enough that one extends one's belief only to someone who is supposed 'really' to believe ... My own unconscious belief is preserved by being delegated; it is repressed by the means of a proxy.
>
> (pp. xxiii–xxiv)

Similarly: we may effectively 'feel' something in this re-routed manner without fully realizing the affective state that conditions our current experience – a case of what Johnston (in Johnston and Malabou, 2013) calls 'misfelt feelings'. We may, for instance, be in love with someone, without having yet realized it, having experienced only – a cliché of romantic fiction – a disproportionate sense of friction or dislike towards the person in question.[27] This idea of a type of latent love, of loving without knowing it, seems, incidentally, a useful way of approaching forms of nationalist affect (the 'love of the nation') that often exist in seemingly 'de-activated' or tacit forms.

Such cases of what we might call 'affective (non)commitment' typically involve a type of passivity and the presence of some Other. Žižek (1989) calls this phenomena 'inter-passivity', and cites the example of canned laughter on TV, which relieves the audience of the duty to laugh. Not only may someone else believe or feel *for me* – the unconscious here being in effect another person – their postulated state of belief (or affect) often allows me to extend a latent feeling in a more power-ful form. This means both that my affects are continually subject to a form of transference (in)to others (i.e. the 'outbound' delegation of affective states), and that many of my powerful affects are only assumed through the mirror of the other, that is, by witnessing and feeling them in/through others (an 'inbound' re-assumption of affect). Hence the reason for the continual Lacanian emphasis on the topic of the 'big Other', the notion, repeatedly stressed so far, that a modicum of externality, or otherness, indeed, of *the socio-symbolic* lies at the very heart of the subjective. Hence also Lacan's idea of 'extimacy': that which is most intimate and revealing of a subject may only be identified or experienced in an ostensibly external form.

Indirect feelings

A Lacanian perspective thus seeks to complicate the idea of affects as merely subjective, as located 'in' individual subjects. It emphasizes instead the externality, the irreducible *inter-subjectivity* of affect.[28] Such a position, counter-intuitive as it may seem, requires further substantiation. Indeed, we may ask why exactly it is that the Other is so crucial in the life of affect? A reflection on psychotherapeutic practice may be in order here. The medium of what is displaced, 'not me', may provide a viable vehicle of exploration for that which may not otherwise be accessed on the 'intra-subjective' plane. It enables the subject to strike some distance from repressed intensities, the 'reals' of experience; furthermore, it affords an expressive modality, it makes the articulation of (particularly *powerful*) affects possible in a more bearable way.

That is to say: I often need the external dimension of an Other to 'get in touch' with losses or joys that would not otherwise remain adequately articulated. What is so crucial here, certainly in instances of extreme affectivity, is the opening up of a gap between the 'real' of engulfing experience and the minimal objectivity of seeing one's own affective state (of loss, trauma, ecstatic experience) realized in the situation of another. Perhaps this accounts for the therapeutic effect of popular narratives wherein an audience is able to feel, via 'artificial' characters, the elation of victory or the desolation of despair in a way that is both one step removed and also nevertheless personally powerful. The subjectively real and the fictional overlap here, as do the artificial and the authentic.

We should draw attention here to two adjoined meanings of the Other in Lacanian terminology, that is, to the Other as both *otherness*, that which is external to the subject, and the Other as *treasury of the signifier*, as encapsulation of the symbolic order as such. In both such meanings the Other enables some expressive possibility relative to the 'real' of affect. Linking unbearable affects to a symbolic framework possesses a 'containing' and a communicative potential. Perhaps part of what is so difficult, so puzzling about intensely negative emotions (feelings of loss, bereavement, depression, etc.), is precisely that they seem to lack the symbolic basis to be effectively shared, 'given shape', adequately expressed, *processed*. Hence the importance, as Leader (2003) argues, of funeral rites, and the often elaborate series of customs, dress-codes and mourning rituals that accompany death in so many societies. We might claim the same about individual affects of joy, celebration, jubilation – they too might often be said to lack an obvious expressive modality, they too might benefit from some or other formal procedure, from a type of commemoration, from an existing narrative template. We return here to the paradox stated at the outset, of the sports fan who feels that accomplishment of his team represents the greatest day of his or her life. We should take this claim seriously, although we might care to phrase it somewhat differently: the team's victory represents the best expressive modality, the most viable societal, trans-subjective form whereby such feelings – private instances of joy, triumph – may be linked to a broader symbolic frame, and thus made real in a social context.

It helps here to introduce an example. An episode of *E.R.*, the 1990s TV show set in a hospital emergency room, deals with the dilemma of a young boy who has recently last his father. The boy has assumed the persona of his comic book hero, Superman, and acts in accordance with this role, ignoring those who do not play along with his act of impersonation. The medical staff is unsure of how to respond to the boy's apparently delusional behaviour, which they take to be his way of reacting to the traumatic loss of his father. Their assumption is that the boy is seeking some escape from the harsh reality of what has transpired, that he has regressed – hopefully only temporarily – into a world of his imagination. The boy's doctor prevaricates in deciding what to do. On the one hand there is the argument that the boy needs to face the painful reality of his father's passing, and cease his apparently childish flight from reality. On the other, there is a sense that the fantasy the child enacts is his own way of coping, and that the staff should play along with the imaginary world that he has constructed for himself, at least insofar as it helps him come to terms with his loss. Adopting a more Lacanian focus on the nature of the boy's symbolic world, we might note something crucial about the role of the character that he impersonates. The character of Superman himself was an orphan, who lost his parents when his home planet of Krypton was destroyed.

In other words, in adopting the guise of Superman, the boy is not simply receding into a world of fantasy; there is something about the Superman story that connects very strongly to the situation he is living through. It is a symbolic construction that enables him some position from which to respond to an unthinkable event.

Furthermore, the Superman story possesses 'symbolic density', by which I mean to stress both that it is a well-known staple of popular culture known to millions, and that it is 'superficial' at least in the sense of being acknowledged as a comic book story. Such a level of realization seems apparent even in the boy himself, although this in no way compromises the value of this 'role playing', which is to say, its symbolic importance to him. A further element of the symbolic density at hand is worth emphasizing: Superman stories involve a familiar ensemble of characters, a series of typical scenarios, oft-rehearsed storylines and situations. To invoke Superman is also to invoke the broader story-framework of which his character is a part. What is so vital about this element of fictional artificiality is that it makes the boy's awful subjective position *communicable*; it transforms it into something others can relate to. After all, which little boy exposed to Western popular culture does not recognize, or have a minimal understanding of, the Superman story? This role is enabling of a type of inter-subjectivity. Whereas otherwise the child may experience only an alienated loneliness of suffering, it is now the case that passing adults and other children may recognize him and respond 'in character' ('Hey Superman! Where is Lois Lane?').

There is, in other words, a mythical quality to this story, which brings with it a framework of understanding that allows the little boy to locate himself relative to a traumatic personal reality. This fictional ensemble of characters and plotlines is a type of symbolic scaffolding that enables the body to give some structure to what would otherwise be overpowering, inchoate and, crucially, *incommunicable*, form of suffering. It gives his experience a meaning, and it provides a set of symbolic co-ordinates within which he may situate himself and his prospective future. Superman was orphaned, but became a hero; Superman had to find his way in a totally foreign environment (Earth) and start a new life, with new parental figures, etc. This would not work if Superman were a literal figure, an actual person. If he was not in some sense figurative, artificial, then the story would not be particularly enabling to the boy. It would be just another story of a child who had lost his parents; it would afford little opportunity for the boy to extrapolate a new identity for himself. That the story is understood or appreciated by others is vital, as is the fact that it brings with it an ensemble of characters and understandings which the child attempts to deploy within his life. The mythical quality to the story means, in other words, that it entails a minimal sociality, a frame of comprehension that others may be able to relate to, and through which they can understand something of his plight, which seems otherwise impossible to communicate.[29]

Two last points should be made before closing. The first runs against the grain of cynical dismissals of the superficiality or shallowness of public affects such as those generated by mega sporting events, commemorative jubilees, etc. Such events provide an expressive vehicle for neglected or unrealised modes of affectivity. They set up a prospective connection between past (and hitherto under-expressed) affective experiences and a properly *trans-subjective* cathartic opportunity.[30] Of course, this does not always mean that we know precisely what it is in our personal histories we are celebrating, rejoicing or commiserating when we are swept up in the euphoria or disappointment of such public spectacles. In such instances we have not just an overlap of the artificial and authentic, but of shared social experience – the trans-subjective – and the 'intra-subjective'.

The second point concerns an apparent contradiction in the argument I have presented above. On the one hand I have suggested that displays in the Other, that is 'shareable' socio-symbolic demonstrations of affect, might be a necessary precondition if certain subjective affects are to be realized at all. Yet I have also suggested that such Other displays (the expressive modality supplied by trans-subjective events) may simply allow the articulation of *what was already latently present* in the individual subject. The category of affect becomes here somewhat virtual; it seems to be both, in certain instances, 'non-existent' prior to its realization through the Other, and yet also *latent*, already silently there, yet made accessible only after the fact of a type of retroactive activation. So, it is not the case that we know from the outset that we are – for example – passionate Brazilian soccer supporters (or, indeed, proud Brazilian citizens). It is rather that through a series of symbolic activities and proxy involvements – many of which maintain a superficial quality, dictated by norms of sports spectatorship, the imagery of advertisers, etc. – that we create the preconditions for types of affect that had hitherto remained latent. It is only subsequently that we then go on to experience such affects – often with surprising enthusiasm and vigour – as natural, spontaneous. It is through such symbolic forms that we effectively became loyal subjects (of the nation, of a given cause). We might put it the following way (and the logic of retroaction is crucial here). There always -*already was* a *latent* ego-ideal love; it was present before we knew what it would become, before we knew what type of subject it would make of us.

Notes

1 The fleeting quality of this unifying group narcissism is nicely captured by the notion of 'the 90 minute nation'. One should note the ambivalence underlying this affective commitment to the team: should they play badly, the latent aggressive quality of this identification becomes all too quickly apparent.

2 For many Lacanians, the answer to such an over-extension of the ego is to be found in the psychological concept of *transitivism* developed by Charlotte Bühler and subsequently adopted by Lacan. One might argue – as I do – that this concept is still too psychological (and ego-based) to be 'properly Lacanian', at least in the sense that it does not take into account the role of the signifier. The purpose of this chapter (and that which follows) is to trace the conceptual development through Freud and into Lacan of ego-based to signifier-based conceptualizations of identification. This, needless to say, is a crucial part of the larger objective of this book, of situating Lacanian theory relative to (and against) psychological conceptualization.

3 Freud's concern with '*massenpsychologie*' had originally been translated by James Strachey as 'Group Psychology'. What this translation fails to express is the scale, breadth and the

variability of a 'mass' which may far exceed the more circumscribed bounds of a 'group'. This shortcoming has been rectified in the 2004 translation of Freud's text, more appropriately entitled: '*Mass psychology and the analysis of the "I"* '.

4 I have purposefully bypassed theorizations of nationalism in this chapter, preferring instead to prioritize a discussion of the *libidinal ties* underlying various mass formations. It is nevertheless worth noting a Lacanian critique of the many constructionist/'post-*Structuralist*' approaches to nationalism. Attempts to deconstruction nationalism as an effect of discursive practices remain inadequate for Lacanian critics such as Stavrakakis (2007) and Žižek (1993) precisely for the reason that they leave unexamined the libidinal facet of the specific *types of enjoyment* that give body to and bond the nation as a product of fantasy.

5 It is worth noting also Lacan's early description of libido (as included in his 1932 doctoral dissertation):

> [Libido is] an extremely broad theoretical entity that goes well beyond the specialized sexual desire of adults. This notion tends rather toward 'desire,' antiquity's Eros understood very broadly – namely, as the whole set of human beings' appetites that go beyond their needs.
>
> (Lacan, 1980, p. 256)

6 An objection could be noted here: groups of different sizes require different types of analysis, surely? The diversity of mass formations is conceded by Freud: 'There. . .[are] natural and artificial masses. . .primitive masses and structured, highly organized masses' (2004, p. 45). Freud's mass psychology focuses on structured masses – the military and the Catholic Church, which suggests that his analysis cannot reliably be extrapolated to fit far larger domains. Reasonable as such an objection sounds it overlooks a crucial consideration. We cannot seek to delimit the functioning of the libidinal economy Freud describes merely on a numerical basis. The question should rather be: is such a libidinal economy in operation in a given social sphere, i.e. does a given community exhibit passionate ties along the lateral and horizontal lines of attachment that Freud's model (as we shall see) specifies? The existence of such a *libidinal structure* is what counts above considerations of scale. Importantly also: such ties give body to a *fantasmatic* rather than an actual or objective community; such an idea of a mass (or Nation) is not thus reducible to strictly rational or quantitative criteria.

7 There is also another meaning to this term which resonates pleasingly with our concerns here: '*nom du père*' is a homonym for ('*non-dupes errent*'), that is, for 'the non-duped err'. That is to say: those who are not duped by symbolic fictions or conventions are in error – they fail to appreciate the structuring force of the symbolic.

8 Lacan calls this 'primitive identification' and it is clearly an imaginary type of identification, which is to say that the wish to be like the image of the father will prepare the way for the Oedipus complex in which the oscillation between love and aggressivity will be irreducible.

9 This is not to say that an identification with a loved figure cannot occur at the same time as sexual attraction to them. In the mode of regressive identification that Freud is describing here these two modes of relation to the object seem to be predominantly successive rather than simultaneous, at least in the conscious mind.

10 This poses the intriguing question of whether South Africans feel national pride in significantly different ways; it seems far more likely in this case that divergent values – and divergent senses of loss – inform what such groups are most proud of in their national identities.

11 Freud (2004) does note however that it is a *painful* cough, suggesting that the guilt occasioned by the repressed wish to replace the mother is thus given an expression in this symptom.

12 This is not to treat the personality features of a given leader as of negligible value; for Freud and Adorno alike, such facets of charisma clearly are of importance. Admittedly, within a given community, some prominent figures clearly are more adept than others

at mobilizing identifications and desires, or indeed, at enacting a master signifier ('hope', 'change', 'authority', etc).

13 This Lacanian clarification throws further light on a feature of Freud's theorization already questioned, namely the necessary failure of the love of the leader. This failure is not simply the result of actual empirical circumstances. It is a result of the fact that *the place* of the leader, that is, the *location* of abstract ideals and laws, cannot be confined to the figure of one human subject. By their very nature, these values cannot be reduced to a romantic love object solely possessed by one person. Furthermore, ego-ideals are the goals the ego strives for; they constitute the benchmark against which it measures itself. As such ego-ideals retain always a minimal externality to the ego, remaining evasive, out of reach, difficult to ever fully attain.

14 One should likewise bear in mind that the values elevated in the form of ego-ideals are not necessarily 'ideal' in any naïve moral sense. Abhorrent values may be elevated to such a position (as is the case of racist/Anti-Semitic values in white supremacist/Fascist ego-ideals). As is typical of Lacanian theory, it is not the *content* of the values themselves which determines their importance as ego-ideals, but *the place* such values come to occupy.

15 Idealistic as this idea was (an imaginary/fantasmatic construction, no doubt), it was repeatedly asserted in the South African press: the country's hosting of the World Cup event engendered a rare sense of cross-racial community, a sense of an encompassing national 'we' not commonly experienced in the country.

16 Despite that the visual is of great significance here – we are after all dealing with phenomena outlined in Lacan's theory of the mirror stage – such imaginary activities should not be reduced to the field of visual/scopic phenomena alone. We need to think of 'the image' in a broader sense encompassing ideas of resemblance, reflection and mirroring, indeed, as a *Gestalt*, that is, as a collection of impressions conveying an identity.

17 Imaginary impressions and historical signifiers will typically be intermingled, as is the case for example of National Anthems sung before international competitions, memories of famous victories and losses, and so on. We may complicate this picture further, by stressing also the role of *jouissance*, that is, the factor of the Lacanian real as connoted by the libidinal enjoyment that typically accompanies such sporting spectacles. Nonetheless, however entangled these Lacanian registers of imaginary, symbolic and real might be, we would expect that facets of each (image, signifier, *enjoyment*) would be apparent in any significant identification, which – to reiterate – cannot stand on the basis of the imaginary alone.

18 As valuable as Rose's differentiation is, one might query her choice of 'introjection' as the term of choice for the operative component of symbolic identifications. As we shall develop in the following chapter, symbolic identifications are perhaps better characterized by reference to operations of signification such as marking, tracing, counting ('introjection' seems still to belong to the register of imaginary identifications of *images*).

19 What is not immediately evident in our foregoing discussion is the evaluative and persecutory nature of the ego-ideal's relation to the ideal-ego. Glowinski (2001) describes this as follows: the ideal-ego remains a narcissistic phenomenon modelled on a love relation with the self. . .it is the part of the ego loved by the Ego-Ideal' (p. 85). The ego-ideal, by contrast, provides the measure of the ideal-ego – it is 'the signifier to which the ideal-ego relates and on which the ego models itself' (p. 85).

> If the ideal-ego satisfies the ego-ideal, the ego-ideal will return the ideal ego's love; in this case, the subject is the beloved of the ego-ideal. But the ego-ideal is . . . exacting . . . demanding . . . it expects satisfaction and perfection, not only love.
>
> (Glowinski, 2001, p. 85)

The ego-ideal, thus understood, is an exacting taskmaster.

20 This has direct clinical implications: Lacanian psychoanalysis continually probes questions of one's symbolic heritage, that is, the values and ideas of one's parents, grandparents and even great-grandparents, along with associated key familial signifiers and the like, i.e. much of what we intuitively consider as beyond the remit of everyday 'psychological' identifications.

21 This postulate holds for vampire fiction. After a person has been turned into a vampire, they no longer have a mirror image. Such a lack of image appears to correspond to the fact that the symbolic (ego-ideal) values of their previous human existence no longer apply. They have transcended this (or any) symbolic value system, and therefore no longer possess an image.

22 Reference was repeatedly made to the gaze of the outside world, which clearly acted as the Other to whom the image of the country was being offered: 'we proved to a sceptical world – and thus ourselves – that we could host a World Cup' (Gevisser, 2010).

23 We could characterize these intersecting trajectories of desire as: transferential desire, desire for signifiers taken from the Other, first; desire at the shared inter-subjective and also trans-subjective levels, second; and the resultant ostensible subjective or personal desire, third. The distinctively Lacan twist here resides in the fact that what I have called 'personal' desire, that is, the desire that we may experience as most pressing and most subjective, is always-already mediated by the Other, that is, by the foregoing factors (of the Other, of the inter-/trans-subjective).

24 It is worth stressing here that there is no contradiction between what appears to be (or what counts as) *my own* desire, and the desire of the Other, for the reason that my own desire can only be carved out of the terrain of the Other's desire. That being said, the progress of an analysis, certainly in the case of neurotics, is ideally dedicated to the 'dialecticization' of such desires, to (certain in Lacan's Seminar VII, *The Ethics of Psychoanalysis*) an interrogation and working through of *what counts* as my desire as part of the ethical endeavour of unearthing (and 'not giving way on') more fundamental (and more repressed) forms of desire.

25 The history of psychoanalysis is not immune to this issue of inherited desire. In Seminar XI Lacan suggests that each psychoanalyst continues a facet of Freud's own inaugural desire – that is to practice psychoanalysis. Admirable as this may sound, it also means that many trainee analysts don't really know why they want to be analysts, and that they have, very possibly, been swept up in an identification with Freud that entails a series of unquestioned aspects. Hence the importance in an analyst's training of the question – seemingly so difficult to answer – 'Why do you want to be an analyst?', or, 'Whose desires other than your "own" might you be serving in your wish to become an analyst?'

26 Similarly pertinent here is Lacan's (1992) comment that the correct assertion is not 'God is dead', but rather 'God is unconscious'. In other words, we can continue to believe without knowing we do, even in fact while strenuously denying that we do.

27 Lacan strongly opposes the idea of unconscious affects (the unconscious being structured like a language, and accessible only via the signifier, that is, symbolic forms). Affects cannot be repressed as such, but they can be disavowed, displaced onto others or disengaged from one signifier and linked to an altogether different signifier (as is the case in obsessional symptoms). If the idea of displaced or disavowed affects sounds odd, consider the case of *jouissance*. One may be intensely aroused by something – stimulated by the painful enjoyments of *jouissance* – as in recounting a horrendous example of torture (this occurs to Freud's patient, the Ratman), without explicitly realizing or acknowledging it. In many such examples of *jouissance* one's reflex reaction is disavowal and or displacement: it is *others* who get off in such a way, never myself.

28 Or, even more accurately, we could speak of the trans-subjectivity of affect, emphasizing thus how affect is routed through not just others but the Other.

29 This illustration gives us one way of approaching Lacan's (2006) pronouncement that 'truth has the structure of fiction'.

30 Those who reject such public displays as facile and superficial are, perhaps, an example of the 'non-duped who err'. In their rejection of the the artificiality of such spectacles they overlook that they provide apt vehicles for the expression of affects not otherwise adequately expressed.

5

THE MARKED SUBJECT

Towards a non-psychological theory of identification

Striking some distance from the largely ego-centred model of identification discussed in the previous chapter, this chapter outlines the basis of a 'non-psychological' theory of identification. In doing so we are tracing a crucial step in the development of Lacanian theory. The two most important concepts in this discussion are the master signifier and the unary trait, both of which remain importantly linked to the foregoing discussion of symbolic ego-ideals. My aim here is for the most part expository. I survey much of the literature in the area, yet endeavour also to provide a more readily accessible overview of these concepts as pinned to practical instances of identification. In respect of the first of these two concepts, I briefly examine the case of Nelson Mandela as a master signifier. In revisiting the unary trait, I take as my impetus a suggestive moment from Alex Ross's history of modern music, *The Rest is Noise.*

I also have a critical objective. In the book's opening chapter I drew attention to how Lacanian theory sometimes becomes detached from the pragmatic concerns of clinical work. This is not only the result of the abstractions and formalizations of the theory – which, as I suggested before, have their clear benefits – but is due also to re-articulations of Lacanian theory in other disciplinary domains. There is, for example, a good deal of excellent literature that explores the Lacanian notion of the master signifier from the perspective of political discourse theory and ideology critique (Laclau, 2007; Laclau and Mouffe, 1985; Stavrakakis, 1997, 1999; Žižek, 1996). While there is much to be commended in literature of this sort, it often neglects salient issues pertaining to the role of master signifiers in the clinical domain. The popularity of the concept of the master (or 'empty') signifier in political discourse analysis and ideology critique has, in other words, proved a double-edged sword. On the one hand it demonstrates how crucial psychical processes are performed via the operations of the signifier enabling thus an effective *de-psychologizing* of such processes of identification. On the other, the use of the master-signifier concept within the political realm to track discursive formations and the functioning of ideology tends to distance the term from application in the case of individual subjects and *as an element in the operation of the unconscious*. In short: the master signifier seems, all too often, more a concept derived from discourse theory than from clinical psychoanalytic practice. A not-dissimilar argument can be made in respect of the unary trait, a concept which is typically investigated in such abstruse formalized terms that often it proves difficult to imagine viably applying it in clinical practice.

Against group psychology

The previous chapter stressed a series of Lacanian re-articulations of Freud's ideas, most pertinently perhaps, the ego-ideal/ideal-ego distinction, and the role and functioning of affect in the situations of group identification. This discussion was marked by a crucial omission: it declined to note how, in advancing upon key terms derived from Freud's mass psychology, Lacan's subsequent theorizations marked not just a departure from, but an implicit critique of, aspects of Freud's thinking on identification.

Bluntly put: Lacan was no advocate of ego-oriented explanations of group phenomena. The more he turned to the role of the signifier and symbolic structure in the 1950s, the more averse he became to thinking identification on the basis to ego-to-ego (imaginary) relations.[1] His writings of the period repeatedly critique explanatory accounts that prioritize an overly biological notion of libido.[2] So while Lacanian theory is clearly influenced by Freud's mass psychology, we should nonetheless be wary of tacitly affirming Lacan's agreement with all that is contained within Freud's analysis. Stressing such differences will help us avoid giving the impression of a seamless transition from Freudian to Lacanian thinking – a not infrequent trend in Lacan scholarship.[3]

Ian Parker is alive to Lacan's reticence to endorse a certain reading of Freud's *massenpsychologie*:

> Lacan urges his audience to 'distrust . . . in the most extreme way . . . everything that marks a community in any genus . . . especially in those which are most original for us' . . . This is precisely what Freud appears to be doing in Group Psychology . . . and it is what Lacan sets himself against . . . There is a general point here . . . it is not the inclusion of the subject in a signifier so they may feel genuinely and fully represented by it . . . Rather, it is that the subject is excluded from the signifier which represents the subject . . . [and moreover, represents the subject] for another signifier.
>
> (2015a, p. 86)

Lacan, in Parker's view, prefers his own account of logical time (discussed in Chapter 3), to the 'group psychology' thesis of a community built on the basis of ego-likenesses or aligned ego-investments. Lacan thus opts for a different (even if tacitly connected) order of theorization, which entails identifications *with signifiers* rather than 'secondary processes of ego-to-ego relations that constitute collectivities' (Parker, 2015a, p. 87).[4]

In short, what really marks the subject, what has the more profoundly constitutive influence is *exclusion from* a group or set, rather than unquestioned membership. It is crucial however not to overlook this critical facet of Lacan's engagement with Freud's *massenpsychologie* for the simple reason that it speaks directly to Lacan's critical stance both on psychology generally and, more specifically, on models of subjectivity based primarily on assumptions of ego identification. By striking distance from facets of earlier Freudian theorizations, we can say – provocatively perhaps – that Lacan was distancing himself not only from the remaining psychological components with Freudian theory, but from those within his own earlier thinking.[5]

'In ways I cannot say'

I stressed, in the previous chapter, the clinical imperative of prioritizing symbolic ego-ideals over imaginary contents in the analysis of identification. Yet this immediately opposes a difficulty. Imaginary contents are omnipresent, they function, after all, as lures; they engage the clinician or analyst at the enticing level of their own ego. Ego-ideals, by contrast, are elusive, difficult to pinpoint, impossible to ever fully enumerate or circumscribe. This is unsurprising. We know, after all, that ego-ideals entail an unconscious dimension. Then again, ego-ideals dictate the most celebrated values within a given culture; they perform a crucial organizing function in the libidinal economy of individuals and groups. Given however that ego-ideals constitute those 'to live or die for' values which surpass in their importance those of the ego itself, it stands to reason that they cannot be *wholly unconscious* either. They must as such remain linked to a series of *available* signifiers – signifiers, in other words, that are accessible to consciousness – even if such signifiers prove to be unsatisfyingly evasive. For this reason it helps to deploy Lacan's notion of the master signifier as a means of understanding the operation of ego-ideals. Let me stress from the very outset that the master signifier must be grasped as an *effect of signification*. We must not fall prey to the illusion that the master signifier is an instantiation of an object or an entity.[6] I stress this because it is part and parcel of Lacan's critique of the psychological: in turning to the signifier and the realm of the symbolic, Lacan aims at a 'de-imaginarization' of psychical contents and a 'de-substantialization' of psychical objects.

If these preliminary comments seem overly theoretical, imagine the following. You are accosted by a camera crew who insist on interviewing you for a live television broadcast. '*What*', the interviewer asks you, '*is it that you most strongly believe?*' Barely pausing, the interviewer continues: '*What would you be prepared to die for?*' True enough, not everyone would be reduced to a state of stumbling inarticulacy by such a situation. Many might quite happily offer an initial response

('My children', 'A better future', 'My country', 'Science', 'Humanity', etc.).[7] Then again, even those who are able to summon up an appropriate response will doubtless be dogged by the inadequacy of their words, by their own inability to fully articulate the reasons for their libidinal investment. Added to this is the inevitable prospect that the words one uses in such situations will seem hopelessly derivative, abstract, formulaic, devoid of any real personalized significance.

Such a situation would be made even more trying should the interviewer press on and on, interrogating each given belief – be it a deeply held personal, political or even spiritual commitment – needling you: '*But why?*', '*Why do you believe* that?' The unavoidable conclusion to such an unrelenting line of questioning would be a circular – and no doubt exacerbated – retort: '*Well, because I do!*' Such a retort is sometimes all that can be offered in order to hold a deluge of questions – and inadequate answers – at bay. This situation calls to mind the age old poetic dilemma: the difficulty of putting into words exactly why one loves one's partner, one's family, one's country, etc. The impossibility of ever fully answering such a question seems self-evident: being in love presents us with a self-justifying condition which always exceeds the reasons I might give for being in love.[8] Indeed, the reasons I love someone (or something) can never be wholly rationalized or exhausted by a string of signifiers, partly because such signifiers refer endlessly to other signifiers without ever 'hitting the real'.[9]

The insufficiency of the signifier

We return here to a problem alluded to in Chapter 3, namely that of the slippage from one inadequate signifier – unable in itself to fix a given meaning – to another, and then another, and so on *ad infinitum* in an indefinite process which fails to arrest the slide of deferred meaning.[10] This scenario is nicely invoked by Lacan's at first curious definition of the process of signification according to which the signifier represents the subject *for another signifier*.[11] There is no naïve psychological realism here. It is not the case that the signifier can transparently represent the subject as he or she really 'is'. It is rather the case that what one 'is', or, more accurately, the signifiers that one uses to portray who one is ('business-like', 'fair-minded', 'decisive', 'dedicated') are, as in the example of a politician's self-portrayals discussed in Chapter 3, related still to other signifiers ('presidential', 'exceptional', etc.).

'The signifier does not provide a guide to reality', insists Miller (forthcoming), 'but presents myriad relations with other signifiers.' A signifier, moreover, is defined by other signifiers, indeed, 'by its relation to the chain of *all* other signifiers'.

> [S]ignifiers slide along, metonymy gets away from real objects, language lives on its own terms, existing in dimensions far removed from signifieds, doing far more than simple describing them. This is where the subject exists; these are the laws to which we are subjected.
>
> (Miller, forthcoming)

In situations such as that alluded to above where more can always be said, our best option is – in effect – *to tie a knot in discourse*. The self-referring quality of a given oft-stressed signifier has to suffice when no over-arching explanation can be given ('*Boys will be boys. . .*'). This, after all, is what self-referential answers do: they don't as much provide sufficient reasons, as loop back on what has already been said, and elevate one signifier over others ('*My* children *mean everything to me*', '*He has his faults, but at the end of the day he was the best choice for* the country', 'Evolution is *unChristian*'). The signifier here over-reaches its signified; it exceeds what it literally signifies to perform a different discursive function: that of drawing a line, halting a sequence of inadequate explanations by the imposition of a master signifier ('*We know it is true because* science *tells us so*').

In this way such responses enable a temporary point of fixity; they ground a point of belief and/or authority. Bracher (1994) has this tautological logic in mind when he explains how speakers use certain signifiers – master signifiers – 'as the last word, the bottom line, the term that anchors, explains or justifies the claims or demands contained within the message' (p. 112). Receivers of communication respond to master signifiers in much the same way: 'whereas other terms and the values and assumptions they bear may be challenged, master signifiers are simply accepted as having a value or validity that goes without saying' (p. 112). Master signifiers often appear then as those incontestable aspects of a discursive position, as those self-validating points of attachment to a broader ideological or personal worldview.

The master signifier in the field of ideology

Helpful as the foregoing illustration may have been, it begs further elucidation. This can be done in two ways: by examining a series of basic themes in political/sociological uses of the term,[12] and then by turning to the more clinical literature. In this way I will provide a basis for understanding the concept both in its societal and subjective areas of application, while also pointing to certain of the tensions arising between these two domains.

Within any discursive network or 'system of signs' there are certain privileged signifiers, what Lacan initially referred to '*points de capiton*' (1993), nodal points, which function to 'button down' meaning and ensure the smooth exchange of signifiers.[13] Such signifiers are evident at the level of everyday speech, typically as those oft-repeated or affectively loaded terms which function to ground an argument or meaning. These signifiers, paradoxically, assume a disproportionate importance in relation to surrounding signifiers. Any number of examples can be supplied here, from master signifiers operating at an overtly political and ideological societal level ('*9–11*', '*Freedom*', '*Our troops*'), to the more idiosyncratic range of master signifiers that operate at the level of a given subject's libidinal economy. Such signifiers play an integrating role, they fashion effects of legibility out of an otherwise indeterminate (and often distressing) set of discursive elements. Indeed, on the 6 June 1956, in a crucial session of his third seminar (on psychosis), Lacan insists:

> Everything radiates out from and is organized by this signifier . . . It's the point of convergence that enables everything that happens in this discourse to be situated retroactively and prospectively.
>
> (1993, p. 268)

A recent definition of the master signifier – which serves us both as a summary overview and as a basis for critical comparison – is found in *The Žižek Dictionary*:

> [B]ecause signifiers refer only to other signifiers, this produces a seemingly endless chain of references . . . [T]his seemingly infinite sequence of referral can be fixed or anchored only through the intervention of a . . . 'nodal point' . . . which 'quilts' them, stops their sliding and fixes their meanings . . . this nodal point . . . in the series of signifiers is the 'master signifier' – a signifier that, although essentially no different from any other signifier, is situated in such a way that it masters the entire sequence of referral by providing a kind of final . . . guarantee of meaning. It is able to do this . . . not because it possesses some special significance . . . but simply because it is able to halt the process of referral by the empty gesture of referring only to itself. This 'reflective' signifier is nothing more than a kind of cul-de-sac in the chain of equivalences. . . . 'beneath' the alleged unity of the field of meaning, there is only a . . . self-referential, performative gesture.
>
> (Gunkel, 2014, pp. 190–191)

This definition, admirable both in its succinctness and its ability to synthesis the literature in the area, is indicative in another way also: no mention is made either of the operation of the unconscious or of the fact that the discursive nodal point of the master signifier represents equally a nodal point *of affect*, a point of passionate investment.

A somewhat different account of how the 'empty signifier' functions in the consolidation of groups is presented in Laclau's *On Populist Reason*. Laclau (2004) notes how under certain circumstances a given signifier, without ceasing to be particular in what it signifies, 'assumes the representation of an incommensurable totality' (p. 70). This signifier is thus 'split between the particularity which it still is and . . . [a] more universal signification' (p. 70). This operation whereby a particular signifier takes up the role of 'incommensurable universal signification' is, for Laclau, that of hegemony. Such a task of hegemonic identity requires an empty signifier in which its 'own particularity' comes to attain an 'unachievable fullness' (p. 71). In contrast to the foregoing definition, Laclau does bring libidinal investment into the picture. The 'fullness' of the master signifier cannot be directly represented, he says, adding that 'a hegemonic totalization requires a radical investment . . . the affective dimension plays a central role' (p. 71).

In the name of Mandela

A name starts to function as a master signifier when, despite the predominance of a consensual meaning, it comes to signify a great many things to a great many people, all of whom remain identified with – or against – what it is thought to signify.[14] The signifier in question – Karl Marx, George Washington, Jesus Christ, Mao Zedong – anchors an array of beliefs and makes a type of (political, religious, ideological) subjectivity possible. In the absence of such a societal master signifier there is no committed or believing subject, no subject of the group, indeed, no viable group or constituency at all.

Mandela as . . .

The name Mandela works in just such a way in post-apartheid South Africa. Evoked by multiple constituencies, Mandela's legacy is pinned to the agendas of divergent interests, and can no longer be assigned any singular meaning. What this means then is that Mandela represents a point of hegemonic convergence in which a variety of incompatible values and identifications overlap. Frederickson's (1990) comment that Mandela succeeded in fulfilling a symbolic role as the 'embodiment of the nation that transcends ideology, party, or group' (p. 28) has by now become a historical commonplace. For some Mandela represents the benign, forgiving father of the nation, the embodiment of hope and racial reconciliation; for others Mandela is the radical protagonist of the armed struggle, the revolutionary icon of the African National Congress; for yet others Mandela is a largely de-politicized figure, the commodity image adorning countless accessories and experiences of the 'new' South Africa. And the list goes on . . .

1 . . . transcendent signifier

The 'magic' of the master signifier in the ideological field is that it is able to knit together different constituencies, appealing equally, albeit in very different ways, to a variety of classes who are otherwise opposed in their political agendas. The point of course has frequently been made that Mandela represents fundamentally different things to Whites and Blacks in South Africa. Such ideological divergences may ultimately be less important than the fact that Whites and Blacks find in Mandela a *shared reference-point*, a common denominator through which their often differing interests may be mediated. Such a master signifier enables communication where previously none may have been possible; it represents the possibility that various social antagonisms might (however temporarily) be overcome. It is in this way that a master signifier makes a type of social bond possible.[15]

2 . . . *empty* signifier

Laclau (2004, 2007) prefers to refer to *empty* as opposed to a *master* signifiers. Doing so draws attention to the fact that master signifiers have no intrinsic or essential meaning. It likewise makes it apparent that master signifiers permit for an endless succession of varying applications and extensions. In the operation of the master signifier, says Stavrakakis:

> a particular signifier is called to incarnate a function beyond its concreteness, it is 'emptied' from its particular signification in order to represent fullness in general and to be able to articulate a large number of heterogeneous signifiers . . . [S]uch an empty signifier . . . serves as a *point de capiton* uniting a whole community.
>
> (1999, p. 80)

We understand then that master signifiers can never be totalized or exhausted; they 'sustain the identity of an ideological field beyond all possible variations of positive content' (Žižek, 1989, p. 87). The signifier Mandela, for example, remains always able to accommodate fresh articulations; it can be appended to a seemingly limitless stream of post-apartheid objects and aspirations. Mandela we might say, is effervescent, an unending signifier. And here the key paradox underlying the concept comes to the fore: the more a master signifier is heaped with imaginary contents and meanings, the more potentially inclusive it becomes.

On the one hand then we have Mandela as an over-arching signifier, the signifier that seemingly encapsulates all that is of value in the post-apartheid context. Yet Mandela is also a kind of nothingness, a signifier devoid of any absolute or definitive meaning, a signifier that exists at the site of the impossibility of ever saying it all. Mandela remains forever indeterminate; one never knows in any final sense what is being invoked when this signifier is being put to use. As one South African journalist put it: 'What Mandela, the symbol of freedom, stands for is so vague that anything can be pegged on him' (Mngxitama, 2014).

3 . . . as positivization of a void

As already intimated, the indeterminacy of Mandela is less important than the fact that a system of signification acquires a centring-point, navigational principle via which all associated signifiers acquire meaning and value. Nonetheless, how are we to make sense of the fact that a master signifier is simultaneously depleted of, and yet overflowing with, meaning, that – differently put – emptiness and symbolic density here coincide? Simply enough, perhaps, by suggesting that the master signifier refers to a signifying operation in which *nothingness has been turned inside-out*. The inability to articulate a final meaning is converted into that *which lies behind the meaning of everything*. The impossibility of saying it all is, in short, transformed into a surplus.

Glynos (2001) makes just this argument in considering how any complex ensemble of discursive elements – constructions of a nation for example, or of a given social mass – come to attain a type of relative closure and meaning. Society, he says, lacks an ultimate signifier with which to make it complete:

[N]othing positive can be said about the 'truth' of society except that it is incomplete – in Lacanian terms, that there is a 'lack in the symbolic Other'. Thus, society exists as a totality only insofar as the social subject *posits* its existence as such through the mediation of empty signifiers.

(2001, p. 197)

It is by virtue of master signifiers, continues Glynos, that *epistemological incapacity* is transformed into a *positive ontological condition*. We use such master signifiers every day, without a second thought ('America', 'women', 'history', 'society', etc.). One might expect that such signifiers would become meaningless. They should, after all, buckle under the weight of the signifying load that has been heaped upon them. Yet this does not happen. What seems to be the impossibility of master signifiers – namely, the fact that no one totallizing or exhaustive meaning can ever be allocated to them – proves, in retrospect, to be very their condition of possibility. A prospective master signifier needs to be impossibly stretched, burdened with the task of 'incommensurable universal signification' (Laclau, 2004, p. 70) before it comes to operate as such. It is only by being over-loaded in this way that a signifier begins to exceed the work of mere signification and becomes self-referential. Hence the initially puzzling idea: master signifiers don't signify anything – other than themselves.

A master signifier is a recursive loop in the functioning of signification itself. The signifying impulse gets caught in a self-affirming pattern, in a repetitive circuit, hence the circular, self-instantiating grounds of such ostensibly 'transcendent' signifiers. It is this endless self-referral of master signifiers that means that they come, paradoxically, to 'count' more than the surrounding signifiers upon which they operate. Lacanian theory thus both extends and yet departs from Structuralism. As Dolar (1999) explains:

[A]ny notion of structure, far from being simply differential, a balanced matrix of permutations (as in Levi-Strauss) necessarily gives rise to a 'master signifier', a structural function that power gets hold of, but which is in itself empty, a pure positivisation of a void.

(p. 87)

4 . . . social fantasy

If we appear to have drifted too far towards abstract theorization, then consider Nuttall's (2013) commentary on the mortality of the former South African president:

With the fact of his late old age comes the sense that [Mandela] marks a deep void at the heart of a place that has always struggled to mask what it feels might be an emptiness at its centre, that has struggled to define itself as a nation and to draw together its many fragments into a sustained sense of commonality, in the wake of a long racist past. We approach alongside him the anxiety or anguish that South Africa is neither a concept nor an idea – just a physical place, a geographical accident.

Mandela, thus approached, is the signifier that covers over the void of meaning – indeed, the historical trauma – that lies at the centre of the political project of post-apartheid South African nationhood. One appreciates how, in late 2013, Mandela's immanent death may have been thought to represent the end of the fantasy, the point at which the concept of South Africa ceased to work as anything other than an imaginary construct. Perhaps it is the case – easy enough to imagine if Mandela's legacy were erased from history – that, following Nuttall (2013) 'South Africa' is no more than the name for a set of historical contingencies to which no grand march of progress can rightly be said to apply.

This allusion to fantasy, to the mythical dimension of Mandela as master signifier, is apt. As Stavrakakis (1999) observes, the symbolic construct articulated via a master signifier 'can function properly only within a certain fantasmatic frame; the empty signifier can function only as an *object petit a*' (p. 81). A master signifier, in other words, is never merely objective in its meaning and value, but is animated by belief, by the imagination of those who have invested in it. There is thus some truth to the idea that Mandela's greatness is a creation of the collective imagination. We might rephrase this idea psychoanalytically by noting that Mandela – and master signifiers more generally – are recipients of intense transference reactions. In speaking of Mandela as master signifier we convey not only that Mandela has become a focal point of multiple subjective investments but the effect of shared social fantasy.

5 . . . and retroactive principle of articulation

We need note here the retroactive dimension of master signifiers. That there is significant meaning – passionate attachments, areas of marked libidinal intensity – is always-already the result of master signifiers ordering the field of signification. This is particularly salient in the case of Mandela, where – in line with the narrative role typically accorded the former president – it is easy to fall prey to the illusion that Mandela was always destined to assume the role of the unifying, 'transcendent' signifier of the post-apartheid nation. Such effects of historical order – indeed, of narrative cohesion – are precisely the consequence of master signifiers knitting together the disarray of contingent signifiers and producing in their place a sense of cogency and inevitability.

As components of ideology, master signifiers don't so much eliminate opposing terms as *re-articulate* them. Rival ideological terms come thus to be reintegrated, arranged in a different set of signifying relations. This is a situation in which nothing new necessarily needs to be added to a field of discursive elements, despite that everything can have changed. In other words, there has been a reshuffling of discursive elements under the ascendancy of a new master signifier. In the TV series *Boston Legal*, an accomplished attorney advises his junior colleague: 'Never let your opponent frame your argument'. The younger attorney had just lost a case against a soldier accused of torturing prisoners in Iraq. What the attorney had taken to be an unimpeachable argument – the moral case against torture under any circumstances – had been re-framed by the defendant's attorney, who, without adding any new substantive content to the trial, opted simply to stress a different master signifier: '*9–11*'.

Such a reshuffling of discursive elements is apparent in the changing historical role of Mandela as master signifier. What had for many years been a crucial signifier of threat within apartheid ideology, a signifier predominantly associated with a series of negative values – 'communist threat', 'anti-White', 'violence', 'terrorist' – eventually came to operate as the focal point of the discourse of the new South Africa. The role of a master signifier in arranging a discursive field is anything but a once-and-for all operation. The effect of master signification is an unending, historical flux of discursive values, a constant realignment of signifiers.

The master signifier and the subject

I stressed above the need to grasp the role of master signifiers not only as elements within the functioning of political discourse, but as components in the psychic operations of subjects. This theoretical context, of how master signifiers operate at the level of the subject, is crucial to an understanding of the concept. A master signifier's strength, in this respect, is not merely linguistic – so we might argue – but also *affective* in nature, a question of the libidinal ties that it underpins.[16] We might put it this way: the operation of master signifiers involves a type of libidinal economy inasmuch as it produces a distribution and arrangement of affects.

Here though we must proceed cautiously. From a Lacanian perspective, after all, linguistic operations are the very stuff of psychical functioning. The question of affective bonds should not thus be seen as extrinsic to the role of signification. 'Affect', as Laclau puts it, 'is not something external, added to the symbolic, but an internal component of it' (Laclau, in Glynos and Stavrakakis, 2010, p. 235). The affective charge of a given signifier or representation *does not* exist *outside of* the realm of signification. Affect should be grasped as the outcome of relations between signifiers, approached as an *internal* component of signification: 'the relation between affect and signification is not a simple addition one' (p. 234). Any rigid demarcation between affect and representation, signifier and *jouissance*, must be brought into question: 'the distinction between affect (cathectic investment) and the symbolic is. . . intra- and not extra-discursive' (p. 239).[17] We must be wary then of perpetuating what from a Lacanian perspective can only be seen as a false dichotomy between the linguistic and the affective.[18]

S1, S2 and the divided subject

Strictly speaking, it makes no sense to speak of a 'master signifier' in a way that implies it can be disengaged from the multitude of other signifiers of which it is a component part. Lacan's quasi-mathematical notion of the 1960s emphasizes this: a master signifier (S1) is always itself contingent on a dispersed array of elements (S2) that come, retroactively, to operate as a bounded field of knowledge. Hence Fink's (1995) description of the master signifier as 'the non-sensical signifier' which is 'brought into the movement of language. . . "dialecticized" through the action of various S2s' (p. 75).

Crucially however, not only does the passage from S2 to S1 (S1 ← S2) render a disorganized set of signifiers legible, it also arranges such a set of signifiers into *practicable* forms of knowledge (*savoir faire*). Such a process, crucially, implies a subject, precisely the subject for whom the relation of knowing thus produced becomes operable (the subject 'who represents a signifier for another signifier'). S1 ← S2 is thus a type of Lacanian shorthand for *subjectification*. This is axiomatic for Lacan: the functioning of the signifier produces the subject, which, in his view, is precisely the effect of signifying relations. Just as S1 cannot be separated from S2 – it wouldn't be a master signifier if this were the case – so the S1 ← S2 relationship, as an instance of signification, cannot be divorced from the subject that is its result. The S1 ← S2 pair, it now becomes apparent, is a triad: its third component is the barred subject.

Let us consider an example that might may bring this idea to life. When the relationship between a master signifier (say, 'Christmas') and an array of ostensibly unrelated signifiers (tinsel, carol-singing, jolly bearded men, roasted chestnuts, mistletoe, the exchange of presents, shepherds assembled around a baby in Jerusalem, etc.) is intuitive and requires no further need of explanation, then a subject of the signifier has already been constituted. This constituted subject is one who spontaneously grasps (and, potentially, *enjoys*) the cultural institution of Christmas as a coherent form of social practice. Crucially however, this produced subject is a *barred* or *non-transparent* subject. It is the subject of the unconscious whose attempts at self-cohesion are constantly derailed by the mechanism of the signifier. Christmas, for example, comes from the field of the Other. So while the subject may identify with this signifier, there is always the prospect that the multiple associated signifiers of Christmas don't quite match up to the subject's expectations such that the event is never quite as fulfilling or satisfying as they had hoped it might be.

The S1 ← S2 relationship needs to be grasped as pertaining to signification in an encompassing sense. Signification here includes not just instances of propositional knowledge, but types of expertise or practical 'know how'. For Lacan, knowledge (S2) in its relation to a master signifier (S1) is meant also in the sense of *savoir faire*. Importantly, both such forms of knowing rely on the rudimentary differentiation between signifiers – that is, a minimal differential element – required by all forms of knowing. So, even in the ostensibly 'pre-linguistic' 'stage' of development, we can see the signifier at work, as for example in the case of the hungry infant fumbling at the mother's breast, trying to find the nipple. There is a rudimentary sort of signification (or comprehension) occurring here; in differentiating the nipple from other parts of the breast the infant 'knows' something: how to go about feeding.

This nascent form of signification plays its part in the production of a (divided) subject of gratification/frustration.

From subjugation to *subjectivization*

From a clinical perspective what matters is not simply to spot a master signifier in the speech of a patient – that is often easy enough – but to query the particular role this signifier is playing for them. We need ask: what task is being performed by this signifier, and, more pointedly, what is being elided, or repressed by the S1 ← S2 relation? The clinical literature makes this point of emphasis quite clear. '[M]aster signifiers', says Bailly (2009), 'have become quite detached from their signifieds', so as to

> carry out the function of changing the meaning of the signifying chain into one that supports the ego. It is one of the main tasks of analysis to . . . bring to light the side of them [master signifiers] hidden in the unconscious.
>
> (p. 64)

'[I]n the analytic situation', says Fink (1995), 'a master signifier presents itself as a dead end, a stopping point . . . [it is] a term, a word, or phrase that puts an end to association, that grinds the patient's discourse to a halt' (p. 135). The contrast between examples drawn from the political literature and the clinic is jarring: in the former, master signifiers represent an apparent overflow of meaning; in the clinic they are typically the point where signification stalls, where meaning closes down.

One of the chief goals of analysis is to shift the relation of domination imposed by S1s, to clear the blockage imposed by such master signifiers, to 'dialectize' those master signifiers which have frozen the subject. It is in line with this conceptualization that Fink refers to the master signifier as 'subjugating the subject' (p. 78), as 'the signifier that commands or [acts as] commandment' (p. 135). It is by bringing master signifiers into relation with other signifiers, signifiers that may shift the given locked (S1 ← S2) relation, by turning 'dead ends . . . into through streets' (p. 78), that one succeeds in 'dialectizing' the master signifier. Returning to our discussion of Mandela, we might ask: what other narratives of the emergence of the post-apartheid nation might be possible; what other accounts and might take us beyond the 'lock-down' of Mandela-associated meanings? More revealing yet, perhaps: why the need to subscribe to the Mandela myth, and what might this myth conceal?

We should pay careful attention to Fink's terminology. The fundamental structure of signification, as we have seen, entails the establishment of a link between a master signifier and other signifiers, a link furthermore which ensures – Fink (1995), notably, uses a neutral term here – that *subjectification* takes place. When the master signifier is isolated, difficult to dialectize, when a S1 ← S2 relationship is locked, says Fink, 'it *subjugates* the subject' (p. 173). If it is possible to shift this

S1 ← S2 relationship, perhaps by making S1 refer to a wider group of S2s, by introducing new S2s, or by challenging S1 with the ascendancy of a new S1, then '*subjectivization* occurs, and a subject of/as meaning results' (p. 173, emphasis added). A successful analysis could be said to pivot on the difference between these two modes of subjectification, that is, on the movement from *subjugation* to *subjectivization*.

To recapitulate:

> [In analysis] one tries to introduce an outside . . . of this S1 . . . If we can bring this S1 into some other kind of relation with [surrounding signifiers] . . . then its status as a master signifier subjugating the subject changes. A bridge is built between it and another linguistic element . . . the analysand is no longer stuck at that particular point of his or her associations . . . A meaning of the master signifier is created . . . the subject is once again split . . . having come to be momentarily in the forging of a link between S1 and S2.
>
> (Fink, 1995, p. 78)

It is the creation of a new relationship between a given S1 and other signifying elements 'which allows for a subjective *position*' (p. 78). What is crucial to grasp here is that this subject *does not* transcend their status as the split subject of the unconscious. The subject cannot bypass or supersede the division which, after all, is, for psychoanalysis, constitutive of the subject as such (hence Fink's reference to the subject being 'once again split'). If anything, the split is realized in a more pronounced way. Yet this is precisely what psychoanalysis is all about, peering deeper into, confronting, the constitutive split that *is* the subject, and considering alternative – less subjugated yet nevertheless divided – forms of subjectivization that become possible in the process.

The 'unenunciated' aspect

Master signifiers then do not only anchor meanings and fix the nodal points of a given discourse. They also *structurally repress* other signified meanings through the subject's insistence that '"this is the way things are", that a given state of affairs is not subject to challenge or dissent' (Parker, 2005, p. 170). The very process of discursive insistence – be it in the endless reiteration of the master signifier or in the self-referring circularity upon which it depends – effectively shuts down differing interpretations and dissent (Parker, 2005).

While, for Bailly (2009) master signifiers are the very backbone of the human subject, 'they are also, perhaps in negative form (in the sense of the negative of a photograph), the stuff of denegation' (p. 61). Master signifiers, furthermore, 'usually mask their opposites . . . they exist in a polarized form' (p. 63). The openly expressed aspect of the master signifier props up an ego – that is, the imagined identity of a subject or community – while the unenunciated aspect remains 'buried in the unconscious . . . constantly pushing up its opposite number' (p. 63). The function of the master signifier is thus to redirect potentially painful or anxiety-provoking signifiers, and to do so in such a way 'that a signifying chain with the opposite, bearable, or even comforting meaning emerges' (p. 63). Clinically, Bailly's injunction is vital: we need to investigate the negated underside of a given master signifier. We must ask: what is it that the master signifier holds at bay and keeps beyond the domain of the thinkable?

How then to understand this unenunciated aspect in respect of the massive proliferation of commemorative practices that took place in South Africa around the time of Mandela's death? The intuitive response would be to say that these significations celebrated Mandela's life, affirmed all that he had achieved. Then again, following the insight that master signifiers often mask their opposites, we might take a different tack. We might question whether this commemorative impulse was propelled by the immanent failure of, or disbelief in, the vision of the integrated South Africa that Mandela championed. Perhaps this multitude of symbolic gestures attempted to affirm such a unified social reality (along the lines of Mandela's 'rainbow nation') precisely in response to mounting evidence of *growing social and political divisions*. Perhaps then the surge of commemorative practices indicated less the truth of the political changes Mandela had secured than the fact that South Africans feared that they *might fail to believe in such changes*. The constant activity of Mandela signification, in other words, can be read as a response to the sense that many of the country's old divisions were resurfacing.[19]

This speculative exercise sheds light on the role of the master signifier both in bolstering ego-affirming fantasies, and in concealing disruptive, anxiety-provoking associations. We can extend this argument by querying how Mandela acts as a site of repression. Posel's (2014) recent discussion of the politics of spectacle in post-apartheid South Africa proves a valuable resource here. A crucial part of Posel's analysis concerns the controversial figure of Julius Malema, the 'angry, unruly bad boy of post-apartheid politics' (p. 32) who Posel positions as a type of 'negative Mandela':

> Malema entered the public sphere as a counterpoint to Nelson Mandela unsettling the iconography of non-racialism, reasserting an angry and confrontational version of race that reinstated the spectre of violent conflagration that Mandela's 'miracle' held at bay.
>
> (p. 32)

While it is certainly the case that the mythic Mandela is both 'the condition and counterpoint of Malema's public persona' (p. 35), Posel's further descriptions suggests something in addition, a type of negation, a return of the repressed:

> If Mandela was the national archetype of adult wisdom, the Black man willing to reconcile and embrace fellow White citizens, Malema styled himself as the quintessentially angry Black man: youthful militant refusing to cow-tow

to his political elders, masculinist 'revolutionary', avowedly confrontational on racial issues.

(p. 39)

While the characterization of Malema as 'the symbolic counterpart' of Mandela is apt, it does not quite do justice to the dynamic underlying the relationship between these signifiers. Malema, we might venture, is the repressed truth of Mandela.[20] Malema emerges as the underside, the return of what was so effectively repressed by Mandela.[21] The remarkable success of Mandela as master signifier may be said to have much to do particularly for White South Africa – with what it kept at bay, namely, all that today is signified by 'Malema'. In this sense, it is not only – to invert Posel's argument – that Mandela be seen as a condition of possibility for Malema, but Malema, or what Malema signifies, that acts as *a condition of possibility for Mandela*.

Master signifiers and repression

My objective in the foregoing discussion has not been to discredit political or sociological applications of the master signifier concept. This literature usefully stresses how master signifiers operate ideologically at the level of discourse to engender effects of hegemony, to weave together a field of discursive elements, and thus to consolidate forms of mass identification. In all of these ways, we stand to benefit from this literature. That being said, much of this literature does run the risk of equating the master signifier with the processes of discursive hegemony in ways which overlook – or underplay – the role of unconscious dynamics of repression.[22]

Reference to the clinical literature shows how the master signifier operates also as a psychical – and not merely discursive – function. It does so moreover at the level of the subject, in accordance with a libidinal economy, to defensively bolster an ego, and to mobilize effects of fantasy and repression. Any adequate analysis of a master signifier needs to consider not only apparent overflows of meaning, but also those points where meaning seizes up and associations are halted; not only how multiple meanings come to be articulated under the ascendancy of a hegemonic signifier, but the various repressed and negated signifiers – the unenunciated and unarticulated – that the master signifier *as ego-function* routinely elides.[23] Simply put: the master signifier is not a properly psychoanalytic concept if it fails to take into account the role of desire, which is inevitably also to consider the unconscious and the multiple defences that arise around it.[24]

What is the unary trait?

A significant portion of the previous chapter was devoted to sketching the paradigmatic differences between imaginary and symbolic identifications. What arises now is the task of properly elaborating the mechanisms underlying the symbolic indeed, the *foundational* modes of identification that pre-empt imaginary identification and lie beyond the horizon of the ego. Van Haute (2002) draws attention to the importance of such a conceptualization. If the subject is to become a member of the symbolic network (or 'community') within a given society, they need to be able to take on a relationship to the big Other. This relationship, moreover, needs to be stable; the big Other must be kept at the right distance: neither threateningly too close, nor so distant that social conventions and meanings become vague and unintelligible. The relation to the Other should, ideally, NOT be characterized by the oscillations between aggression and narcissism so typical of imaginary inter-subjectivity. Differently put: *non-psychotic* subjectivity requires that we maintain a relationship with the Other that is not of a predominantly imaginary sort.[25] Imaginary identification, after all, reduces the other to an equal, and thus fails to recognize the alterity (the *otherness*, the 'unidentifiable with') quality of the Other.[26] So, how then is the subject to relate to this Other which resists imaginary domestication and retains its 'non-subjective' quality? Lacan's answer: via an isolated trait, the *trait unaire*.

Before proceeding any further, let us offer an illustration of the unary trait. In *The Rest is Noise*, his history of twentieth-century music, Alex Ross (2007) considers the paradox underlying one of Adolf Hitler's political inspirations. In 1906 Hitler attended a Vienna performance of Wagner's opera *Tristan*, and was riveted by what he saw. That Hitler idolized Wagner is well known; it is likewise well documented that Hitler claimed a performance of Wagner's *Rienzi* inspired him to enter politics. What is less commonly noted, as Ross stresses, is that the conductor of the 1906 production that so transfixed Hitler was none other than the famous Jewish composer Gustav Mahler. There was, as Ross puts it,

> a strange displacement going on . . . given that a Jew occupied the podium during what was may have been the most tremendous musical experience of Hitler's life. Was Mahler a tormenting symbol of Jewish power amid Hitler's failures? Or did the young man identify with Mahler's aura, his ability to command forces with a wave of his arms? In photographs, certain of the Führer's oratorical poses seem vaguely characteristic of Mahler's conducting – the right hand raised in a clenched, rotated fist, the left hand drawing back in a clawlike motion.
>
> (p. 341)

That Hitler may have identified with Mahler makes for a striking example of the partiality of certain identifications.[27] It demonstrates that identification with a signifier in the field of the Other might effectively bypass the requirements of imaginary resemblance (the need to identify with the other as a whole or an image). Ross's speculations seem at first to miss the mark precisely for this reason (positing thematic or imaginary identifications with Mahler's aura, etc.), but then he latches onto the role of the trait-of-identification of the composer's pose. It is this singular feature which provides the foothold for a different order of identification, an identification-of-difference enabled by the repetition of a key signifier.

The mark of difference

I mentioned at the outset of this chapter that Lacan was critical of much in Freud's *massenpsychologie*. A crucial exception was Freud's reference to '*ein einziger Zug*'. In speaking of those 'opportunistic' identifications which presume no tie of love or affection to the object of identification, Freud famously comments that the identification in question 'is a partial and extremely limited one and only borrows a single trait ("*ein einziger Zug*") from the person who is its object' (Freud, SE 18, p. 107/p. 136). Here, as elsewhere, we see how adept Lacan is at refurbishing a Freudian idea, building upon a discrete but crucial Freudian qualification with the conceptual tools of structural linguistics.

This is an inspired move. This idea of a single, limited trait chimes perfectly with the differential quality with which Saussure qualifies the relationship between signifiers. This is a relationship, to reiterate, which is not of substance or image, but of *pure difference*. It is important thus to note that 'unary' is not 'unitary' in a sense implying a *unifying* function. Lacan borrows the term from set theory, in which it refers to the attribute *of consisting or involving a single element*.[28] What is 'unary' cannot be said to be unique on the basis of any ostensibly positive content or inherent properties. This being said, the unary element remains unique albeit in a distinct sense: it is singular inasmuch as it can always be differentiated from similar – indeed, often *identical* – marks or traces in a given set or sequence. What is in question is a difference of pure *relation* rather than of kind; we are concerned with *signifying* as opposed to qualitative difference.

Take the example of a repeated drum beat. The sound of each beat could be exactly the same. However, despite that they are in this respect identical, each beat is nevertheless crucially different by virtue of the fact that each has a different place in the resulting sequence. Each strike of the drum shares this elementary feature: it has a *different* position in the progression of beats, in the chain of repetitions. What matters is not any intrinsic quality of the beats (as played louder or softer, in a more muffled and echoing way, etc.): their 'unary' quality depends on the fact of a chain, a sequence of, we might say, *a counting:* this is what makes the elements different to one another.

From object to mark

Let us now run through several defining features of the unary trait. Unary trait identifications, first, involve the taking on of an isolated and typically unremarkable quality of the Other (it is precisely in this sense, after all, that they are 'unary', in the sense of being *composed of a single element*). The qualification of the unary trait as a *signifier* is again vital: what is in question is not the *meaning* of the trait (meaning being within the domain of the imaginary):

> The child identifies ... not with the other as a whole as *Gestalt* but only
> with a detail that is insignificant in itself. Lacan says that these 'specific traits'
> are 'emblems' of the power of the Other ... They are signifiers in which
> the power of the Other takes on a concrete form, or in which this power
> is represented in a concrete way.
>
> (Van Haute, 2002, p. 95)

So, in the case of the young psychoanalytic trainee who takes on a 'single trait'
of the influential analyst whose career they hope to emulate, the trait in question
will typically be of a meaningless sort (a signifier detached from any definitive
signification), such as how the senior figure raises their eyebrow when asking a
question, or modulates their voice when expressing concern. It would be missing
the point if we tried to read meaning into the trait (the upturned eyebrow as
connoting inquisitiveness, etc.). To reiterate: the unary trait is a formal feature (a
mark, a trace) that has no positive meaning.

A transference relation

Unary trait identifications, second, entail a hierarchical dimension. This hierarchical aspect is evident in many of the examples sprinkled across the literature, of
children identifying with parental figures, students with teachers, analysands with
analysts, etc.[29] Although this power-differential often goes largely unremarked upon
as such, it is indispensable to the operation of the unary trait. How so? Well, such
a differential signals the presence of the Other (the 'subject supposed to know'),
which in turn implies a transference relation, that is, a relationship of love and/or
authority. The presence of the Other also indicates the place of symbolic ego-ideals.
The identification with a unary trait taken from the field of the Other thus plays
a pivotal role in constituting ego-ideals for the subject. Lacan insists on this point
in a rather cryptic passage from *The Subversion of the Subject*, where he stresses the
role of 'the locus of the Other' before challenging his audience to

> [t]ake just one signifier as an insignia of this omnipotence ... of this wholly
> potential power, of this birth of possibility, and you have the unary trait which
> filling in the ... mark the subject receives from the signifier ... [results] in
> the first identification that forms the ego-ideal.
>
> (2006, p. 684)

Foundational identification

A third feature comes to light here. Unary trait identifications play a foundational
role for the subject. Take for instance Bracher's (1994) description of the *trait unaire*
'as the earliest significance through which the child experiences itself':

[the master signifier] constitutes the subject's primary identification. . . . [a] primary identification [that] continues throughout the subject's existence to exercise a decisive influence on the subject's desire, thought, perception, and behaviour.

(p. 111)

We should be wary here of slipping into the presumptions of developmental psychology. As we saw in Chapter 3, Lacan's sense of psychic temporality follows the logic of structures rather than any idea of developmental phases or sequences. It adheres, furthermore, to the logic of Freud's (1950) deferred action (*nachträglichkeit*), that is, it is a *retroactive* rather than an obviously linear causality. It is not simply then a case of locating a given unary trait which has formed the nucleus of myriad subsequent identifications. The unary trait is better approached as a logical presumption, a necessary structural precursor to symbolic identifications that have already occurred.

While unary traits do undoubtedly play a crucial role in the emergence of the subject as such, they should not be seen as applying exclusively to early childhood. Rather than stressing the 'primal' or 'originary' quality of the unary trait – qualifications, which while accurate, imply a 'once only' action that is consigned to an early critical period in the life of the subject – we should think of unary traits along the lines of proto-identifications, that is, as setting the groundwork for the very possibility of identification. They make the paradigm of identification possible. Hence Johnston's (2008) characterization: unary traits work as 'co-ordinates shaping the contours of identification' (p. 213). Clearly then – and as was implicit in our foregoing examples – unary trait identifications also take place later in life, precisely when a structural shift in identification occurs.

Insignia of the Other

The unary trait does not emerge in a simply random way, or from just any instance of signification. As we have already seen: it must be derived from the field of the Other, first, and under conditions of transference, second. There is thus something akin to an intimate connection as Parker (2007) stresses between the unary trait and the Other. What is extracted from the Other is not an object however - this is our fourth defining feature - but a symbolic element. Hence Lacan's characterization of the unary trait as a type of *insignia* or *emblem*. It perhaps helps to reiterate that the Other cannot be 'imaginarised', which is to say that it cannot be incorporated as a whole, as an image.

This pertains to whatever is taken from the Other as the basis of a unary trait identification: it surpasses the dimensions of an imaginary object; it is severed from the range of *imaginary* associations with the Other. The trait, after all, is a *signifier*, not an image. More accurately, as Lacan (1979) asserts, the unary trait is the transition point between imaginary object and pure symbolic element. This is the case with emblems, insignia, which bear the imprint of an origin, while nevertheless remaining abstract enough to support difference, that is, to allow for a degree of singularity in those that wear them.

We need guard against presuming that unary trait identifications involve a transmission of themes or a series of parallel similarities between the Other and identifying subject. Hitler's apparent assumption of Mahler's pose, for example, neglects all other aspects of the composer's person, although crucially it occurs under the spell of transference with this Other. So even though something is snatched from the Other – an insignia, an emblem – this very process, as discussed above, enables singularity: it puts an end to the alienating destiny of being wholly subsumed within, or determined by the Other. Lacan (1979) accordingly asserts that the unary trait is what allows a distinction to be made between two elements *beyond an identity of resemblance*.

The singularity of the subject

The unary trait, says Hewitson (2014), marks the point of intersection between the imaginary and the symbolic:

> [it] allows the subject to effect a movement that situates him in the latter rather than the former. The unary trait marks the point at which an imaginary identification with . . . [Freud's] *einziger Zug* . . . can start to function instead as a signifying identification. Lacan's innovation on Freud's initial insight was to move us beyond thinking of these unary traits as merely imaginary traits, and conceive of them as purely formal marks . . . *Ein einziger Zug* is a signifier that can give to the subject a place in the symbolic order. It provides . . . a singularity, a uniqueness, that is the opposite of the pathological coincidence of self and other that is a feature of the imaginary register.

Identification with the unary trait engenders difference and instantiates something new. Hence Lacan's assertion that the unary trait is 'an emblem of . . . omnipotence . . . of [a] wholly potential power . . . [the] birth of possibility' (2006, p. 684). In Seminar IX, Lacan similarly invokes the *einziger Zug* precisely as a 'support for difference'; as entailing 'the power of radical otherness'; and as establishing the singularity of the subject (lesson of 6 December 1961). The unary trait, says Van Haute (2002), anchors the subject

> in an order that transcends him . . . this identification establishes an attachment to the Other that does not fail to recognize her alterity, and this is precisely how the Other can (continue to) function as a representative of an order that essentially transcends the subject . . . identification with the 'specific trait' determines desire without immediately reducing it to a pure duplication of the (imaginary) other . . . the [unary] trait is a sort of fixed point marking the place from which the subject can become something.

(p. 96)

This then is our fifth crucial feature of the unary trait: it enables the singular subject to come into being.

A non-psychological trait

Eyers (2012) highlights the type of symbolic agency that now becomes possible in this view of the subject. 'Lacan', he says, 'finds a certain *active* quality in the unary trait, such that the nascent subject actively *finds* or *marks* the trait it requires to become amenable to symbolic logic' (p. 58). In what serves as an adept recapitulation of many of the key aspects of the concept discussed thus far, Eyers describes the unary trait as

> a primitive marker of being absolutely distinct from any sense of subjective 'personhood', even as it might provide the minimal grounds for the later development of such an Imaginary sense of self . . . [As] well as marking the birth of the subject, the unary trait marks the beginnings of the Symbolic – as something both radically intertwined with the emergence of subjectivity and radically *opaque* to that emergent subjectivity – and the extent to which Lacan will insist on the indivisibility of this trait, this 'beginning' that will persist, and which can only reinforce the sense in which signification is a material process of inscription quite separate from Imaginary forms of subjective intentionality.
>
> (p. 58)

The is a non-egoic intentionality, distinct both from imaginary processes and from the symbolic (the Other's/signifier's) constitution of the subject. The unary trait, thus conceptualized, is at the same time a type of historical marking which underlies the very emergence of the subject (and the symbolic *for* the subject) and a marker of the subject's existence that pre-empts subsequent imaginary forms. Eyers repeatedly emphasizes the materiality of the process. Instances of inscription, 'writing', marking are stressed so as to ensure we do not fall prey to viewing this as a type of 'internal' or predominantly psychological process.

Likewise concerned with the non-psychological status of the unary trait – our final defining feature – is Moncayo (2012) who warns the unary trait is not akin to a character trait as it is known in the psychology. 'Lacan's unary trait is more of a trace or a stroke than a trait in psychological or genetic sense', he insists, adding that we need conceive of the unary trait as more than anything else, a *trace*,[30] 'a singularity, a state or an instance in time' (Moncayo, 2012, pp. 20–21). For this reason Moncayo prefers the terminology of the 'unary trace' to the 'unary trait', a move which goes some way to de-substantializing (indeed, de-psychologizing) the concept altogether.[31] Johnston (2008) likewise stresses the role of the unary trait as a 'bare insignia or mark', a 'maximally minimal trait', that 'succeeds at being an inscription/trace that evokes the presence of subjectivity without relying on reference to a wealth of concrete empirical features' (2008, p. 218). The operation of the unary signifier is thus better characterized as *linguistic* than as in any way psychological, as subsisting in the *trace* or *inscription* rather than in any type of psychological substance.

Symbolic inscription

As an illustration of the unary trait as mode of inscription, we might picture a prisoner, scratching lines on the wall of his cell. We might also take up Lacan's example in Seminar XI (1979) and imagine the prehistoric cave-dweller who engraves marks on a piece of ivory as a means of recording their kills. What is in question in these examples is not the making of an image, but the keeping of a tally, an act of historical inscription. These marks belong to the register of history rather than to that resemblance. This being said, this minimal mode of transcription amounts to more than merely a 'counting the count'. Why?

In the prisoner's scratches, the neanderthal's carvings, we have an elementary differentiating sequence, in which the first mark, initially in isolation, is followed by a second and a third and so on, each of which takes its place in a subsequent chain. Such a symbolic order – a chain of signifiers – poses the question of this subject's position, their place. The act of counting entails the presumption of the subject, the subject that is 'counted into' the sequence they record.[32]

Here we need to proceed carefully. It is tempting to see these marks as retaining an indexical quality (like a palm-print on a window or a footprint in mud which is itself the evidence that someone made them). While there is no doubt a degree of the indexical at play here, Lacan's point is more nuanced. The idea is not simply that markings bear the imprint of the marker (a point that Lacan does admittedly explore with reference to the unary trait in Seminar X[33]). For after all, a mode of imaginary presence is still implied by the notion of the indexical marker, by the idea that the marker is the maker of the markings. Lacan's assertion is rather that a differentiating sequence, precisely as a rudimentary symbolic system, produces a subject not simply *within* but *by* its signifying operations.[34] The idea is to get away from the imaginary dimension of reference, indeed, to isolate *differentiality* itself as the underlying mechanism of formative symbolic identifications.[35] This, importantly, is why Lacan's most effective examples of the unary trait involve the subject being, as we have already said, 'counted into' the sequence they record. This is the unary trait functioning at its purest, ensuring identification through nothing but operations of difference.

There is, however, arguably some room for leeway here. We know that the symbolic can never be completely exorcised of all traces of the imaginary, and that Lacan speaks of the unary trait as a *transition point* between imaginary and symbolic forms (as in the case of bearing the insignia of the Other). We might argue then that many unary trait signifiers still function at least partly as *traces*, as *markers of existence* which retain some minimal imprint of their makers. Numerous prospective examples spring to mind: the school-boy carving his name into a desk, the couple inscribing joined initials on a park-bench, the tags of the graffiti artist.[36] In each case such markings impart a symbolic existence to those who made them. This is the 'meta-referential' context to any such mark: 'I was here', 'We were here', or, more minimally, 'I was', 'We were', or, reduced even further: 'A subject was'.[37]

A powerful illustration of a signifier imparting a symbolic existence to its maker is to be found in reference to the so-called Dakota Uprising of 1862. In December of that year, in the middle of the Civil War, the US Government executed 30 Sioux warriors who were said to have participated in the massacre of 800 Whites. Many of those who witnessed the execution described an unforgettable moment that occurred just before the men were put to death. As they were waiting to be hanged, each of the condemned men shouted: 'I am here!' Such an act of signification, while in one sense clearly redundant, is perhaps best understood along the lines described above, that is, as a means of marking the symbolic existence of the subject. Arguably, unary trait identification always involves this dimension of the symbolic *act*.[38] The unary trait must as in the case of Hitler's re-use of Mahler's gesture be enacted, *performed* by the subject who will both thus be differentiated and 'singularized' as a result.

The (linguistic) subject of singularity

We have covered a considerable distance since broaching the topic of identification at the beginning of the previous chapter. The notions of the master signifier and the unary trait are, as I have tried to show, of crucial significance in Lacan's journey away from imaginary (ego-based) and thereby psychological conceptualizations of identity. In the case of both such conceptualizations identification is less a psychological achievement or process than a linguistic function, an effect of the signifier in the *marking* of the subject.

It is important to underline exactly why the theorization of the unary trait (in particular) represented such a crucial advance for Lacanian theory. It enabled Lacan to move beyond the well-worn psychoanalytic vocabulary of incorporation and introjection, and to supplement his own terminology of resemblance and reflection as the key processes of identification. In contrast to Lacan's earlier emphasis on illusory totality, remarks Rose (1986), we are now called upon to see identity as a function of *repeated difference*. It is via reference to the structure of linguistic insistence that Lacan provides the basis for a

> potentially structuralist concept of identity, where each element is distinct from its own origin, different at each new instance of its repetition and identical only in its opposition to all other elements in the signifying chain.
> (Rose, pp. 184–185)

Identification here – as I hope is by now clear – occurs not on the basis of object-resemblance, but according to the differential functioning of language. When the subject repeats a key signifier drawn from the Other, this gesture is different to its point of origin; it is more than an echo or a miming of what has gone before.

This is how identification in respect of the Other occurs: not on the basis of incorporated images, but through a differential mode of marking through which the subject is realized as something new.

Lacan's conceptual achievement is worth highlighting. Up until the early 1960s he had never tired of emphasizing the agency of the language ('the signifier') over and above that of the subject. He had just as relentlessly stressed that the subject was the subject-of-lack, subject *to* language, alienated, in fact, both by the imaginary regime of images and the by the symbolic order (the Other). The question had become unavoidable: in way was the subject not mere epiphenomenon? How was this subject to be differentiated from insubstantiality?

We can see now then how, with the notion of the unary trait, Lacan seemingly achieved two apparently irreconcilable goals. He continued to insist that the subject was both the effect *of*, and contingent *upon*, the signifier emerging in the domain of the Other. Nevertheless, focusing on the differentiating function of signifiers and on the unary trait as the basis for the singularity of the subject, he succeeded in showing that this subject-as-effect-of-the-signifier is something more than a merely derivative entity, an ontological void. We are left then with an intriguing depiction of how subjectivity emerges not by means of psychology defined in the sense of imaginary operations (via the role of objects or images), but on the basis of a differentiating function, that is, as a result of the operation of language. Hence the at first seemingly implausible Lacanian idea: the subject emerges as an effect of the signifier.

Notes

1 The objection can of course be made that the importance of the symbolic (and 'symbolic efficacy') is already apparent in Lacan's formulations of the mirror stage, and is not new as such.

2 This critique is most apparent in Lacan's *Beyond the "Reality Principle"*. While he uses the term libido there to refer to "the metabolism of the sexual functions in man" (2006, p. 73), and as a means of understanding the dynamic investment made in images, he nevertheless rejects what he calls the substantialist hypothesis that teats libido as a type of matter or (presumably) biological endowment.

3 The fact that one could write a Lacanian critique of Freud's 'libidinal economy of the mass' should not distract us from the fact that there are, similarly, contrary shifts of emphasis and theorization apparent within the corpus of Lacan's own work. There is no need to apologize for such apparently contradictory shifts as they emerge between – or within – the relative domains of Freudian and Lacanian theory. The critical revision of earlier concepts is an indication both that we need to be vigilant regards the dogmas of existing theory and that psychoanalytic conceptualization needs to be attentive to the historical contingencies of the clinic.

4 Hoens (2016) likewise draws attention to Lacan's divergence from Freud in respect of group formations. For Lacan, 'a group does not need to depend on a leader or an ideal in order to show . . . organization and coherence'. Lacan questioned 'the necessity of a "point" (leader, ideal. . .) outside of yet required for, any mutual, "horizontal" identification'.

5 Despite differences of conceptual emphasis, Stavrakakis (1999) usefully highlights a vital link between Freud's mass psychology and Lacanian theory: 'In Freud's view . . . what can unite thousands or millions of people is the relation – and the libidinal investment

of this relation – of each one of them to a leader . . . or an idea occupying the position of a *point de capiton* [or master signifier] . . . a common point of reference' (p. 78).

6 This is an all too often error of perspective that slips into uses of Lacanian theory (most notably perhaps in relation to the notion of the phallus). We know, we *insist* that the-Name-of-the-Father, a master signifier, the phallus, etc., are not substantial (or imaginary) entities but are precisely *signifiers*, yet as soon as we think of clinical case material there is the temptation to 'imaginarise' such signifiers. This is certainly the case – as we will see – in investigating Mandela as signifier, where there is a constant tendency to think of Mandela as the man, the heroic figure, rather than as the signifier that has come to represent him (for yet other signifiers).

7 One might expect, in line with Freudian theory, that a series of parental values might feature here, even if they are not explicitly identified as such.

8 In such moments – such is the Lacanian thesis – it is typically the imperfections of the object that come most immediately to mind. Such points of lack are distinctive of the object and prove that it has come to function as *objet a* (object cause of desire) for us. Hence Lacan's oft-cited description of being loved by another as *giving something one doesn't have to someone who doesn't want it*. In other words: to be loved means giving one's lack to another who, ideally, would prefer not to have their own lack filled in this way, because this is what sustains their desire. As Miller (2008) notes of love, 'It's not giving what you possess, goods and presents; it's giving something else that you don't possess, which goes beyond you . . . To do that you have to assume your lack, your "castration"'.

9 The only appropriate response to such a question, avers Leader (1996), a question which invokes the structural impossibility of saying it all, is an answer in which this impasse is transposed into a formal (or grammatical) failing of language itself. The appropriate response then, to the question 'How much do I love you?' would be something like: 'Big'.

10 This is the process which, as noted in Chapter 3, results in the establishment of the big Other as the posited authority that can halt this infinite regress of signifiers.

11 In 'The subversion of the subject', Lacan puts it this way: 'My definition of the signi-fier (there is no other) is as follows: a signifier is what represents the subject to another signifier' (2006, pp 693–694).

12 This, incidentally, provides a supplementary perspective on the topic of mass identifi-cation discussed in the last chapter.

13 As Neill (2011) observes, the basis of the master signifier concept is to be found in Lacan's (1993) earlier notion of the 'quilting point', the *point de capiton*, that is, the signifier that halts the otherwise endless movement of signification (of metaphoric substitution and metonymic combination).

14 I include counter-identification as itself a form of identification here, such that even rejections of the historical figure or master signifier in question may be said to maintain a tacit (indeed, *negative*) identification with what is being rejected.

15 Historically, this much seems difficult to dispute: Mandela more than any other signifier, proved capable of lending moral purpose and meaning to South Africa's political transition, to the multiple contradictions underlying the post-apartheid era. This is perhaps what proved so anxiety-provoking for many South Africans about Mandela's declining health in late 2013: the prospect that the country would lack a crucial 'race mediator', i.e. a political figure who not only speaks powerfully to black and white groupings, but who also enables them to speak with and to one another.

16 This link between master signifiers and affect is worth stressing, not only because it refers back to the topic of the foregoing chapter – the libidinal dynamics of mass identification – but also because it helps avoid the impression that we are dealing with two wholly different theories of identification, one, Freud's, which deals with libidinal ties, and another, Lacan's which focuses entirely on the role of signifiers and language.

17 Laclau continues:

Affect is not some vague emotion external to signification, for it can only constitute itself on the basis of overdetermining a signifying chain . . . the signifier 'rat' [in Freud's case of the Raman] is so affectively overcharged because it evokes – overdetermines – a plurality of currents of unconscious thoughts – money, sex, the father, and so on.

(Laclau, in Glynos and Stavrakakis, 2010, p. 235)

Furthermore:

the distinction between affect and the symbolic is intra- and not extra-discursive [and] is perfectly compatible with maintaining that some elements of a discursive formation may be highly cathected while others are not . . . What is being denied is the idea . . . that this unevenness in cathectic investment should be explained by the action of a force fully outside the discursive field.

(p. 239)

Such a view, says Laclau, risks positing a radical opposition between the symbolic and what lies outside the symbolic, an opposition which conflicts with the basic premises of Lacanian theory.

18 One of the reasons why Lacan's work on the signifier cannot be thought of as merely linguistic, is that he takes into account the dimension of *the drive*. This not only means that using the signifier entails libidinous gratification, but that what sets our use of signifiers in motion is a fundamental deadlock (a 'real'). Stijn Vanheule and I have addressed this point elsewhere: We need to take into account both the forms of libidinal enjoyment produced in and through speech, and the fact that such linguistic processes are set in motion by an impasse, an impossibility at the level of communication and signification. Indeed, the master signifier only obtains its privileged position in discourse because it comes as an answer to this fundamental deadlock . . . Lacan posits that inside discourse a libidinous element fuels the use of the master signifier . . . a passionate attachment that simultaneously drives and yet defies communicability (Hook and Vanheule, 2016).

19 This gives us a Lacanian response to the question of what it is we hope to attain with the building of monuments. The sheer number of Mandela-related monuments and commemorations in South Africa is a clear signal that the country was fortifying a mode of belief, concretizing a cherished set of ideals and subjective/societal investments. That is, we don't erect monuments simply to celebrate and affirm what we already know. We build and sustain monuments so that we will continue to know and believe what may otherwise be erased through various forms of uncertainty or doubt. We build monuments to make the Other believe.

20 There is a nice formal bridge here at the level of the signifier, which will not go unnoticed by Lacanians: Mandela and 'Malema' are near homonyms.

21 While Posel doesn't explicitly utilize the term, the concept of repression clearly informs her analysis: juxtaposing the spectacular public life of Julius Malema . . . with that of Nelson Mandela draws attention to . . . the 'haunting' presence of the past . . . If the mythic Mandela championed the project of 'national reconciliation' – his symbolic powers put to the work of performing 'non-racialism' – Malema emerged as the symbolic counterpoint, marking the limits of this project: a ghostly reminder of the abiding racial wounds that have endured (2014, p. 35).

22 It is not difficult to understand why this is so: discourse analysis, in adherence with the later Foucault's (1990) emphasis on the *productions* as opposed to *suppressions* of discourse, has long since proved averse to the concept of repression, seeing it as a concept freighted with problematic 'psychological' (and psychoanalytic) presumptions. Lacan approaches the issue differently: the concepts of repression and the unconscious are to be retained, but theorized precisely via the operations of the signifier.

23 True enough, the psychoanalytic dimension of the concept is not neglected by all political theorists. Stavrakakis (1997) and Glynos (2001), to note just two examples, remain attentive to the dynamics of repression and the fantasy-inducing aspects of master signifiers, aspects notably absent, as noted above, in definitions such as that provided by Gunkel (2014).

24 There is a further consideration here: clinical work with a given master-signifier would not fail to investigate the various double meanings and homonymic displacements associated with such a term. Perhaps the most famous example of such verbal bridges in Freud's work concerns the signifier '*ratten*' in the Ratman case. As Laclau (2004) points out, associations occur here both at the level of the signified ('rat' becomes associated with 'penis' because both can spread diseases) and at the level of the signifier (the German 'ratten' means instalments, '*speilratten*' means gambling, both of which become entwined within the Ratman's complex). Given that this is how the unconscious works – in operations of the signifier – this type of investigation is essential in any consideration of the master signifier as element in psychical economy.

25 The 'imaginarization' of the Other is one way of conceptualizing psychosis, hence Rogers' (2016) reference to the 'Imaginary Other' in her description of psychotic experience.

26 I am referring of course to the trans-subjective dimension of the Other as existing beyond the level of inter-subjectivity as discussed in Chapters 1 and 3.

27 It suggests – reiterating a point made in the previous chapter – that identification can occur in the absence of any loving libidinal attachment, indeed, even in a context of racist (or Anti-Semitic) animosity.

28 'Unary' is thus preferable to 'single' in stressing the 'extreme reduction . . . of all the opportunities for qualitative difference' (Lacan, Seminar IX, 29 November 1961).

29 This consideration goes some way to explaining the predominance of the *paternal* identifications cited by Freud, which are to be understood not only in the literal or delimited sense of the term but as connoting broader factors of authority and/or power.

30 While I appreciate Moncayo's (2012) objective in making such a change, I prefer to retain the notion of 'trait' for the reason that unary traits do indeed operate as traits in the sense at least of acting as fixing-points of subsequent identifications. Nonetheless, Moncayo is certainly right to reiterate that such traits are made possible by the signifier's operation of differentiation rather than by any psychological substance.

31 Interestingly, in light of our foregoing discussion, Moncayo adds also adds that 'Strictly speaking, the ideal ego and the ego-ideal are unary traces or instances and moments rather than substantial entities' (2012, p. 42). Both ideal-ego and ego-ideal, continues Moncayo, stand in for the subject and do so in the face of the void of inherent or substantial identity.

32 Neill (2011) makes the same point: 'The subject is both the one who puts the notch on the cave wall and the one who signifies something . . . he is both the sender and receiver of the same message' (p. 18).

33 Lacan explores this indexical dimension with reference to Robinson Crusoe's discovery of footprints in the sand of what he had hitherto imagined to be a deserted island (see Parker, 2007).

34 It helps here perhaps to recall our earlier description of how the S2 to S1 relationship brings into being the split subject of the signifier.

35 That is to say, the subject of *singularity* is implicated more by the making of the mark and its *differential placement within a symbolic system*, than what it stands for.

36 In respect of graffiti: what matters here, from the Lacanian perspective we are developing, is not so much the artistic prowess of the artist, or even the facts of a particularly daring or accomplished image, but the historic mark constituted by their being made, and being made by someone. The mark – even if it is part of an elaborate array of markings – plays its part in making a subject. Interestingly, this facet of the subject's own inscription in their aesthetic production became a feature of Abstract Expressionism, where the 'gestural mark', i.e. the evidence of the artist's own hand, came to ensure the distinctiveness and authenticity of the work (beyond any appeal to expertise of technique, etc.). One Lacanian lesson here is that however impressive the aesthetic production on display might be, the content of the image can be viewed as of secondary importance. The image can be seen as a means to an end, the imaginary prop supporting the work's more primary function as a collection of marks by means of which the subject is afforded symbolic singularity.

37 An example of how the subject being imbued a symbolic existence by virtue of a marking signifier can be found in the biography of Robert Sobukwe, the radical Pan-Africanist opponent of the apartheid order, condemned by the South African government to 6 years of solitary confinement on Robben Island. In a 1957 article in the *Africanist*, he includes what at first seems a peripheral anecdote:

> There is a song they sing in the deserted villages of Africa. It goes:
>
> *Noraa sikhona, noma sesifile*
> *Bakusala besho, bethi sasikhona!*
>
> (While we live, and even after we are gone,
> They will remain saying, WE ONCE WERE!)
> That . . . is the meaning of our struggle!
>
> (Sobukwe, 2013. p. 465)

The temporality of such a signification – the future anterior of what 'will have been' – suits the role of the unary trait as a *historical* marker reaching simultaneously toward the future. Furthermore, the context of this reflection – that of political resistance – nicely highlights how such a 'marking of existence' plays its part in setting the subject apart from the determining authority of the Other.

38 While this dramatic example of a symbolic act of historical inscription is not necessarily an instance of the unary trait as such, it nonetheless illustrates an irreducible aspect of the concept: it marks the existence of a singular subject.

6

ON THE SUBJECT OF PSYCHOLOGY

The vanishing subject

In an overview of Lacanian theory in the context of child analysis, Leonardo Rodriquez (1999) pinpoints what during the 1950s Lacan took to be the overarching agenda of a psychoanalytic treatment:

> for Lacan the aim of analysis was the *realisation* of the subject, which is only possible in speech, in the utterance of the truthful word. The subject constitutes him-/herself *in* and *as* what he/she says in analysis to his/her listener, the analyst. In gaining access to that primary language in which desire is written (albeit always incompletely), in talking it aloud, the subject does not simply learn about what is said there. More importantly, the operation itself is constitutive of him-/herself as a subject.
>
> (p. 116)

This clinical objective can be interestingly juxtaposed with the conclusions that Malcolm Bowie (1991) reaches on the nature of the Lacanian subject:

> 'The subject' is no longer a substance endowed with qualities, or a fixed shape possessing dimensions, or a container awaiting the multifarious contents that experience provides: it is a series of events within language, a procession of turns, tropes and inflections.
>
> (p. 76)

These two descriptions challenge many of our understandings of what a subject is. They both refute the assumption, commonplace to much psychology, of a self-reflexive subject – such as the participant of psychotherapy intent on gaining insight

– who might directly access the underlying elements of their subjectivity. More counter-intuitively yet in both the above accounts, the subject lacks the minimal continuity or permanence that is fundamental in many of our basic assumptions as to what 'subjectivity' is.

The Lacanian subject is not a permanent or constant entity; it is an episodic, or vanishing phenomena. It is the subject *as event* which – like the unconscious itself – fades and resurfaces, proving not just elusive but essentially discontinuous. This subject is not in fact an 'entity' at all, certainly not in any substantial sense. It is rather a flash, a pulse, a spark, a type of truth-possibility. Utterly contingent on the productions of speech that, paradoxically, it itself produces, this subject is at once constituted *in* and *as* speech. In this sense the subject encompasses an irreconcilability: it *is* the disjunction (the 'real') evinced between *the act of speaking* (enunciation) and *what is spoken* (statement), two facets of speech which can never quite be fully reconciled. At once something that is constituted (by speech) and self-constituting (in speaking) this subject-as-rift is nothing other than the *barred subject of the unconscious* which psychoanalysis endeavours to treat.

Having conducted a number of excursions into Lacanian theory in the previous chapters, it is time now, in this concluding chapter, to return to Lacan's critique of the psychological. My objective here is not to systematically work through Lacan's various criticisms. I want rather to register aspects of this critique and thus provide a retrospective backdrop to the preceding exposition of Lacanian concepts. My agenda is neither to evaluate Lacan's critique of the psychological, nor to adopt a defensive position in respect of the discipline of psychology. After all, Lacan's various criticisms of psychology – apposite as they often are – are perhaps less instructive regards what they tell us about psychology itself than they are in respect of how they encourage us to revise our understanding of the subject.[1]

There are, admittedly, several excellent existing studies that explore Lacan's critique of psychology (Pavón-Cuéllar, 2013, forthcoming; Parker, 2003, 2015c). While I will be guided in several respects by this literature, I will steer a different course. My approach adopted here – which aims to extend a series of emerging themes noted in the foregoing chapters – pivots on Lacan's notion of the subject. This proves an appropriate focus for this concluding chapter insofar as the Lacanian subject, in its inseparability from the unconscious and in its radical incommensurability with the ego, remains arguably the primary concept in the differentiation of Lacanian psychoanalysis from the terrain of the psychological.

Psychology's objects and objectifications

In Seminar I, Lacan pauses to consider the nature of the subject: 'What do we call the subject?' he asks, before answering: 'Quite precisely, what in the development of objectivation, is outside the object' (1988a, p. 194). This oblique definition provides a useful starting point for us: it situates the subject decisively beyond the imaginary impetus to 'objectivate', something that Lacan sees everywhere in the domain of the psychological.

The meaning of this term ('objectivation'), like so many others that Lacan deploys, is not immediately apparent, and it is worth pausing for a moment to offer a clarification. In what follows I will treat 'objectivation' as a compound concept entailing two aspects of psychological conceptualization that Lacan takes issue with. First, there is the objectifying tendency to treat aspects of psychic life and subjects as thing-like, as objects of knowledge and/or intervention. Such a tendency has clear connotations of control and/or influence, something rejected by both Freud and Lacan as profoundly anti-psychoanalytic. Second, there is the epistemological and scientific goal of *objectivity*, an objective that is similarly ill-suited to psychoanalysis inasmuch as the latter prioritizes a subjectivism of experience, or more importantly yet, the *psychical* over 'objective'. In referring to Lacan's 'anti-objectivism' below (a less clumsy term than 'anti-objectivation') I have both such meanings in mind.

Considering the relationship between psychoanalysis and criminology, Lacan stresses – in a clear swipe at psychology – that 'Psychoanalysis stops short at the objectification of the Id and proclaims the autonomy of an irreducibly subjective experience' (2006, p. 120). Lacan (2006) similarly describes himself as taking on 'nothing less than the status of the psychological object' (p. 131), preferring to such an approach a description of a 'phenomenology of the psychoanalytic relationship as it is experienced between doctor and patient' (p. 131). The writings of the 1950s make this much clear: psychoanalysis is – or should be – opposed to any form of psychological objectification:

> Psychoanalytic experience . . . proceeds entirely in . . . [the] subject-to-subject relationship, which means that it preserves a dimension that is irreducible to any psychology considered to be the objectification of individual properties.
> (Lacan, 2006, p. 176)

The objectifying tendency that Lacan associated with psychology, had, by the early 1950s, begun to spread to psychoanalysis. Even the notion of the unconscious, he averred, had been 'substantialized', and done so at the loss of adequate attention being paid to the immediacy of speech. The concepts of 'ego', 'id' and 'super-ego' were likewise being applied not so much as instances of psychical functioning but as psychical entities, as objects, a fact which amounted to a denial of the lived – and potentially transformative – reality of the unconscious as event. Malone and Friedlander (2000b) bring this Lacanian critique to bear on contemporary forms of American psychology:

> psychology's objectivistic, objectifying procedures do not and cannot provide us with adequate answers . . . We cannot afford to characterize subjectivity in terms of (a set of) fixed properties or attributes, for instance, rationality, need for attachment, etc. We must reject the vision of an isolated subject as the atavistic shadow of American ideology and psychology's experimental method.
> (p. 6)

For Lacan, the attempt to engender objects, to circumscribe and delimit the subject as a knowable entity, to create 'identities' of knowledge, remains an imaginary process, an instance of *méconnaissance*. Parker (2015c) puts it well when he notes that 'Lacan relentlessly *de-substantializes* phenomena that are usually reified by the discipline [of psychology] . . . that are rendered as if they were observable and empirically verifiable things' (p. 25).

'Apparatuses of objectivity'

There are multiple facets to Lacan's critique of psychological objectification, the first of which – Lacan's dismissal of the reification of various apparent 'subjective attributes' which come to be transformed into psychological objects of knowledge – links back to his historical critique of the discipline in his paper *Beyond the Reality Principle*.[2] Lacan (2006) takes issue there with the classificatory framework of late nineteenth-century psychology, which, in grouping its phenomena 'into sensations, perceptions, images, beliefs, logical operations, judgements and so on' had stooped to incorporating a series of concepts 'borrowed unchanged from scholastic psychology, which had itself borrowed it from centuries of philosophy' (p. 59). Such a derivative conceptual framework falls short, for psychoanalysis, in providing an adequate conception of psychical reality. These phenomena (sensations, perceptions, etc.) are not, according to Lacan

> objective things discovered in 'psychical reality' by psychological research, but, rather, ideological or theoretical deposits . . . residues of 'centuries of philosophy' . . . 'products of a sort of conceptual erosion' that detaches, isolates, solidifies, reifies and objectifies them, presenting them as a 'guarantee of truth', as undeniable evidence for psychology, as if they were objective things.
>
> (Pavón-Cuéllar, forthcoming)

Adapting concepts from the history of philosophy and scholastic psychology will not, for Lacan, suffice. A discrete area of scientific endeavour, after all, needs to develop the concepts and instruments that have been developed *within its own domain* and which are best suited to what it undertakes to study. Derivative ideas inherited from other disciplines cannot compete with concepts and methods developed through the dedicated clinical work of *attending to the speech of patients*. In short: the wrong concepts have been prioritized in the historical development of psychology. This is a problem confounded by the fact that in imposing such concepts upon the empirical field, psychology has screened out more salient clinical phenomena.

In its eagerness to model itself upon existing natural sciences and to assume their conceptual priorities and methods (experimentation, measurement, the isolation of cause-effect relations) the emerging discipline of psychology came to exclude a series of phenomena existing outside the operations of rational knowledge.

'[B]eliefs, delusions, assents, intuitions and dreams' (2006, p. 63) came to be thought of as insubstantial, epiphenomenal, of little negligible importance for the discipline. This is a reiteration of Lacan's longstanding argument against positivist psychology. In 1933 he had declared that 'institutional psychology [is] . . . the last advent of positivist science' (1988c, p. 4). A positivist psychology which views 'the psychological' as a collection of verifiable objects and processes that must be observable, positively identified and demonstrated, preferably through experimentation. Of course the postulate of the unconscious does not sit well in such a paradigm. To trace the effects of the unconscious is, after all, to investigate what is *not there* (at least in the sense of what is consciously present, for we are concerned with what is *repressed*).

Lacan's critical reflections on psychology date back to his earliest published work. In 1933 he was already lamenting how scientific psychology, having fallen in line with a positivist science, had assumed a 'naive confidence in . . . mechanistic thought' (p. 4). Lacan's argument against mechanistic psychological theory took issue with a series of related assumptions, such as the cause-effect model of explanation preferred by the natural sciences. Such a model called for the clear and definitive identification of linear and verifiable causative relations, which as I have just noted, is something clearly ill-suited to psychical reality of the unconscious, where such links are complex, over-determined and typically less than obvious or transparent. Aside from Lacan's insistence that psychical processes cannot be fixed as objects, this set of presumptions clearly implies a deterministic and reductionist account of human behaviour.

Many of Lacan's criticisms of psychology as necessitating observable, empirical objects and a positivist natural science methodology can be interestingly articulated with a psychology as a *human* science critique (Brooke, 2016; Giorgi, 1970) which similarly argues that in modelling itself on natural sciences, psychology lost sight of the most essential features of the subject.[3] Although clearly mounted from a phenomenological as opposed to a psychoanalytic perspective, Giorgi's (1970, 2000) arguments about the inappropriate use of natural science methods and concepts resonates with Lacan's own critique. Giorgi (1970) asks: 'is the subject matter of psychology identical to . . . or radically different from that of the natural sciences?' before suggesting that in the latter eventuality 'ought not psychology then conceive of itself and [be] practice[d] . . . in a way that is different from the way that the natural sciences are conceived and practiced?' (p. 2). Elsewhere, he argues that

> Natural scientific psychology . . . imitated the methods and procedures of the natural sciences even though it meant a reductionistic understanding of what it meant to be human . . . [Psychology's] ambition to be a natural science was an ideological commitment that was forced upon its subject matter. Its desire to be a natural science actually preceded an examination of its subject matter and by adopting and imitating pre-existing natural scientific methods and criteria, its methods preceded its problems.
>
> (Giorgi, 2000, pp. 234–235)

Lacan hence condemns psychology for having failed in its scientific aspirations: by relying on hand-me-down concepts and methodological presumptions from the natural sciences and scholastic psychology, it has failed to do justice to the distinctive phenomena of psychical reality. The broader disciplinary edifice of psychology has, for the most part, missed both the distinctive materiality of the psychical (the domain of speech and language) and the psychical and inter-subjective *relativity* of its objects by insisting on maintaining an 'apparatus of objectivity' (2006, p. 59) in how human psychology is approached.

Lacan's general argument then – which encapsulates much of his early critique of psychology – is that

> Psychical phenomena are . . . granted no reality of their own: those that do not belong to 'true' reality [as defined by the natural/physical sciences] have only an illusory reality . . . The role of psychology is merely to reduce psychical phenomena to this system [of the established sciences] and to *verify* the system . . . It is insofar as this psychology is a function of this truth that it is not a science.
>
> (2006, p. 63)

Such a pseudo-scientific form of 'psychologism' can be said 'to constitute a radical misrepresentation of human nature' which, as Lacanian commentator Burgoyne (forthcoming) stresses, 'threatens a loss of access to the causes of human suffering'. Lacan (2006) is harsher yet: such a form of psychologism[4] is guilty of 'reifying human beings', indeed, of perpetrating 'a new alienation of man' (p. 177), of producing '*homo psychologicus*' (p. 178), that is, a thoroughly psychologized species of humanity. It is for the above reasons that Lacan goes to such pains to insist on the *non-psychological* nature of the subject, underscoring in Seminar I that 'By [the] *being of the subject*, we do not mean its psychological properties, but what is hollowed out in the experience of speech, which constitutes the analytic situation' (1988a, p. 230).

If there is any doubt that Lacan's critique is of current relevance, consider Murray's (2016) comments:

> Representations of human life as mechanical are even evident in . . . psychology *now*, in the twenty-first century. A popular contemporary example is cognitive behavioural therapy (CBT), which 'forces' patients to relinquish . . . self-destructive thoughts and 'trains' them to adopt more positive ones . . . The attribution of mechanism to human nature does indeed instruct many modern psychological descriptions . . . [T]here were very influential psychological theories that *predated* CBT that held that humans react to stimuli in a way that is both 'natural' and 'automatic' . . . In them, human psychology is taken to resemble animal behaviour in reacting mechanistically to instinctive impulses. Behavioural psychology . . . still takes . . . this kind of positivistic and causal view of the human as a sort of animal that is also a sort of machine.
>
> (pp. 90–93)

Subject made object

For Lacan, psychology's 'objectivistic' ethos necessarily fails the subject. A variety of issues – political, conceptual, ethical – spring to the fore here, perhaps the most pressing of which concerns the claim that applied psychology amounts to a normalizing endeavour, a type of adaptive engineering. Reflecting on how psychoanalysis had been taken up in America, Lacan laments how the mindset 'known as behaviourism. . . . dominates psychological notions in America' (p. 204) before regretting how

> the conception of psychoanalysis in the United States has been inflected towards the adaptation of the individual to the social environment, the search for behaviour patterns, and all the objectification implied in the notion of 'human relations'. And the indigenous term, 'human engineering', [which] strongly implies a privileged position of exclusion with respect to the human object.
>
> (p. 204)

Added to this criticism is an epistemological concern. We should recall here the anti-objectivism of phenomenology adapted by Lacan (discussed in Chapter 2) and applied to the notions of the unconscious and the subject. Just as consciousness cannot be rendered in the concepts and categories used to understand physical objects, so the unconscious – and indeed the subject – cannot be viewed as types of substance or indeed as objective or positive categories. The implications of this for clinical practice are clear: we cannot reduce the patient to a general type (an object), or to a series of object properties viewed externally, from 'a position of exclusion' (Lacan, 2006, p. 204).

Verhaeghe's (2001) characterization of psychoanalysis as a *science of the particular*, as a treatment modality attentive to the singularity of its patients, is pertinent here. To neglect this imperative, to fall back on categorical or objectifying understandings of the patient and their presenting problems is to compromise the curative potential of psychoanalysis. It is to fail the subject by remaining inattentive to the particularity of their desire.[5] It likewise detracts from the agency of those non-object-like potentialities (of speech, of the unconscious) that the subject effectively *is*. More bluntly put, such objectifications (of the patient, of their attributes, of categorical psychological knowledge) relegate the psychotherapeutic process either a type of human engineering or to an imaginary knowledge-gathering exercise, to – and here one senses Lacan's (2006) evident disdain – a 'mere psychology' (p. 451).

From phenomenology to the signifier

The influence of phenomenology is apparent in early Lacan not only in terms of anti-objectivism and the prioritization of inter-subjectivity. Phenomenology leaves also a methodological trace in Lacan's work. The classical phenomenological procedure involves the suspension – or 'bracketing' – of preconceived notions and constructs, the attempt to attend as faithfully as possible to the phenomena in question without imposing preconceived notions or judgements. This means avoiding the encumbrances of pre-existing objects of knowledge. 'In adopting this perspective', says Miller (1996b), 'what Lacan found to be the fundamental datum of analytic experience was language' (pp. 16–17). So, whereas the phenomenologist treats *experience* as primary, Lacan insists on the irreducible role of language and *speech*. Speech, he insists, is the fundamental phenomena of psychoanalytic practice; it is to be engaged *as speech*, not as a conduit to a different – or somehow more substantial – facet of psychical reality.

Clinically, this means not replacing what patients say with something else (the objectification of imposed themes, the analyst's own ostensibly 'objective' descriptions), or working on the basis of a different order of suppositions (the patient's body language, their affects, or how those apparent affects rebound off the clinician) (Miller, 2011). Psychology's inevitable tendency to objectification – which for Lacan typically coincides with its inability to appreciate the significance of speech – is again stressed when he refers to

> the privileged attention paid to the function of non-verbal aspects of behaviour in the psychological manoeuvre, a preference. . . . for a vantage point from which the subject is no longer anything but an object.
>
> (2006, p. 177)

Psychology is accused of inevitably looking behind or beyond the phenomena of speech, of attempting to grapple with something else (feelings, evolutionary adaptations, behavioural patterns, cognitive structures, etc.) that is ostensibly 'more primary' than spoken language itself. It is in view of such objectifications, by virtue of neglecting the primacy of speech, that psychology runs aground for it is in such verbal and symbolic productions – and these alone – that we access the subject of the unconscious. Ultimately it is for this reason – paying inadequate attention to the role of the signifier, that is the functioning of language and speech – that 'psychology is the field of the "imaginary", in the sense of the illusory' (Lacan, 2006, p. 65).[6]

The structure of inter-subjectivity

If psychical life is wholly over-written by symbolic operations, by 'the signifier', and if these operations are in essence social, which is to say, evinced in functions of symbolic exchange, then psychical life is never so much a matter of objects as *of symbolic inter-subjectivity*. The prioritization of inter-subjectivity in Lacan's work of the 1950s is not merely the result of a debt to phenomenology. A pragmatic reason plays its part here too. Simply put: psychoanalysis can work no other way. Why so? Well, first, the fact that psychoanalysis relies on spoken interaction, on exchanges of speech ensures that psychoanalytic practice retains a basically dialectical inter-subjective character. Second, given that the clinician is a focus of transference, their role in the analytic exchange is never merely neutral or 'objective'. Third – and here again we distinguish psychoanalysis from mechanistic/behavioural forms of psychology – psychoanalysis does not

> presume that given symptoms have the same 'objective' meaning for all subjects . . . From a Lacanian point of view, the symptom . . . always has a meaning . . . This meaning is always subjective rather than objective and it will be different for different subjects.
>
> (Murray, 2016, p. 95)

In this respect, Lacan is indebted to the dynamic (and phenomenological) psychiatry of Ludwig Binswanger: particularity and subjective meaning will always thus be preferred to objectivity and categorical (objectifying) explanations.

We can further specify the inter-subjectivity of the psychoanalytic encounter. What occurs in analysis is neither objective nor purely subjective, but is – as was explored in Chapter 3 – of the order of a subjectivity *premised on another subjectivity*. 'Lacan', notes Miller (1996b), 'emphasized the fact that a patient speaks *to* someone' (p. 17), and that 'speaking *to* someone is more important that speaking *about* something' (p. 19). Or, in Lacan's own words: 'analytic experience . . . comes upon the simple fact that language, prior to signifying something, signifies to someone' (Lacan, 2006, p. 66).

So, even though it may appear that what the analysand says has no apparent meaning, it will nevertheless be animated by an unconscious intention, a fact which means that the analyst must remain alive to the fact that what is said in analysis is frequently 'expressed but not understood by the subject' (Lacan, 2006, p. 66). That is to say, each of the inter-subjective factors stressed above – the factor of dialectical exchange, the non-objectivity of transference, the role of an Other – are crucial by virtue of the structural role they play in bringing out the unconscious:

> [W]hat happens in an analysis is that the subject, strictly speaking, is con-stituted through a discourse to which the mere presence of the psychoanalyst, prior to any intervention he may make, brings the dimension of dialogue.
>
> (Lacan, 2006, p. 176)

Working within the structure of psychoanalytic discourse as described above thus necessitates the fundamental rule (of free association), the role of the Other, and a gravitation towards unconscious truth. 'In short', concludes Lacan, 'psychoanalysis is a dialectical experience', a 'notion [which] should prevail when raising the question of the nature of the transference' (p. 177). Transference, the unconscious, the emergence of the subject: each of these is contingent on the structure of inter-subjectivity constituted by the psychoanalytic treatment. We might note here, parenthetically, that by invoking the factor of the transference, and the unconscious transmission triggered by the presence of an Other, Lacan is also implying that the structural inter-subjectivity discussed here might be better understood – as in Chapter 3 – along the lines of the *trans-subjective*.[7]

We may summarize the foregoing arguments by stressing once again that objectifying and objectivistic relations – inseparable for Lacan from psychology as such – misapprehend the nature of the subject. Such approaches impede attempts to elicit the unconscious and to locate the subject in an appropriately transformative dimension. Such 'psychologistic' approaches, furthermore, necessarily fail in engaging the subject inasmuch as they substitute their own categorical forms of knowledge for a more open-ended relation of *not-knowing*.

Ignoratia docta

Lacan's attempt to think beyond the parameters of objectivation involves a distinctively psychoanalytic epistemology, or more appropriately perhaps, a *negative-epistemology*, a type of *not-knowing*.[8] Such a stance is explicitly premised *against understanding*, for, as Fink (2014a) warns, the process of understanding

> can be seen to reduce the unfamiliar to the familiar, to transform the radically other into the same, and to render the analyst hard of hearing. Our ability ... to detect the unconscious ... is compromised by our emphasis on understanding and can be rectified only by taking as our fundamental premise that we do *not* understand ... The emphasis on understanding can also do a disservice to analysands who observe themselves and to explain their feelings and behaviours to themselves and others in sophisticated terms without necessarily changing.
>
> (pp. 24–25)

This critique of understanding is explicitly tied to psychology by Lacan: '[M]aking-things-understood is and always has been the real stumbling block in psychology' (2014, p. 18). In Seminar II Lacan (1988b) approvingly cites Plato's *Meno*, a Socratic dialogue, using this classical reference to argue that

> Psychoanalysis is a dialectic ... The art of conversation of Socrates ... is to teach the slave to give his own speech its true meaning ... In other words, the position of the analyst must be that of an *ignorantia docta* [learned ignorance] which does not mean knowing ... but [which] is capable of being formative for the subject ... [T]hese days ... there is a great temptation to transform the *ignorantia docta* into ... an *ignorantia docens* [taught ignorance]. If the psychoanalyst thinks he knows something, in psychology for example, then that is already the beginning of his loss, for ... in psychology nobody knows much, except that psychology itself is an error of perspective on the human being.
>
> (1988a, p. 278)

It is in our inability to grasp 'what the realization of the being of man is' (p. 278) – that is, the emergence of the unconscious in the subject – that we are put into an erroneous perspective, namely, that of 'the psychological'.

Lacan's eschewal of understanding must be viewed alongside the correlating methodological principles of non-omission and non-systemization. Speaking of how 'analytical experience' is constituted, Lacan asserts that

> its first condition is formulated in a law of non-omission, which promotes everything that 'is self-explanatory', the everyday and the ordinary, to the status of the interesting . . . usually reserved for the remarkable; but it is incomplete without the second condition, the law of non-systematization, which, positing incoherence as a condition of analytic experience, presumes significant all the dross of mental life – not only the representations in which scholastic psychology sees only non-meaning (dream scenarios, presentiments, daydreams, and confused or lucid delusions), but also the phenomena that are not even granted a civil status in it . . . since they are altogether negative (slips of the tongue and bungled actions).
>
> (2006, p. 65)

What Lacan speaks of here – the embracing of incoherence, a methodological prioritization of non-omission – clearly does not harmonize with the goals of a positivistic natural science psychology focused on clearly defined dependent and independent variables and causative relations. This methodological incompatibility is furthered when we consider the objectives of psychology as a behavioural science that rules out of hand any 'internal' psychological functioning (and thereby most certainly 'the dross of mental life') not verifiable within the field of behavioural action.

The absent object

As early as the 1930s Lacan was insisting both on the '*relativity*' of the object and upon the role of psychical reality – or, indeed, desire – in the 'making' of this object. In a clinical discussion of a man routinely aroused by the refusal of a woman – a nicely grounded example of the point at hand – Fink (1997) observes that

> it seems to the outside observer that his desire is incited by the object – that it is correlated with a specific object . . . But as soon as that association is broken, as soon as it becomes impossible for him to imbue the object at hand with the trait or characteristic that turns him on – refusal – we see that what is crucial is not the object, the specific woman he gets involved with, but the trait or characteristic that arouses his desire.
>
> (p. 51)

This brief vignette is indicative of a more general Lacanian postulate:

> Desire is not so much drawn towards an object (Desire → Object) as elicited by a certain characteristic that can sometimes be read into a particular love object . . . For a while, the object is seen as 'containing' the cause, as 'having' the trait or feature that incites this analysand's desire . . . *Human desire, strictly speaking, has no object.*
>
> (Fink, 1997, p. 51)

This is an 'object error' that imaginary misrecognition is prone to: the assumption that objects are the animating principles of our desires, when in fact objects function rather as screens upon which the travails of desire are played out. Lacan's notion of *objet a* is thus decidedly not an object at all; it is instead the non-object *cause* of desire that various imaginary objects come again and again to be conflated with. This conceptualization is faithful to Freud (1915), who had long since asserted that the object is contingent and dispensable relative to the aims of the drive. And it translates into a constant injunction in Lacan: apparent 'objects' must be dissolved in their pretend substantiality and viewed instead as – at best – stop-off points, temporary locations in the itinerary of (metonymic) desire.

To this we must add the fact that absence – lack, loss – over-determines the apparent presence of the object:

> What Lacan has emphasized is the *radical*, absolute character of the loss of the object, in that this object (at the level of drive as well as desire) is constituted *as forever lost*: it is not that the subject once had it and then lost it, but rather that the subject can only 'have' it as lost, as a pure lack . . . Thus, for Lacan, the object relation is the relation with the lack of the object.
>
> (Rodriquez, 1999, p. 122)

This, then, is how the notion of the object is rethought by Lacan: as first and foremost *lack*, lack as it is present in desire, as the wish to have once again what one never really possessed. We should note again here the obvious distinction: whereas psychology adheres to notions of objective 'reality', psychoanalysis insists that reality is always infused with, over-written by psychical reality (fantasy).[9] So, while it is true that the subject may have experienced the painful loss of 'actual' material objects, these are only pale imitations of the always-already lost object of fantasy:

> the analytic experience shows . . . that the multiple losses through which the subject goes in his/her life derive their significance qua losses from the essential lack that forms the subject: lack of object, lack of any guarantee of satisfaction, lack-in-being (*manqué-*. . .).
>
> (1999, p. 122)

This crucial postulate in Lacanian theory – the primacy of lack over substance – both distinguishes Lacanian psychoanalysis from psychology and relates back to Lacan's conceptualizations of the subject. The triumvirate of lacks noted above (of object, *jouissance* and being) indicates that for Lacan each such aspect of the subject is best grasped not within the parameters of the object – that is, as an entity capable of a clear ontological status – but rather according to a trajectory of lack. The ego can accordingly be conceptualized as simultaneously caught up within and formed by the wishful illusion of its own substantiality.

The culture of the ego

In Seminar I Lacan (1988a) warns his audience that there is a fundamental error in cleaving 'to the idea that the subject's ego is identical to the presence that is speaking to you' (p. 250). This is the problem when an 'objectifying case of mind' (i.e. a psychologizing approach) slides

> from the ego defined as the perception-consciousness system – that is, as the system of the subject's objectifications – to the ego conceived of as the correlate of an absolute reality and thus, in a singular return of . . . psychologistic thought, to once again take the ego as the 'reality function'.
>
> (Lacan, 1998a, p. 251)

Multiple problems converge here for Lacan. A particular objectifying dimension within human psychical functioning – the agency of the ego – has erroneously come to be understood *as the subject*, as the focus of psychological (even *psychoanalytic*) attentions over and above the unconscious itself. Worse yet, this reified construct of the ego has come to be seen as 'autonomous', as the psychical representative of reality.

Such a simplistic notion of 'reality' cannot go unopposed by Lacan. Rather than it being the case that reality exists as the objective order of things to which the ego has – or must be – adapted, reality is itself the outcome of ego's defensive, misrecognitions. 'The point', Lacan argues, 'is not to adapt [a patient] to it [reality], but to show him that he is only too well adapted to it, since he [as ego] assists in its very fabrication' (2006, p. 498).

In Seminar II Lacan is as strident as he is forthright in contesting the ego-subject conflation. The subject, he remarks, 'is decentred in relation to the individual [as ego]' (1988b, p. 9). The year before, Lacan had defined the ego as 'that set of defences, of denials, of dams, of inhibitions, of fundamental fantasies which orient and direct the subject' (1988a, p. 17). This characterization is now extended: 'The ego isn't a superior power, nor a pure spirit, nor an autonomous agency, nor a conflict-free sphere' (1988b, p. 326). The work of retrieving unconscious desire, furthermore, lies beyond 'that circle of certainties by which man recognizes himself as ego' (1988b, p. 8).

Psychology, again, has much to answer for here. The Freudian conceptualization of the ego, claims Lacan, is genuinely upsetting, revolutionary; it threatens to abolish preceding conceptualizations of the psyche. Despite this – and, indeed, as a reaction to it – 'a notion of the ego has re-emerged', one which 'tends towards the re-absorption . . . of analytic knowledge within general psychology' (1988b, pp. 3–4). It is not difficult to understand why such a reversion to an essentially pre-Freudian conceptualization has occurred. The ego, as the epicentre of unique individuality, as *the* point of reflexive capacity within the domain of experience, is a seductive and seemingly self-evident concept:

> The notion of the ego today draws its self-evidential character from a certain prestige given to consciousness insofar as it is a unique, individual, irreducible experience. The intuition of the ego retains, in so far as it is centred on experi-ence of consciousness, a captivating character, which one must rid oneself of in order to accede to our conception of the subject. I try to lead you away from its attraction with the aim of . . . [showing] where, according to Freud, the reality of the subject is. In the unconscious, excluded from the system of the ego, the subject speaks.
>
> (Lacan, 1988b, p. 58)

For Lacan in the early 1950s the concept of ego had become perhaps the biggest single obstacle to the practice of a genuinely Freudian psychoanalysis. His work of the time provides ample demonstration of how a questionable philosophical/ psychological concept leads to highly problematic clinical practices. The ethical shortcomings of such a conceptualization are nowhere better illustrated than in Lacan's lambasting of psychoanalytic ego psychology:

> In centring analytic intervention on the dissipation of [behavioural] patterns . . . the analyst has no other guide than his own conception of the subject's behaviour. He attempts to normalize it – in accordance with a norm that is coherent with his own ego. So this will always be a modelling of one ego by another ego. . .[Th]e subject's ego. . . . must become an ally of the analyst. What does this mean – . . . that the subject's new ego is the ego of the analyst . . . the normal end of the treatment is identification with the ego of the analyst.
>
> (1988a, p. 285)

Aside from the obvious political objections one may have to such clinical goals – which seem unavoidably to rely on conformity to social norms – they are further-more sure to end in failure. That is to say, such agendas (modelling, normalization, identifying with the analyst's ego) are necessarily alienating. They install a rela-tionship of dependence upon the person of the analyst and the social norms that this analyst is thought to embody, and they result in a leading away of the patient from their own desire. Lacan's attack against the clinical centring of the ego quickly expands into a more expansive critique of forms of knowledge that are rooted in, and promote, the productions of the imaginary.

Psychology as discipline of the imaginary

From the beginning of Lacan's work, the image – the principle vehicle of imaginary identifications – is characterized as deceptive, as maintaining a seductive, captivating and ultimately alienating hold on the subject. The image thus understood is the very medium of the ego. As we know from Chapter 1: the image is a vessel not only of idealizing self-love, projection and aggressive conflict, but of misrecognition or *méconnaissance*. It is a place where the gratifying image of what one thinks one already knows – or of what one wants to believe one *is* – is preferred above the prospect of the more destabilizing truths of unconscious desire.

Why do I again stress Lacan's critique of the psychical function of the image here? Well, because there is an echo in Lacan's various attacks on the psychological that must not escape us. Psychology is repeatedly criticized for its objectifying qualities, and much the same is alleged of the self-objectifying ego's captivation in images. Psychology itself is thus likened to the ego, viewed, indeed, *as itself as egoic*. It pays to reiterate that a primary function of the imaginary is to make an object where there is none (as in the case of the ego), and that this object-making imperative is one of the most fundamental reasons why psychological conceptualization amounts to an imaginary operation.

Here we should recall the elementary features of Lacan's mirror stage. The mirror stage involves the imaginary process of the subject looking at, and as intrigued by, an image that they subsequently come to take on as themselves (as the basis of their ideal-ego). Such an image gives the subject an illusory sense of substantiality and identity; affirms them in a persistent relation of misrecognition (*méconnaissance*); enables them to believe that they can reliably know and gain mastery over themselves; and forms a basis with which to (narcissistically) love and be fascinated by themselves.

The claim then is not simply that psychology in some way parallels processes of the ego. The claim is rather that psychology is a disciplinary (indeed, *epistemic*) re-enactment of the *méconnaissance* exemplified in the mirror stage. Hence, no doubt, Lacan's declaration on 7 July 1954 (in Seminar II) that 'psychology . . . is an error of perspective on the human being' (1988a, p. 278). The imaginary foundation of psychology as a domain of knowledge production seems, in retrospect, inevitable. Any epistemic formation which takes the psychological terrain of the ego as its primary object will invariably be tainted by the tendencies and suppositions of the imaginary. More simply put: the study of the ego is likely to be affected by the ego itself. Lacan advances much the same argument when he cautions that '[O]bjectification in psychological matters is subject, at it very core, to a law of misrecognition [*méconnaissance*] that governs the subject not only as observed, but also as observer' (2006, p. 349). Evidence for this reading of psychology as 'discipline of the imaginary' is to be found in the many mythical objects and assumptions that psychology produces, and which Lacan goes about listing in Seminar III:

> The myth of unity of the personality, the myth of synthesis, of superior and interior functions . . . all these types of organization of the objective field, constantly reveal . . . misrecognition of the most immediate experience.
>
> (1993, p. 8)

The subject of structure, not development

Lacan's anti-objectivism and his antipathy to psychology's ego-affirmations are matched in vehemence by his opposition to the development assumptions that permeate so much of the discipline. He declares psychoanalysis 'diametrically opposed to everything . . . inspired by a psychology that calls itself genetic' (2006, p. 116). The vigour with which he takes up cudgels against the developmental paradigm is, perhaps, initially surprising, given the layperson's typical association of Freudian theory and the notion of psychosexual (oral, anal, genital, phallic) stages of development. Nevertheless, Lacan is less than reticent in proclaiming:

> [T]here is no psychogenesis. . . . [T]here is precisely nothing that could be further from psychoanalysis in its whole development, its entire inspiration and its mainspring, in everything it has contributed, everything it has been able to confirm for us in anything we have established.
>
> (1993, p. 7)

This is not to ignore the importance of the subject's history, a point that Rodriquez (1999) anticipates: 'Psychoanalysis deals with history, rather than maturational development. And history, oral or written, is grounded in language' (p. 114).[10] This enables us to nuance the point at hand. Lacan eschews forms of genetic (i.e. *developmental*) psychology that approach children as existing somehow outside of or anterior to language. Attempts to assess children's aptitudes in comparison to 'purely abstract register of adult mental categories' are denigrated for not appreciating how children

> from their very first manifestations of language, use syntax . . . with a level of sophistication that the postulates of intellectual 'genesis' would . . . reach only at the height of a metaphysician's career.
>
> (pp. 116–117)

Any psychology which claims to 'reach the child's reality' in this manner – via the study of developmental progressions – is dismissed as 'idiotic' (p. 117).[11] Much the same argument is made in Seminar I:

> [O]ne cannot make judgements concerning the acquisition . . . of language
> on the basis of . . . the mastery revealed by the appearance of first words
> . . . Everyone knows the degree of diversity shown by the first fragments of
> language as they appear in the child's elocution. And we . . . know how
> striking it is to hear the child give expression to adverbs, particles, words, to
> *perhaps* or *not yet*, before having given expression to . . . the minimal naming
> of an object.
>
> (Lacan, 1988a, p. 54)

What initially seems an isolated argument about the acquisition of language –
Lacan's position being that one doesn't learn language one word at a time or in a
nominalist manner, by naming objects – opens up into a more substantial thesis
regards the predominance of structure. Prior to any learning by the subject – and
in marked contrast to psychological notions of a pre-linguistic (or preverbal)
existence – language is always-already there. The notion of structure thus undercuts
the search for psychological origins:

> [T]here is no origin of structure: we cannot think unless language is already
> there. Language is an order . . . a whole composed of interrelated elements.
> A differential order must be conceived of as a whole, the different component
> elements being interrelated.
>
> (Miller, 1996a, p. 13)

This throws into perspective a question of agency that remains crucial in Lacan's
disagreement with psychology's focus on the properties, skills, attributes and
acquisitions of the individual. It is not how subjects use language, and attain a degree
of agency in this way; it is rather the case of how *the agency of language* (the symbolic,
the signifier) itself over-rides conscious ego-productions and determines its speaking
subjects. So, although clinical psychoanalysis needs to accommodate the singularity
of its subjects – the particularity of their speech, their desire – it is largely
uninterested in the 'individuality' of their apparent psychological attributes,
concerned rather with how the agency of the symbolic as spoken *through* and *by*
them is at once formative and transformative of whom they are *as subjects*. Hence
Lacan's declaration: one needs to 'grasp clearly the autonomy of the symbolic
function in the realizing of the human' (1988a, p. 54).

The myth of immediate experience

Lacan, as I have noted in foregoing chapters, repeatedly exhibits a fascination with
logical forms and linguistic functioning. Indeed, he routinely over-rides the
intuitive attraction of psychologistic accounts, preferring structural modes of
explanation that remain almost completely antithetical to psychology. In his essay
on logical time, for example, Lacan (2006) prioritizes 'the essential logical form'
to the 'so-called existential form . . . of the psychological "I"' (p. 170). Why so?
Badiou's reflections on the topic prove illuminating:

> [Lacan] inserts himself into the structuralist galaxy not only because he had recourse ... to logico-mathematical formalisms, but also because he renounced the reflexive subject as the centre of all experience. From his analytic perspective, the subject hinges on an irreflexive and ... transindividual structure: the unconscious, which for Lacan depends entirely on language. The science of the unconscious therefore replaces the philosophy of consciousness.
>
> (2014, p. 8)

Lacan's opposition to elementary facets of phenomenology becomes here apparent:

> From its invention by Husserl, phenomenology folded the thought of the subject back onto a philosophy of consciousness. It is rooted in lived experience, immediate and primitive. The subject is confounded with consciousness ... It is not by chance that phenomenologists ... accord so much importance to perception: it is the most elementary experience of this direct and intentional relationship consciousness has with the world.
>
> (Badiou in Badiou and Roudinesco, 2014, p. 6)

Consciousness, perception, subjective experience, reflexivity: these are suspect psychological concepts inasmuch as they imply autonomy from, and primacy in respect of, the broader determining structure of language. Badiou continues:

> Moreover – and in this sense French phenomenology is also an inheritor of traditional psychology – the subject is apprehended as an interiority, seen from the point of its feelings, its emotions, and so on. The result is a heavy focus on the reflexive ego or self and the sphere of intimacy or inwardness.
>
> (2014, p. 7)

The psychoanalytic subject is thus the 'irreflexive' subject of trans-individual and symbolic *structure*, rather a subject than of development or accumulated knowledge and experience. The signifier (the operations of language and the symbolic) is not extrinsic to but constitutive of the subject. Moreover, psychological or philosophical assumptions regarding the interiority of the individual are themselves *symptomatic* rather than foundational, certainly so given that the ego 'is only a privileged symptom, the human symptom *par excellence*' (1988a, p. 16).

The 'de-natured' subject

Once we have grasped the idea of the subject as *subject of structure*, then a further component dimension of psychology quickly becomes untenable: the idea of humans as 'natural'. Lacan takes up this line of criticism by noting that human psychology amounts to an extension of animal psychology:

[T]he psychological is, if we try to grasp it as firmly as possible . . . the ethological, that is, the whole of the biological individual's behaviour in relation to his natural environment. There you have a legitimate definition of psychology. There you have a real order of relations, an objectifiable thing, a field with quite adequately defined boundaries.

(1993, pp. 7–8)

Such a conflation of human and animal psychology is apparent in the presumption – underwriting so much of twentieth and twenty-first centuries psychology – that humans can be studied by focusing predominantly on their behavioural, evolutionary, biological or non-verbal forms as occurring beyond the remit of language and symbolic/interaction. In doing this however, in treating humans as 'natural', psychology is for Lacan in perpetual error. 'It has to be said of human psychology', offers Lacan, 'what Voltaire used to say about natural history, which was that it's not as natural as all that and that, frankly, nothing could be more anti-natural' (1993, pp. 7–8).

The human is not all of nature; to be human is to exceed natural parameters. Whereas 'animals are strictly riveted to the conditions of the external environment', the same cannot be said of humans, who are 'sufficiently open' (p. 322), that is, *under*-determined by nature. One has to assume a biological gap in the human, insists Lacan (1993), which is to say that a fundamental discontinuity characterizes the subject's relation to nature. The subject is derailed from an existence as purely biological entity by the intrusion of language and the symbolic:

The subject . . . is something other than an organism which adapts itself. It is something else . . . it's entire behaviour speaks of something other than the axis we grasp when we consider it as a function of an individual.

(Lacan, 1988b, p. 9)

The problem with biologising modes of explanation is that they misconstrue what it is to be a human subject. True enough, to be human is to be a biological entity. However, to be a human in the world of language, culture and symbolic structures is to be biological in a way that is paradigmatically different from the instinctual domain of animals where imaginary adaptation reigns supreme. To be human, by contrast, is always-already to have been plunged into the domain of the signifier which necessarily over-writes and exhaustively (re)articulates any ostensibly 'pre-symbolic' aspects of subjectivity.

Constitutive disequilibrium: against adaptation

A brief digression into Freudian theory should suffice to make it clear why Lacan was so ill disposed to what he considers the essentially *psychological* concept of adaptation. As is well known, Freud's theorization of neurosis – and indeed, of subjectivity in general – is underpinned by the irresolvable conflict (or 'real') that he sees as existing between the imperatives of culture and nature (cf. Freud, 1930). This theme is perhaps most famously explored in *Civilization and its Discontents* (1930), where this 'irresolvability' is folded back into the subject them-selves, into their own 'natural' functioning, so much so that Freud maintained that 'there is something inherent in the function [of sex] itself [that denies] us total satisfaction' (p. 54).

The anti-naturalism of this position soon becomes apparent, and it provides an important corrective to the idea that psychoanalysis is all about sex. The prioritization of *sexual* drive and sexuality in the unconscious is not about some naïve preoccupation with sex; it arises because of the impossibility of (a 'natural' form of) sexuality ever attaining full satisfaction in and of itself. From a Lacanian perspective, we may offer multiple reasons why this is so – the never-ending metonymic extensions of desire, the troublesome link between sexual *jouissance* and trauma – yet the important point to grasp here is that human sexuality has been de-naturalized, split from within by its own constitutive impossibility. For Freud (1930), this factor of impossibility is likewise evident within culture: '*unbehagen in der kultur*' ('discontent within civilization') characterizes the impossibility of balancing individual enjoyments and the renunciations expected of the social contract. The fact that culture is always already divided from within echoes thus both the constitutively divided subject and the fraught nature of human sexuality itself.[12]

It is precisely this – the *a priori* disequilibrium of the subject – which so much of psychology and American psychoanalysis had effectively disavowed, that Lacan is determined not to neglect. From a Lacanian standpoint the notion of adaptation is itself an instance of *méconnaissance*, a wishful denial of the 'primal' incompatibility of the subject identified by Freud:

> What does analysis uncover – it if isn't the fundamental, radical discordance of forms of conduct essential to man in relation to everything which he experiences? The dimension discovered by analysis is the opposite of anything which progresses through adaptation . . . There is a radical difference between any investigation of human beings even in the laboratory, and what happens in animals . . . The animal fits into its environment. There's adaptation . . . animal learning displays the characteristics of an organized and finite mode of becoming perfect. How different it is . . . in man! . . . In man it is the wrong form which prevails.
>
> (Lacan, 1988b, p. 86)

For Lacan the conceptualization of a homeostatic relation – between an organism and the environment, or within the organism itself – must be ruled out in the case of the human. Conceiving the subject via the idealized notion of natural harmony avoids completely the radical break from the instincts that characterizes the subject. It fails, in other words, to register the trajectory of drives, the factor of painful libidinal enjoyment (*jouissance*) and the excessive, self-destructive component of the death drive.[13]

Psychology, treated here as inseparable from such biological, physiological, evolutionary and developmental perspectives – in fact, any psychology premised on the notion of adaptation – is roundly rejected by Lacan: 'there is no compromise possible with psychology' (2006, p. 588).

Lacan's issue with such perspectives is not only conceptual: it has a direct bearing on clinical practice. We are reminded of Lacan's critique of ego psychology. Once the aim of a psychoanalytic treatment is associated – however implicitly – to adaptation, then the analyst invariably becomes the model of such a process. Given Freud's declaration that psychoanalysis is opposed to any suggestive model of cure, ethical clinical practice is simply not viable under such conditions. To trade an emphasis on the 'non-resolvable' nature of subject for assurances of adaptation is to sell the subject into a play of influence and social conformity (via the clinical ideal of adaptation). For Lacan it is, furthermore, a betrayal of the essentially subversive nature of psychoanalysis.

There is no subject

There are several conclusions that can be drawn from Lacan's anti-objectivism, from his anti-developmental, anti-adaptation and anti-ego psychology tirades against the discipline. The most basic of these can be stated simply enough: the more psychology confers an object status on what it studies, the more such psychical phenomena are misrecognized, 'imaginarized'. Psychical life, simply put, does not fit within the conceptual parameters of the object, but is better grasped in structural terms, that is, within the terms of signifying, symbolic operations. The futility of trying to grapple with the Lacanian subject from within psychology can be highlighted by referring to Evans's (1996) comment that Lacan's concept of the subject concerns those aspects of the human being that 'that cannot be (or should not be) objectified, reduced to a thing, nor studied in an objective way' (p. 195).

The same holds for developmental, biological and non/pre-linguistic approaches to the human. Such approaches contribute to the psychologizing advance of *homo psychologicus* and to the reduction of psychical life to the parameters of the psychological. It is precisely this move – which, as we have seen, entails a range of adjoined epistemological, ethical and political implications – that ensures that the de-natured and essentially divided subject, incommensurable both to its environment and to itself, falls from view. Approaches that pivot on the notion of a centralized and reality-conditioned ego, which prioritize imaginary-affirming concepts of experience, consciousness and reflexivity, likewise fail to grasp the subject.

The foregoing discussion has shed further light on the early Lacan's minimal definition of the subject (that which is 'outside the object' (1988a, p. 194)). One appreciates now that such a negative definition is consonant with a non-objectifying approach: the potentiality of this subject of the unconscious requires just such a bracketing of objectifying (and indeed biological, developmental, natural 'scientific') preconceptions and imaginary understandings alike. Hence also the related notion that the Lacanian subject should be treated as void of any definitive contents. We have also thus opened up a series of perspectives – appropriately enough at this closing juncture – which segue into the middle and later period of Lacan's teaching: the ideas of the 'real' of the subject, the subject as void, the role of the death drive and *jouissance* within the subject.

This means then that the multiple failures of psychological conceptualization to adequately grasp this subject are not only intellectual or philosophical errors, errors of theorization, they represent also missed curative – which is to say *ethical* – opportunities: they amount to modes of failing the subject. Throughout this book I have tried to show how Lacan's teaching traces an ever more assertive and systematic excision of all facets of the psychological. This chapter has demonstrated how that this exclusion of the psychological is particularly pronounced when it comes to the topic of the subject. Indeed, given psychology's multiple 'objectivations', along with its inability to bring the de-natured and divided subject of speech and the signifier into view, we can understand why, for Lacan, there is no – and can be no – *subject* of psychology.

Notes

1 And indeed for how they clarify Lacan's aspirations for a properly Freudian form of psychoanalytic practice.
2 David Pavón-Cuéllar's (forthcoming) extensive commentary on Lacan's paper is the best single source to consult in this respect.
3 This is not to underplay the conflicts between many phenomenological ideas underlying the human science approach and Lacan's (often apparently anti-humanistic) psychoanalytic conceptualizations.
4 'Psychologism' understood here as the reduction of the psychical to psychological categories modelled on the natural sciences.
5 I mean desire here in its unconscious or repressed forms, the desire that may be separated – in the form of object a – from alienation in the Other, as discussed by Lacan (1979) in Seminar XI's distinction between alienation and separation.
6 It is the psychological insistence on the broader conceptual category of *thought* that uselessly complicates the question of language for Lacan, says Pavón-Cuéllar:

> Simplicity vanishes when psychologists try to go beyond words, away from the signifiers of language, and make them thinkable at the level of meaning, signification, cognition, information, or mental processes. At this level, the speaking subject fades.
> (forthcoming)

7 Pavón-Cuéllar (forthcoming) makes a nice observation in respect of how Lacan's emphasis on the structure of inter-subjectivity will be transformed in his later work:

> We may conjecture that, in the development of Lacanian theory, this early relativism of interpersonal relations would pave the way for the future structuralism of signifying relations, of an 'intersignifiance' that explicitly excludes any kind of interpersonal 'intersubjectivity'.

8 The obvious reference-point in Freud would be the idea of negative capability.
9 Hence Lacan's assertion:

I have opposed the psychologizing tradition that distinguishes fear from anxiety by virtue of its correlates in reality. In this I have changed things, maintaining of anxiety – *it is not without an object*. What is that object? The object *petit a*.

(Lacan cited in Eyers, 2012, p. 31)

10 Rodriquez's (1999) subsequent qualification is worth noting:

Events themselves, traumatic or not, enter into the psychoanalytic scene only as realities of discourse. Similarly, maturation, developmental and psychosexual stages cannot be conceived of as residing outside language, since it is language itself, through the concrete transmission of speech, that constitutes them as 'factors' or 'structural components'.

(p. 115)

11 Lacanian theory is anti-developmental not only because it eschews notions of maturational sequence or because it prefers an analysis of logical structures, but also, as Parker (2003) remarks, because it attends to the time of the unconscious, temporalities of deferred action/retroaction (*nachträglichkeit*) over and above presumptions of linear time.

12 This idea of structural discordance (or 'non-unifiability') is of course a vital antecedent for, an early Freudian form of, the subsequent Lacanian notion of 'the real'.

13 I have, regrettably, not been able to do justice to this crucial Freudian concept (of the death drive) here. See however Hook (2016) for a Lacanian account of the death drive.

REFERENCES

Adorno, T. (1991) *The Culture Industry*. London and New York: Routledge.

Adorno, T. (2003) *Negative Dialectics*. New York: Continuum.

Ahmed, S. (2004) *The Cultural Politics of Emotion*. Edinburgh: Edinburgh University Press.

Austin, J. L. (1962) *How to Do Things With Words*. Oxford: Oxford University Press.

Badiou, A. (2009). *The Theory of the Subject*. London: Bloomsbury.

Badiou, A. and Roudinesco, É. (2014) *Jacques Lacan Past and Present: A Dialogue*. New York: Columbia University Press.

Bailly, L. (2009) *Lacan*. Oxford: Oneworld.

Benvenuto, B. and Kennedy, R. (1986) *The Works of Jacques Lacan an Introduction*. London: Free Association Press.

Billig, M. (1976) *Social Psychology and Intergroup Relations*. London: Academic Press.

Billig, M. (1999). *Freudian Repression: Conversation Creating the Unconscious*. Cambridge: Cambridge University Press.

Billig, M. (2006) 'Lacan's misuse of psychology: evidence, rhetoric and the mirror stage', *Theory, Culture and Society*, 23(4), 1–26.

Bonilla-Silva, E. (2003) *Racism Without Racists: Color-blind Racism and the Persistence of Racial Inequality in the United States*. New York: Rowman.

Borch-Jacobsen, M. (1991) *Lacan the Absolute Master* (translated by D. Brick). Stanford, CA: Stanford University Press.

Bouasse, H. (1934) *Optique et Photométrie dites Géométriques*. Librairie Delgrave: Paris.

Bowie, M. (1991) *Lacan*. Cambridge, MA: Harvard University Press.

Bracher, M. (1994) 'On the psychological and social functions of language: Lacan's theory of the four discourses', in M. Bracher, M. W. Alcorn, R. J. Corthell and F. Massardier-Kenney (eds) *Lacanian Theory of Discourse*. New York University Press: New York.

Branney, P. (2008) 'Subjectivity, not personality', *Social and Personality Psychology Compass*, 2(2), 574–590.

Branney, P., Gough, B. and Madrill, A. (2009) 'The other side of social psychology?', *Annual Review of Critical Psychology*, 7, 187–204.

Braunstein, N. A. (2003) 'Desire and jouissance in the teachings of Lacan', in J. Rabaté (ed.) *The Cambridge Companion to Lacan*. Cambridge: Cambridge University Press.

Burgoyne, B. (forthcoming) 'Presentation on transference', in C. Neill, D. Hook and S. Vanheule (eds) *Reading the Écrits – A Guide to Lacan's Works. Between the Imaginary and the Symbolic*. London: Routledge.

Brooke, R. (2016) 'Some common themes of psychology as a human science', in C.T. Fisher, L. Laubscher and R. Brooke (eds) *The Qualitative Vision for Psychology: An Invitation to a Human Science Approach*. Pittsburgh: Duquesne University Press.

Butler, J. (2000) 'Critically queer', in P. Du Gay, J. Evans and P. Redman (eds) *Identity: A Reader*. London: Sage.

Butler, R. (2014) 'The act', in R. Butler (ed.), *The Žižek Dictionary*. Durham: Acumen.

Chiesa, L. (2007) *Subjectivity and Otherness: A Philosophical Reading of Lacan*. Cambridge, MA: MIT Press.

Coelho, N. E. and Figueiredo, L. C. (2003) 'Patterns of intersubjectivity in the constitution of subjectivity: dimensions of otherness', *Culture and Psychology*, 9(3), 193–208.

Coetzee, J. M. (2013) *The Childhood of Jesus*. London: Jonathan Cape.

Cohen, J. (2005).*How to read Freud*. London: Norton.

Darmon, M. (2014) 'Unary trait', Gale dictionary of psychoanalysis, www.answers.com/topic/unary-trait (accessed 21 March 2014).

Dashtipour, P. (2009) 'Contested identities: using Lacanian psychoanalysis to explore and develop social identity theory', *Annual Review of Critical Psychology*, 7, 320–337.

Dashtipour, P. (2012) *Social Identity in Question: Construction, Subjectivity and Critique*. London: Routledge.

Davies, B. and Harré, R. (2001) 'Positioning: the discursive production of selves', in M. Wetherell, S. Taylor, and S. J. Yates (eds) *Discourse Theory and Practice: A Reader*. London: Sage/Open University Press.

Dawes, N. (2013). Mandela: the long Goodbye. *Mail and Guardian*, 28 June.

Dolar, M. (1993) 'Beyond interpellation', *Qui Parle*, 6(2), 73–96.

Dolar, M. (1999) 'Where does power come from?', *New Formations*, 35, 79–92.

Dolar, M. (2008) 'Introduction: the subject supposed to enjoy', in A. Grosrichard *The Sultan's Court*. London: Verso.

Domhoff, G. W. (2005) 'Refocusing the neurocognitive approach to dreams: a critique of the Hobson versus Solms debate', *Dreaming*, 15, 3–20.

Dor, J. (1998) *Introduction to the Reading of Lacan: The Unconscious Structured Like a Language*. New York: Other Press.

Dor, J. (1999) *The Clinical Lacan*. New York: Other Press.

Durrheim, K. Mtose, X. and Brown, L. (2010). Race Trouble: Race, Identity and Inequality in Post-Apartheid South Africa. Durban: University of KwaZulu-Natal Press.

Emerson, P. and Frosh, S. (2009) *Critical Narrative Analysis in Psychology: A Guide to Practice*. London and New York: Palgrave.

Evans, D. (1996) An Introductory Dictionary of Lacanian Psychoanalysis. London and New York: Routledge.

Ettinger, B. L. (2002) 'Trans-subjective transferential borderspace', in B. Massumi (ed.) *A Shock to Thought: Expression after Deleuze and Guattari*. London and NY: Routledge.

Ettinger, B. L. (2006) 'Matrixial trans-subjectivity', *Theory, Culture and Society*, 23, 2–3, 218–222.

Eyers, T. (2012). *Lacan and the Concept of the 'Real'*. London and New York: Palgrave.

Fanon, F. (1952/1986) *Black Skin, White Masks*. London: Pluto.

Felman, S. (1987) *Jacques Lacan and the Adventure of Insight*. Cambridge, MA: Harvard University Press.

Fink, B. (1995) *The Lacanian Subject Between Language and Jouissance*. Princeton: Princeton University Press.

Fink, B. (1996) 'Logical time and the precipitation of subjectivity', in R. Feldstein, B. Fink and M. Jaanus (eds) *Reading Seminars I and II: Lacan's Return to Freud*. New York: SUNY Press.

Fink, B. (1997) *A Clinical Introduction to Lacanian Psychoanalysis: Theory and Technique*. Cambridge: Harvard University Press.

Fink, B. (2006) 'Translator's endnotes', in J. Lacan (ed.) *Écrits: The First Complete Edition in English*. New York and London: W. W Norton and Company.

Fink, B. (2014) *Against Understanding: Cases and Commentary in a Lacanian Key*. London and New York: Routledge, vol. I

Fischer, C., Brooke, R. and Laubscher, L. (eds) (2016) *Invitation to Psychology as a Human Science*. Pittsburgh: Duquesne University Press.

Flynn, G. (2012) *Gone Girl*. London: Weidenfeld and Nicolson.

Forrester, J. (1990) *The Seductions of Psychoanalysis*. Cambridge: Cambridge University Press.

Foster, D. (2012) *After Mandela: The Struggle for Freedom in Post-Apartheid South Africa*. London and New York: Liveright.

Foucault, M. (1977) *Discipline and Punish: The Birth of the Prison*. New York: Random House.

Foucault, M. (1990) *The History of Sexuality Volume 1: An Introduction*. London: Vintage.

Frankfurt, H. G. (2005) *On Bullshit*. Princeton, NJ: Princeton University Press.

Frears, S. (dir.) (2006) *The Queen*. Prod. A. Harries. Granada productions. Miramax Films. Manchester.

Frederickson, G. (1990) The Making of Mandela. *New York Review of Books*, 27 September.

Freud, S. (1911) 'Formulations on the two principles of mental functioning', in S. Freud (1966–1974) *The Standard Edition of the Complete Psychological Works of Sigmund Freud* (translated by J. Strachey). London: Hogarth, vol. XIV.

Freud, S. (1912) 'Totem and taboo', in S. Freud (1966–1974) *The Standard Edition of the Complete Psychological Works of Sigmund Freud* (translated by J. Strachey). London: Hogarth, vol. XIII.

Freud, S. (1914) 'On narcissism: an introduction', in S. Freud (1966–1974). *The Standard Edition of the Complete Psychological Works of Sigmund Freud* (translated by J. Strachey). London: Hogarth, vol. XIV.

Freud, S. (1915) 'Instincts and their vicissitudes', in S. Freud (1966–1974) *The Standard Edition of the Complete Psychological Works of Sigmund Freud* (translated by J. Strachey). London: Hogarth, vol. XIV.

Freud, S. (1917) 'Mourning and melancholia', in S. Freud (1966-1974) *The Standard Edition of the Complete Psychological Works of Sigmund Freud* (translated by J. Strachey). London: Hogarth, vol. XIV.

Freud, S. (1918) 'From the history of an infantile neurosis', (The 'Wolf-Man') in S. Freud (1966–1974) *The Standard Edition of the Complete Psychological Works of Sigmund Freud* (translated by J. Strachey). London: Hogarth, vol XIIV.

Freud, S. (1921) 'Group psychology and the analysis of the ego', in S. Freud (1966–1974) *The Standard Edition of the Complete Psychological Works of Sigmund Freud* (translated by J. Strachey). London: Hogarth, vol. XVIII.

Freud, S. (1927) 'The future of an illusion', in S. Freud (1966–1974) *The Standard Edition of the Complete Psychological Works of Sigmund Freud* (translated by J. Strachey). London: Hogarth, vol. XXI.

Freud, S. (1930) 'Civilization and its discontents', in S. Freud (1966–1974) *The Standard Edition of the Complete Psychological Works of Sigmund Freud* (translated by J. Strachey). London: Hogarth, vol. XXI.

Freud, S. (1950) 'Project for a scientific psychology', in S. Freud (1966–1974) *The Standard Edition of the Complete Psychological Works of Sigmund Freud* (translated by J. Strachey). London: Hogarth, vol. I.

Freud, S. (2004) *Mass Psychology and Other Writings*. London: Penguin.

Frosh, S. (2008) 'Desire, demand and psychotherapy: on large groups and neighbours', *Psychotherapy and Politics International*, 6, 185–197.

Frosh, S. (2010). *Psychoanalysis Outside the Clinic*. London & New York: Palgrave.

Frosh, S., Phoenix, A, A., and Pattman, R. (2000) ' "But it's racism I really hate": young masculinities, racism and psychoanalysis', *Psychoanalytic Psychology*, 17, 225–242.

Frost, D. and Zelnick, B. (2007) *Frost/Nixon*. London: Pan-Macmillan.

Garfinkel, H. (1967) *Studies in Ethnomethodology*. Englewood Cliffs, NJ: Prentice Hall.

Gergen, K. (1985) 'The social constructionist movement in modern psychology', *American Psychologist*, 40(3), 266–275.

Gevisser, M. (2010) 'We did it, we showed the world!', *The Guardian*, 10 July, http://theguardian.com/football/2010/jul/10/south-africa-unites-over-football (accessed on 10 December 2013).

Gherovici, P. & Steinkholer, M. (2015). 'Introduction', P. Gherovici & M. Steinkholer (eds) *Lacan on Madness: Madness, Yes You Can't*. London & New York: Routledge.

Gillespie, A. and Cornish, F. (2009) 'Intersubjectivity: towards a dialogical analysis', *Journal for the Theory of Social Behaviour*, 40(1), 19–46.

Gillespie, A. and Richardson, B. (2011) 'Exchanging social positions: enhancing intersubjective coordination within a joint task', *European Journal of Social Psychology*, 41(5), 608–616.

Giorgi, A. (1970) *Psychology as a Human Science*. New York: Harper and Row.

Giorgi, A. (2000) 'The idea of human science', *The Humanistic Psychologist*, 28, 1–3, 119–137.

Glynos, J. (2000) 'Sex and the limits of discourse', in D. R. Howarth, A. J. Norval and Y. Stavrakakis (eds) *Discourse Theory and Political Analysis: Identities, Hegemonies and Social Change*. Manchester and New York: Manchester University Press.

Glynos, J. (2001) 'The grip of ideology: a Lacanian approach to the theory of ideology', *Journal of Political Ideologies*, 6(2), 191–214.

Glynos, J. and Stavrakakis, Y. (2010) 'Politics and the unconscious – an interview with Ernesto Laclau', *Subjectivity*, 3, 231–144.

Glowinski, H. (2001) 'Ideal ego', in H. Glowinski, Z. Marks and S. Murphy (eds) *A Compendium of Lacanian Terms*. London: Free Association Books.

Goffman, E. (1959) *The Presentation of Self in Everyday Life*. New York: Doubleday.

Goffman, E. (1967) 'On face-work: an analysis of ritual elements in social interaction', in *Interaction Ritual: Essays on Face-to-Face Behaviour*. New York: Random House.

Goldman Baldwin, Y. (2016). Lacanian psychoanalysis as a human science in C.T. Fisher, L. Laubscher and R. Brooke (eds) *The Qualitative Vision for Psychology: An Invitation to a Human Science Approach*. Pittsburgh: Duquesne University Press.

Grigg, R. (2001a) 'Discourse', in H. Glowinski, Z. M. Marks and S. Murphy (eds) *A Compendium of Lacanian Terms*. London: Free Association.

Grigg, R. (2001b) 'Signifier', in H. Glowinski, Z. Marks and S. Murphy (eds) *A Compendium of Lacanian Terms*. London: Free Association Books.

Grose, A, (2014) 'The unconscious from Freud to Lacan', in A. Gessert *Introductory Lectures on Lacan*. London: Karnac.

The Guardian (2010) 'The rainbow nation's verdict', 10 July, http://theguardian.com/football/2010/jul/10/south-africa-unites-over-football (accessed on 10 December 2013).

Gunkel, D. J. (2014) 'Master signifier', in R. Butler (ed.) *The Žižek Dictionary*. Durham: Acumen.

Habermas, J. (1984) *The Theory of Communicative Action*. Boston, MA: Beacon Press, vol. I.

Harré, R. and van Langenhove, L. (eds) (1999). *Positioning Theory: Moral Contexts of International Action*. Oxford: Blackwell.

Heidegger, M. (1927) *Being and Time* (translated by J. Macquarrie and E. Robinson). London: SCM Press.

Hensher, P. (2008) *The Northern Clemency*. London: Harper Perenial.

Hewitson, O. (2014) 'Shades of subjectivity', http://lacanonline.com/index/2013/07/shades-of-subjectivity-iii/ (accessed 4 February 2017).

Hoens, D. (2016) 'Logical time and the assertion of anticipated certainty', in C. Neill, D. Hook and S. Vanheule (eds) *Reading the Écrits – A Guide to Lacan's Works: Between the Imaginary and the Symbolic*. London: Routledge, vol. I.

Hollinghurst, A. (2011) *The Stranger's Child*. London: Picador.

Hook, D. (2008) 'Absolute other: Lacan's Big Other as adjunct to critical social psychological analysis', *Social and Personality Psychology Compass*, 2(1), 51–73.

Hook, D. (2011) *A Critical Psychology of the Postcolonial: The Mind of Apartheid*. London and New York: Routledge.

Hook, D. (2013) 'Towards a Lacanian group psychology: the prisoner's dilemma and the trans-subjective', *Journal for the Theory of Social Behaviour*, 43(2), 115–132.

Hook, D. (2013b) 'Tracking the Lacanian unconscious in language', *Psychodynamic Practice*, 19(1), 38–54.

Hook, D. (2016) 'Of symbolic mortification and 'undead' life: Slavoj Zizek on the death drive', *Psychoanalysis & History*, 18(2), 221–256.

Hook, D. and Vanheule, S. (2016) 'Revisiting the master signifier, or: Mandela and repression', *Frontiers in Psychology*, January, http://journal.frontiersin.org/article/10.3389/fpsyg.2015.02028/full#note1a (accessed on 2nd December 2016).

Jakobson, R. (1960) 'Linguistics and poetics', in T. Sebeok (ed.) *Style in Language*. Cambridge, MA: M.I.T. Press.

Johnston, A. (2004) 'The cynic's fetish: Slavoj Žižek and the dynamics of belief', *Psychoanalysis, Culture and Society*, 9, 259–283.

Johnston, A. (2005) *Time Driven: Metapsychology and the Splitting of the Drive*. Evanston, IL: Northwester University Press.

Johnston, A. (2008) *Žižek's Ontology: A Transcendental Materialist Theory of Subjectivity*. Evanston, Il: Northwestern University Press.

Johnston, A. and Malabou, C. (2013) *Self and Emotional Life*. New York: Columbia University Press.

Kotso, A. (2008) *Žižek and Theology*. London and New York: Continuum.

Lacan, J. (1961–1962) *Seminar IX: Identification* (translated by Cormac Gallagher from unpublished seminar transcripts).

Lacan, J. (1979) 'The neurotic's individual myth', *Psychoanalytic Quarterly*, 48, 405–425.

Lacan, J. (1980) *De la Psychose Paranoïaque dans ses Rapports avec la Personnalité*. Paris: Seuil.

Lacan, J. (1981) *The Seminar of Jacques Lacan, Book XI: The Four Fundamental Concepts of Psychoanalysis*. London: W.W. Norton.

Lacan, J. (1988a) *The Seminar of Jacques Lacan, Book I: Freud's Papers on Technique, 1953–1954* (edited by Jacques-Alain Miller, translated with notes by John Forrester). New York and London: W.W. Norton.

Lacan, J. (1988b) *The Seminar of Jacques Lacan, Book II: The Ego in Freud's Theory and in the Technique of Psychoanalysis, 1954–1955* (edited by Jacques-Alain Miller, translated by Sylvana Tomaselli). New York and London: W.W. Norton.

Lacan, J. (1992) *The Seminar of Jacques Lacan, Book VII: The Ethics of Psychoanalysis, 1959–1960*. London: W.W. Norton.

Lacan, J. (1993) *The Seminar of Jacques Lacan, Book III: The Psychoses, 1955–1956* (edited by Jacques-Alain Miller, translated by Russell Grigg). New York and London: W.W. Norton.

Lacan, J. (1998) *The Seminar of Jacques Lacan, Book XX, Encore: On Feminine Sexuality, the Limits of Love and Knowledge, 1972–1973* (edited by Jacques-Alain Miller, translated by Bruce Fink). New York and London: W.W. Norton.

Lacan, J. (2006) *Écrits: The First Complete Edition in English* (translated with notes by Bruce Fink, in collaboration with H. Fink and R. Grigg). New York and London: W.W Norton.

Lacan, J. (2007) *The Seminar of Jacques Lacan, Book XVII: The Other Side of Psychoanalysis* (translated by R. Grigg). New York and London: W.W. Norton.

Lacan, J. (2013) *On the Names-of-the-Father.* Cambridge: Polity.

Lacan, J. (2014) *Anxiety: The Seminar of Jacques Lacan, Book X* (edited by Jacques-Alain Miller, translated by A.R. Price). Cambridge: Polity Press.

Lacan, J. (2016) *Transference: The Seminar of Jacques Lacan, Book VIII.* Polity Press: Cambridge.

Laclau, E. (2004) *On Populist Reason.* London: Verso.

Laclau, E. (2007) *Emancipations.* London: Verso.

Laclau, E. and Mouffe, C. (1985) *Hegemony and Socialist Strategy.* London: Verso.

Laplanche, J. & Pontalis, J.B. (1978) *The Language of Psychoanalysis.* London. W.W. Norton.

Latour, B. (1996) 'On interobjectivity', *Mind, Culture and Activity*, 3(4), 228–245.

Leader, D. (1992) 'Some notes on obsessional neurosis', Lecture given at Leeds Metropolitan University, December 1992, www.jcfar.org/past_papers/Some%20Notes%20on%20 Obsessional%20Neurosis %20-%20Darian%20Leader.pdf (accessed 12 June 2012).

Leader, D. (1996) *Why Do Women Write More Letters than They Post?* London: Faber and Faber.

Leader, D. (2000) 'The schema L', in B. Burgoyne (ed.) *Drawing the Soul: Schemas and Models in Psychoanalysis.* London: Rebus Press.

Leader, D. (2003) 'Psychoanalysis and the voice', The Centre for Freudian Analysis and Research Web Journal, www.cfar.org.uk/pdf/voice.pdf (accessed 2 December 2016)

Leader D. (2008) *The New Black: Mourning, Melancholia and Depression.* London: Hamish Hamilton.

Leader, D. and Corfield, D. (2007) *Why Do People Get Ill?* London: Hamish Hamilton.

Leader, D. and Groves, J. (1995) *Lacan for Beginners.* London: Icon.

Lévi-Strauss, C. (1974) *Structural Anthropology* (translated by C. Jacobson and B. G Schoepf). London and New York: Basic Books.

Lewis, P., Newburn, T., Taylor, M., Mcgillivray, C., Greenhill, A., Frayman, H. and Proctor, R. (2011). *Reading the Riots: Investigating England's Summer of Disorder*, The London School of Economics and Political Science and The Guardian, London, UK, http://theguardian. com/uk/series/reading-the-riots (accessed 15 April 2014).

Lewis, M. (2008) *Derrida and Lacan: Another Writing.* Edinburgh: Edinburgh University Press.

Lodge, T. (2006) *Mandela: A Critical Life.* Oxford: Oxford University Press.

Macey, D. (1993) *The Lives of Michel Foucault.* London: Vintage.

Macey, D. (1998) *Lacan in Contexts.* London: Verso.

Malone, K. R. (2012) 'Subjectivity and alterity', *Journal of Theoretical and Philosophical Psychology*, 32(1), 50–66.

Malone, K. R. and Friedlander, S. R. (ed.) (2000a) *The Subject of Lacan: A Lacanian Reader for Psychologists.* New York: SUNY Press.

Malone, K. R. and Friedlander, S. R. (2000b) 'Introduction', in K. R. Malone and S. R. Friedlander (eds) *The Subject of Lacan: A Lacanian Reader for Psychologists.* New York: SUNY Press.

Malone, K. R. and Roberts, J. L. (2010) 'In the world of language but not of it', *Theory and Psychology*, 20(6), 835–854.

Marks, M. P. (2004) *The Prison as Metaphor: Re-examining International Relations.* New York: Peter Lang.

McKaiser, E. (2012) *A Bantu in my Bathroom.* Johannesburg: Macmillan.

Mead, G. H. (1934) *Mind, Self and Society from the Standpoint of a Social Behaviourist.* Chicago: University of Chicago Press.

Miller, J. A. (1977) 'Suture (Elements of the logic of the signifier)'. *Screen*, 18, 4, Winter 1977–78, 24–34.

Miller, J. A. (1996a) 'An introduction to Seminars I and II: Lacan's orientation prior to 1953 (I)', in R. Feldstein, B. Fink and M. Jaanus (eds) *Reading Seminars I and II: Lacan's Return to Freud*. SUNY Press: New York.

Miller, J. A. (1996b) 'An introduction to seminars I and II: Lacan's orientation prior to 1953 (II)', in R. Feldstein, B. Fink and M. Jaanus (eds) *Reading Seminars I and II: Lacan's Return to Freud*. New York: SUNY Press.

Miller, J. A. (1996c) 'An introduction to Seminars I and II: Lacan's orientation prior to 1953 (III)', in R. Feldstein, B. Fink and M. Jaanus (eds) *Reading Seminars I and II: Lacan's Return to Freud*. New York: SUNY Press.

Miller, J. A. (2008) On love, Lacan.com, www.lacan.com/symptom/?page_id=263 (accessed 10 May 2014).

Miller, M. J. (2011) *Lacanian Psychotherapy: Theory and Practical Applications*. London and New York: Routledge.

Miller, M. J. (forthcoming) 'Psychoanalysis and its teaching', in C. Neill, D. Hook and S. Vanheule (eds) *Reading the Écrits – A Guide to Lacan's Works*. London: Routledge.

Moghaddam, F. M. (1997) *The Specialized Society: The Plight of the Individual in the Age of Individualism*. Westport, CT: Praeger.

Moghaddam, F. M. (2003) 'Interobjectivity and culture', *Culture and Psychology*, 9, 221–232.

Moghaddam, F. M. (2006) 'Interobjectivity: the collective roots of individual consciousness and social identity', in T. Postmes and J. Jetten (eds) *Individuality and the Group: Advances in Social Identity*. Thousand Oaks, CA: Sage.

Moncayo, R. (2008) *Evolving Lacanian Perspectives for Clinical Psychoanalysis*. London: Karnac.

Moncayo, R. (2012) *The Emptiness of Oedipus: Identification and Non-identification in Lacanian Psychoanalysis*. London and New York: Routledge.

Muller, J. P. and Richardson, W. J. (1982) *Lacan and Language: A Reader's Guide to Écrits*. New York, NY: International Universities Press.

Mngxitama, A. (2014) 'How Malema became Mao'lema', *Mail and Guardian*, 13 March.

Mngxitama, A. and Kaganof, A. (2013) *From a Place of Blackness*. Melville: Sankara Publishers.

Mulhall, S. (1996) *Heidegger and Being and Time*. London and New York: Routledge.

Murray, M. (2016). *Lacan: A Critical Introduction*. London: Pluto Press.

Neill, C. (2011) *Lacanian Ethics and the Assumption of Subjectivity*. London and New York: Palgrave.

Neill, C. (2013) 'Breaking the text: an introduction to Lacanian discourse analysis', *Theory and Psychology*, 23 (3), 334–350.

Neill, C. (2014) *Without Ground: Lacanian Ethics and the Assumption of Subjectivity*. London and New York: Palgrave.

Neill, C. (forthcoming) 'The mirror stage as formative of the I function as revealed in psychoanalytic experience', in C. Neill, D. Hook and S. Vanheule (eds) *Reading the Écrits – A Guide to Lacan's Works: Between the Imaginary and the Symbolic*. London: Routledge.

Newman, S. (2004) 'New reflections on the theory of power: a Lacanian perspective', *Contemporary Political Theory*, 3, 148–167.

Nobus, D. (2000) *Jacques Lacan and the Freudian Practice of Psychoanalysis*. London and New York: Routledge.

Nobus, D. (2017) 'Life and death in the glass: A new look at the mirror stage', in D. Nobus (ed.) *Key Concept in Lacanian Theory*. London: Karnac.

Nobus, D. and Quinn, M. (2005) *Knowing Nothing, Staying Stupid: Elements for a Psychoanalytic Epistemology*. London and New York: Routledge.

Nuttall, S. (2013) 'The mortality of Nelson Mandela', *Mail and Guardian*, 5 April.

Owens, C. (2009) 'Lacan for critics!', *Annual Review of Critical Psychology*, 7, 1–4.

Parker, I. (1992) *Discourse Dynamics*. London and New York: Routledge.

Parker, I. (2001) 'Lacan, psychology and the discourse of the university', *Psychoanalytic Studies*, 3, 67–77.

Parker, I. (2003) 'Jacques Lacan: barred psychologist', *Theory and Psychology*, 13, 95–115.

Parker, I. (2005) 'Lacanian discourse analysis in psychology: seven theoretical elements', *Theory and Psychology*, 15(2), 163–182.

Parker, I. (2007a) 'The phallus is a signifier', the Symptom, 8, http://lacan.com/symptom8_articles/parker8.html (accessed 4 February 2017).

Parker, I. (2007b) 'Identification: signifiers, negation and the unary trait in *Seminar XI*', *Journal for Lacanian Studies*, 5(1), 36–52.

Parker, I. (2010) *Lacanian Psychoanalysis Revolutions in Subjectivity*. London and New York: Routledge.

Parker, I. (2015a) *Psychology After the Unconscious*. Hove and New York: Routledge.

Parker, I. (2015b) *Psychology After Psychoanalysis*. Hove and New York: Routledge.

Parker, I. (2015c) *Psychology After Lacan*. Hove and New York: Routledge.

Parker, I. and Pavón-Cuéllar, D. (eds) (2012). *Lacan, Discourse, Event: New Analyses of Textual Indeterminacy*. London and New York: Routledge.

Pavón-Cuéllar, D. (2009) 'Untying the real, imaginary and symbolic: a Lacanian criticism of behavioural, cognitive and discursive psychologies', *Annual Review of Critical Psychology*, 7, 33–51.

Pavón-Cuéllar, D. (2010) *From the Conscious Interior to an Exterior Unconscious: Lacan, Discourse Analysis and Social Psychology*. London: Karnac.

Pavón-Cuéllar, D. (2013) 'Lacan and social psychology', *Social and Personality Psychology Compass*, 7(5), 261–274.

Pavón-Cuéllar, D. (forthcoming) 'Beyond the reality principle', in C. Neill, D. Hook and S. Vanheule (eds) *Reading the Écrits – A Guide to Lacan's Works: Between the Imaginary and the Symbolic*. London: Routledge.

Pfaller, R. (2005) 'Where is your hamster? The concept of ideology in Slavoj Žižek's cultural theory', in Boucher, G., Glynos, J. and Sharpe, M. (eds) *Traversing the Fantasy Critical Responses to Slavoj Žižek*. London and New York: Ashgate Press.

Piaget, J. (1970) *Structuralism*. New York: Basic.

Pinker, S. (2007) *The Stuff of Thought*. London and New York: Allen Lane.

Pluth, E. (forthcoming) 'Remarks on Daniel Lagache's Presentation: "Psychoanalysis and Personality Structure"' in C. Neill, D. Hook and S. Vanheule (eds) *Reading the Écrits – A Guide to Lacan's Works: Between the Imaginary and the Symbolic*. London: Routledge.

Pluth, E. and Hoens, D. (2004) 'What if the other is stupid? Badiou and Lacan on "logical time"', in P. Hallward (ed.) Think *Again: Alain Badiou and the Future of Philosophy*. London: Continuum.

Posel, D. (2014) 'Julius Malema and the post-apartheid public sphere', *Acta Academica*, 46(1), 32–54.

Rodriquez, L. S. (1999) 'Lacan's subversion of the subject', in L. S. Rodriquez (ed.) *Psychoanalysis With Children*. London: Free Association.

Rodriguez, L. S. (2004) 'Diagnosis in psychoanalysis, paper presented at the Centre for Freudian Analysis and Research', London, 24 January, http://cfar.org.uk/pdf/diagnosis.pdf (accessed 4 February 2017).

Rose, J. (1986/2005) *Sexuality in the Field of Vision*. London: Verso.

Rose, N. (1985) *The Psychological Complex: Psychology, Politics and Society*. London: Routledge and Kegan Paul.

Rose, N. (1998) *Inventing Ourselves: Psychology, Power* and Personhood. Cambridge: Cambridge University Press.

Rose, N. (1999) *Governing the Soul: The Shaping of the Private Self.* London: Free Association.

Ross, A. (2007) *The Rest is Noise: Listening to the Twentieth Century.* London: Harper.

Roudinesco, É. (2014) *Lacan: In Spite of Everything.* London: Verso.

Salecl, R. (1998) *(Per)versions of Love and Hate.* London and New York: Verso.

Sammut, G., Daanen, P. and Sartawi, M. (2010) 'Interobjectivity: redefining objectivity in cultural psychology', *Culture and Psychology*, 16(4), 451–463.

Samuels, R. (1996) 'From Freud to Lacan', in R. Feldstein, B. Fink and M. Jaanus (eds) *Reading Seminars I and II: Lacan's Return to Freud.* New York: SUNY Press.

Saussure, F. (1974) *Course in General Linguistics.* London: Fontanna.

Shannon, C., and Weaver, W. (1949) *The Mathematical Theory of Communication.* Urbana: University of Illinois Press.

Sharpe, M. (2004) *Slavoj Žižek: A Little Piece of the Real.* Aldershot: Ashgate Press.

Sharpe, M. and Boucher, G. (2010) *Žižek's Politics.* Edinburgh: Edinburgh University Press.

Sheridan, A. (1981) 'Translator's note', in J. Miller (ed.) *The Seminar of Jacques Lacan, Book XI: The Four Fundamental Concepts of Psychoanalysis.* London: W.W. Norton.

Sobukwe, R. (1975) *Letter to Nell Marquard of 4th May.* Robert Sobukwe papers, Africana Library, Johannesburg: Wits University.

Sobukwe, R. M (2013) 'Forward to 1958!', in T. G. Karis and G. M. Gerhart (eds) *From Protest to Challenge: A Documentary History of African Politics in South Africa, 1882–1990.* Auckland Park: Jacana, vol. III

Soler, C. (1996) 'The symbolic order (I)', in R. Feldstein, B. Fink and M. Jaanus (eds), *Reading Seminars I and II Lacan's Return to Freud.* Albany, NY: State University of New York Press.

Stavrakakis, Y, (1997) 'Green ideology: a discursive reading', *Journal of Political Ideologies*, 2(3), 259–279.

Stavrakakis, Y. (1999) *Lacanian and the Political.* London and New York: Routledge.

Stavrakakis, Y. (2007) *The Lacanian Left.* Edinburgh: Edinburgh University Press.

Stavrakakis, Y. (2008) 'Subjectivity and the organized other: between symbolic authority and fantasmatic enjoyment', *Organization Studies*, 29(7), 1037–1059.

Sullivan, G. (2014) *Emotions of Collective Pride and Group Identity: New Directions in Theory and Practice.* London and New York: Routledge.

Swales, S. S. (2012). *Perversion.* London and New York: Routledge.

Thom, C. (1981) 'The unconscious structured as a language', in C. McCabe (ed.) *The Talking Cure.* New York, NY: St Martin's Press.

Van Haute, P. (2002) *Against Adaptation: Lacan's "Subversion" of the Subject.* New York: Other Press.

Vanheule, S. (2011). *The Subject of Psychosis: A Lacanian Perspective.* London & New York: Palgrave.

Vanheule, S. and Verhaeghe, P. (2009) 'Identity through a psychoanalytic looking glass', *Theory and Psychology*, 19(3), 391–411.

Verhaeghe, P. (2001) *Beyond Gender: From Subject to Drive.* New York: Other Press.

Verhaeghe, P. (2004) *On Being Normal and Other Disorders.* New York: Other Press.

Von Scheve, C. and Salmela, M. (2014) *Collective Emotions: Perspectives from Psychology, Philosophy and Sociology.* Oxford: Oxford University Press.

Vygotsky, L. (2004) 'Sign operations and organization of mental processes', in R. W. Reiber and D. K. Robinson (eds) *The Essential Vygotsky.* New York: Kluwer Academic Press.

Wallon, H. (1931) 'Comment se développe chez l'enfant la notion de corps propre', *Journal de Psychologie*, 16, 121–510.

Webster, J. (2015) 'Variations on the standard treatment', in C. Neill, D. Hook and S. Vanheule (eds) *Lacan's Ecrits: A reader's Guide*, vol. I.

Webster, J. (forthcoming) 'Variations on the standard treatment', in C. Neill, D. Hook and S. Vanheule (eds), *Reading the Écrits – A Guide to Lacan's Works: Between the Imaginary and the Symbolic*. London: Routledge.

Weir, R. (1962) *Language in the Crib*. The Hague: Mouton.

Wetherell, M. (1998) 'Positioning and interpretative repertoires: conversation analysis and post-structuralism in dialogue', *Discourse and Society*, 9(3), 387–412.

Wertsch, J. V. (1985) *Vygotsky and the Social Formation of Mind*. Cambridge, MA: Harvard University Press.

Wilden, A. (1968) 'Lacan and the discourse of the Other', in J. Lacan *Speech and Language in Psychoanalysis* (translated with notes by A. Wilden). Baltimore and London: John Hopkins University Press.

Žižek, S. (1989) *The Sublime Object of Ideology*. London and New York: Verso.

Žižek, S. (1993) *Tarrying with the Negative: Kant, Hegel, and the Critique of Ideology*. Durham, NA: Duke University Press.

Žižek, S. (1996) *The Indivisible Remainder: On Schelling and Related Matters*. London and New York: Verso.

Žižek, S. (1997) *The Plague of Fantasies*. London and New York: Routledge.

Žižek, S. (2002) 'Introduction: between the two revolutions', in S. Žižek (ed.) *Revolution at the Gates*. London and New York: Verso.

Žižek, S. (2005) *Interrogating the Real* (eds) R. Butler and S. Stephens. New York and London: Continuum.

Žižek, S. (2006) *How to Read Lacan*. London: Granta.

Žižek, S., Aristodemou, M. and Frosh, S. (2010) '*Unbehagen* and the subject: an interview with Slavoj Žižek', *Psychoanalysis, Culture and Society*, 15, 418–428.

INDEX

Printed in Great Britain
by Amazon

21891907R00123